Yemen Immigration Laws and Regulations Handbook: Strategic Information and Basic Laws

by Cram101
Textbook NOT Included

Table of Contents

Title Page

Copyright

Foundations of Business

Management

Business law

Finance

Human resource management

Information systems

Marketing

Manufacturing

Commerce

Business ethics

Accounting

Index: Answers

Just The Facts101

Exam Prep for

Yemen Immigration Laws and Regulations Handbook: Strategic Information and Basic Laws

Just The Facts101 Exam Prep is your link from
the textbook and lecture to your exams.

**Just The Facts101 Exam Preps are unauthorized and comprehensive reviews
of your textbooks.**

All material provided by CTI Publications (c) 2019

Textbook publishers and textbook authors do not participate in or contribute to these reviews.

Just The Facts101 Exam Prep

Copyright © 2019 by CTI Publications. All rights reserved.

eAIN 438699

Foundations of Business

A business, also known as an enterprise, agency or a firm, is an entity involved in the provision of goods and/or services to consumers. Businesses are prevalent in capitalist economies, where most of them are privately owned and provide goods and services to customers in exchange for other goods, services, or money.

An _____ is a contingent motivator. Traditional _____ s are extrinsic motivators which reward actions to yield a desired outcome. The effectiveness of traditional _____ s has changed as the needs of Western society have evolved. While the traditional _____ model is effective when there is a defined procedure and goal for a task, Western society started to require a higher volume of critical thinkers, so the traditional model became less effective. Institutions are now following a trend in implementing strategies that rely on intrinsic motivations rather than the extrinsic motivations that the traditional _____ s foster.

Exam Probability: **Medium**

1. *Answer choices:*

(see index for correct answer)

- a. Incentive
- b. hierarchical perspective
- c. functional perspective
- d. Character

Guidance: level 1

:: Business ::

The seller, or the provider of the goods or services, completes a sale in response to an acquisition, appropriation, requisition or a direct interaction with the buyer at the point of sale. There is a passing of title of the item, and the settlement of a price, in which agreement is reached on a price for which transfer of ownership of the item will occur. The seller, not the purchaser typically executes the sale and it may be completed prior to the obligation of payment. In the case of indirect interaction, a person who sells goods or service on behalf of the owner is known as a salesman or saleswoman or salesperson, but this often refers to someone _____ goods in a store/shop, in which case other terms are also common, including salesclerk, shop assistant, and retail clerk.

Exam Probability: **High**

2. *Answer choices:*

(see index for correct answer)

- a. Shareholder rebellion
- b. Intangible asset finance
- c. Selling
- d. Procurement PunchOut

Guidance: level 1

:: Employment ::

The _____ is an individual's metaphorical "journey" through learning, work and other aspects of life. There are a number of ways to define _____ and the term is used in a variety of ways.

Exam Probability: **High**

3. *Answer choices:*

(see index for correct answer)

- a. Temporary duty assignment
- b. In-basket test
- c. Ontario Disability Employment Network
- d. Alternative employment arrangements

Guidance: level 1

:: Management ::

A _____ is an idea of the future or desired result that a person or a group of people envisions, plans and commits to achieve. People endeavor to reach _____ s within a finite time by setting deadlines.

Exam Probability: **High**

4. *Answer choices:*

(see index for correct answer)

- a. Goal
- b. Millennium software
- c. Provectus IT Inc
- d. Reverse innovation

Guidance: level 1

:: Macroeconomics ::

A foreign _____ is an investment in the form of a controlling ownership in a business in one country by an entity based in another country. It is thus distinguished from a foreign portfolio investment by a notion of direct control.

Exam Probability: **Medium**

5. *Answer choices:*

(see index for correct answer)

- a. Microsimulation
- b. Austrian business cycle theory
- c. Direct investment
- d. Asset-based economy

Guidance: level 1

:: Organizational theory ::

_____ is the process of groups of organisms working or acting together for common, mutual, or some underlying benefit, as opposed to working in competition for selfish benefit. Many animal and plant species cooperate both with other members of their own species and with members of other species.

Exam Probability: **Low**

6. *Answer choices:*

(see index for correct answer)

- a. Organizational communication
- b. Strategic Choice Theory
- c. Institutional complementarity
- d. Cooperation

Guidance: level 1

:: Evaluation ::

_____ is the practice of being honest and showing a consistent and uncompromising adherence to strong moral and ethical principles and values. In ethics, _____ is regarded as the honesty and truthfulness or accuracy of one's actions. _____ can stand in opposition to hypocrisy, in that judging with the standards of _____ involves regarding internal consistency as a virtue, and suggests that parties holding within themselves apparently conflicting values should account for the discrepancy or alter their beliefs. The word _____ evolved from the Latin adjective integer, meaning whole or complete. In this context, _____ is the inner sense of "wholeness" deriving from qualities such as honesty and consistency of character. As such, one may judge that others "have _____" to the extent that they act according to the values, beliefs and principles they claim to hold.

Exam Probability: **High**

7. *Answer choices:*

(see index for correct answer)

- a. Evaluation Assurance Level
- b. Academic equivalency evaluation
- c. Teaching and Learning International Survey
- d. Integrity

Guidance: level 1

:: ::

A _____ is any person who contracts to acquire an asset in return for some form of consideration.

Exam Probability: **Low**

8. *Answer choices:*

(see index for correct answer)

- a. personal values
- b. Sarbanes-Oxley act of 2002
- c. Buyer
- d. empathy

Guidance: level 1

:: Problem solving ::

In other words, _____ is a situation where a group of people meet to generate new ideas and solutions around a specific domain of interest by removing inhibitions. People are able to think more freely and they suggest as many spontaneous new ideas as possible. All the ideas are noted down and those ideas are not criticized and after _____ session the ideas are evaluated. The term was popularized by Alex Faickney Osborn in the 1953 book Applied Imagination.

Exam Probability: **Low**

9. *Answer choices:*

(see index for correct answer)

- a. Failure analysis
- b. Curiosity
- c. Self-organising heuristic
- d. Brainstorming

Guidance: level 1

:: Logistics ::

_____ is generally the detailed organization and implementation of a complex operation. In a general business sense, _____ is the management of the flow of things between the point of origin and the point of consumption in order to meet requirements of customers or corporations. The resources managed in _____ may include tangible goods such as materials, equipment, and supplies, as well as food and other consumable items. The _____ of physical items usually involves the integration of information flow, materials handling, production, packaging, inventory, transportation, warehousing, and often security.

Exam Probability: **High**

10. *Answer choices:*

(see index for correct answer)

- a. Merge in transit
- b. Logistics in World War I

- c. Logistics
- d. DASH7

Guidance: level 1

:: Marketing ::

> _____ comes from the Latin neg and otsia referring to businessmen who, unlike the patricians, had no leisure time in their industriousness; it held the meaning of business until the 17th century when it took on the diplomatic connotation as a dialogue between two or more people or parties intended to reach a beneficial outcome over one or more issues where a conflict exists with respect to at least one of these issues. Thus, _____ is a process of combining divergent positions into a joint agreement under a decision rule of unanimity.

Exam Probability: **Low**

11. *Answer choices:*

(see index for correct answer)

- a. Market development
- b. Negotiation
- c. Buy one, get one free
- d. Generic trademark

Guidance: level 1

:: Scientific method ::

In the social sciences and life sciences, a _____ is a research method involving an up-close, in-depth, and detailed examination of a subject of study, as well as its related contextual conditions.

Exam Probability: **Low**

12. *Answer choices:*

(see index for correct answer)

- a. Preference test
- b. Causal research
- c. pilot project
- d. explanatory research

Guidance: level 1

:: Human resource management ::

_____ is the corporate management term for the act of reorganizing the legal, ownership, operational, or other structures of a company for the purpose of making it more profitable, or better organized for its present needs. Other reasons for _____ include a change of ownership or ownership structure, demerger, or a response to a crisis or major change in the business such as bankruptcy, repositioning, or buyout. _____ may also be described as corporate _____, debt _____ and financial _____.

Exam Probability: **Low**

13. *Answer choices:*

(see index for correct answer)

- a. Diversity Icebreaker
- b. Organizational ethics
- c. Attendance management
- d. Sham peer review

Guidance: level 1

:: Competition (economics) ::

_____ arises whenever at least two parties strive for a goal which cannot be shared: where one's gain is the other's loss .

Exam Probability: **Low**

14. *Answer choices:*

(see index for correct answer)

- a. Level playing field
- b. Transfer pricing
- c. Blindspots analysis
- d. Competition

Guidance: level 1

:: Market research ::

A _____ is a small, but demographically diverse group of people and whose reactions are studied especially in market research or political analysis in guided or open discussions about a new product or something else to determine the reactions that can be expected from a larger population. It is a form of qualitative research consisting of interviews in which a group of people are asked about their perceptions, opinions, beliefs, and attitudes towards a product, service, concept, advertisement, idea, or packaging. Questions are asked in an interactive group setting where participants are free to talk with other group members. During this process, the researcher either takes notes or records the vital points he or she is getting from the group. Researchers should select members of the _____ carefully for effective and authoritative responses.

Exam Probability: **Low**

15. *Answer choices:*

(see index for correct answer)

- a. Zyfin
- b. Sagacity segmentation
- c. Product Intelligence
- d. Focus group

Guidance: level 1

:: Project management ::

Some scenarios associate "this kind of planning" with learning "life skills". _____s are necessary, or at least useful, in situations where individuals need to know what time they must be at a specific location to receive a specific service, and where people need to accomplish a set of goals within a set time period.

Exam Probability: **Low**

16. *Answer choices:*

(see index for correct answer)

- a. ISO 21500
- b. Project governance
- c. Effort management
- d. Schedule

Guidance: level 1

:: ::

_____ is the administration of an organization, whether it is a business, a not-for-profit organization, or government body. _____ includes the activities of setting the strategy of an organization and coordinating the efforts of its employees to accomplish its objectives through the application of available resources, such as financial, natural, technological, and human resources. The term "_____" may also refer to those people who manage an organization.

Exam Probability: **Low**

17. *Answer choices:*

(see index for correct answer)

- a. co-culture
- b. information systems assessment
- c. Management
- d. corporate values

Guidance: level 1

:: Television commercials ::

_____ is a phenomenon whereby something new and somehow valuable is formed. The created item may be intangible or a physical object.

Exam Probability: **Medium**

18. *Answer choices:*

(see index for correct answer)

- a. Reassuringly Expensive
- b. Creativity
- c. Time Sculpture
- d. Orange Man

Guidance: level 1

:: Business ::

A _____ is a mathematical object used to count, measure, and label. The original examples are the natural _____ s 1, 2, 3, 4, and so forth. A written symbol like "5" that represents a _____ is called a numeral. A numeral system is an organized way to write and manipulate this type of symbol, for example the Hindu–Arabic numeral system allows combinations of numerical digits like "5" and "0" to represent larger _____ s like 50. A numeral in linguistics can refer to a symbol like 5, the words or phrase that names a _____ , like "five hundred", or other words that mean a specific _____ , like "dozen". In addition to their use in counting and measuring, numerals are often used for labels , for ordering , and for codes . In common usage, _____ may refer to a symbol, a word or phrase, or the mathematical object.

Exam Probability: **Low**

19. *Answer choices:*

(see index for correct answer)

- a. Functional sourcing
- b. absolute value
- c. Number
- d. Open-book contract

Guidance: level 1

:: Rhetoric ::

_____ is the pattern of narrative development that aims to make vivid a place, object, character, or group. _____ is one of four rhetorical modes, along with exposition, argumentation, and narration. In practice it would be difficult to write literature that drew on just one of the four basic modes.

Exam Probability: **Low**

20. *Answer choices:*

(see index for correct answer)

- a. Description
- b. Pars pro toto
- c. Anatomy of Criticism
- d. Climax

Guidance: level 1

:: Money ::

In economics, _____ is money in the physical form of currency, such as banknotes and coins. In bookkeeping and finance, _____ is current assets comprising currency or currency equivalents that can be accessed immediately or near-immediately. _____ is seen either as a reserve for payments, in case of a structural or incidental negative _____ flow or as a way to avoid a downturn on financial markets.

Exam Probability: **Low**

21. *Answer choices:*

(see index for correct answer)

- a. Money clip
- b. Cash
- c. Coin of account
- d. Slang terms for money

Guidance: level 1

:: ::

Business is the activity of making one's living or making money by producing or buying and selling products. Simply put, it is "any activity or enterprise entered into for profit. It does not mean it is a company, a corporation, partnership, or have any such formal organization, but it can range from a street peddler to General Motors."

Exam Probability: **Medium**

22. *Answer choices:*

(see index for correct answer)

- a. information systems assessment
- b. surface-level diversity
- c. similarity-attraction theory
- d. Firm

Guidance: level 1

:: Real estate valuation ::

_____ or OMV is the price at which an asset would trade in a competitive auction setting. _____ is often used interchangeably with open _____ , fair value or fair _____ , although these terms have distinct definitions in different standards, and may or may not differ in some circumstances.

Exam Probability: **Medium**

23. *Answer choices:*

(see index for correct answer)

- a. Days on market
- b. Zoopla

- c. Highest and best use
- d. Chartered Surveyor

Guidance: level 1

:: Classification systems ::

_____ is the practice of comparing business processes and performance metrics to industry bests and best practices from other companies. Dimensions typically measured are quality, time and cost.

Exam Probability: **Low**

24. *Answer choices:*

(see index for correct answer)

- a. Virus classification
- b. Motion picture rating system
- c. Climate classification
- d. Benchmarking

Guidance: level 1

:: Supply chain management ::

_____ is the process of finding and agreeing to terms, and acquiring goods, services, or works from an external source, often via a tendering or competitive bidding process. _____ is used to ensure the buyer receives goods, services, or works at the best possible price when aspects such as quality, quantity, time, and location are compared. Corporations and public bodies often define processes intended to promote fair and open competition for their business while minimizing risks such as exposure to fraud and collusion.

Exam Probability: **High**

25. *Answer choices:*

(see index for correct answer)

- a. ISO/PAS 28000
- b. Materials management
- c. Universal Product Code
- d. CTSI-Global

Guidance: level 1

:: Reputation management ::

_____ or image of a social entity is an opinion about that entity, typically as a result of social evaluation on a set of criteria.

Exam Probability: **Medium**

26. *Answer choices:*

(see index for correct answer)

- a. Reputation system
- b. Sybil attack
- c. personal brand
- d. 123people

Guidance: level 1

:: ::

> Culture is the social behavior and norms found in human societies. Culture is considered a central concept in anthropology, encompassing the range of phenomena that are transmitted through social learning in human societies. _____ universals are found in all human societies; these include expressive forms like art, music, dance, ritual, religion, and technologies like tool usage, cooking, shelter, and clothing. The concept of material culture covers the physical expressions of culture, such as technology, architecture and art, whereas the immaterial aspects of culture such as principles of social organization, mythology, philosophy, literature, and science comprise the intangible _____ heritage of a society.

Exam Probability: **High**

27. *Answer choices:*

(see index for correct answer)

- a. process perspective

- b. Cultural
- c. interpersonal communication
- d. hierarchical

Guidance: level 1

:: ::

> _____ or accountancy is the measurement, processing, and communication of financial information about economic entities such as businesses and corporations. The modern field was established by the Italian mathematician Luca Pacioli in 1494. _____ , which has been called the "language of business", measures the results of an organization's economic activities and conveys this information to a variety of users, including investors, creditors, management, and regulators. Practitioners of _____ are known as accountants. The terms "_____" and "financial reporting" are often used as synonyms.

Exam Probability: **Medium**

28. *Answer choices:*

(see index for correct answer)

- a. process perspective
- b. hierarchical
- c. Accounting
- d. interpersonal communication

Guidance: level 1

:: ::

Some scenarios associate "this kind of planning" with learning "life skills". Schedules are necessary, or at least useful, in situations where individuals need to know what time they must be at a specific location to receive a specific service, and where people need to accomplish a set of goals within a set time period.

Exam Probability: **Low**

29. *Answer choices:*

(see index for correct answer)

- a. Scheduling
- b. open system
- c. surface-level diversity
- d. similarity-attraction theory

Guidance: level 1

:: Marketing ::

_____ or stock is the goods and materials that a business holds for the ultimate goal of resale.

Exam Probability: **Medium**

30. *Answer choices:*

(see index for correct answer)

- a. In-game advertising
- b. Cross merchandising
- c. Inventory
- d. Green marketing

Guidance: level 1

:: Management ::

In organizational studies, _____ is the efficient and effective development of an organization's resources when they are needed. Such resources may include financial resources, inventory, human skills, production resources, or information technology and natural resources.

Exam Probability: **High**

31. *Answer choices:*

(see index for correct answer)

- a. Value proposition
- b. One in, one out policy
- c. Responsible autonomy

- d. Resource management

Guidance: level 1

:: Business law ::

A _____ is an arrangement where parties, known as partners, agree to cooperate to advance their mutual interests. The partners in a _____ may be individuals, businesses, interest-based organizations, schools, governments or combinations. Organizations may partner to increase the likelihood of each achieving their mission and to amplify their reach. A _____ may result in issuing and holding equity or may be only governed by a contract.

Exam Probability: **Low**

32. *Answer choices:*

(see index for correct answer)

- a. Industrial relations
- b. Retained interest
- c. Limited liability company
- d. Stick licensing

Guidance: level 1

:: Financial accounting ::

_____ is a financial metric which represents operating liquidity available to a business, organisation or other entity, including governmental entities. Along with fixed assets such as plant and equipment, _____ is considered a part of operating capital. Gross _____ is equal to current assets. _____ is calculated as current assets minus current liabilities. If current assets are less than current liabilities, an entity has a _____ deficiency, also called a _____ deficit.

Exam Probability: **Medium**

33. *Answer choices:*

(see index for correct answer)

- a. Deferred Acquisition Costs
- b. Intangibles
- c. Advance payment
- d. Working capital

Guidance: level 1

:: Debt ::

_____, in finance and economics, is payment from a borrower or deposit-taking financial institution to a lender or depositor of an amount above repayment of the principal sum, at a particular rate. It is distinct from a fee which the borrower may pay the lender or some third party. It is also distinct from dividend which is paid by a company to its shareholders from its profit or reserve, but not at a particular rate decided beforehand, rather on a pro rata basis as a share in the reward gained by risk taking entrepreneurs when the revenue earned exceeds the total costs.

Exam Probability: **High**

34. *Answer choices:*

(see index for correct answer)

- a. Credit crunch
- b. Interest
- c. gearing
- d. External debt

Guidance: level 1

:: Production economics ::

In microeconomics, _____ are the cost advantages that enterprises obtain due to their scale of operation, with cost per unit of output decreasing with increasing scale.

Exam Probability: **High**

35. *Answer choices:*

(see index for correct answer)

- a. Hicks-neutral technical change
- b. Economies of scale
- c. Synergy
- d. Marginal product

Guidance: level 1

:: Statistical terminology ::

_____ is the magnitude or dimensions of a thing. _____ can be measured as length, width, height, diameter, perimeter, area, volume, or mass.

Exam Probability: **Low**

36. *Answer choices:*

(see index for correct answer)

- a. Iterated conditional modes
- b. Size
- c. Nuisance parameter
- d. Deviation

Guidance: level 1

:: Business law ::

A _____ is a business entity created by two or more parties, generally characterized by shared ownership, shared returns and risks, and shared governance. Companies typically pursue _____ s for one of four reasons: to access a new market, particularly emerging markets; to gain scale efficiencies by combining assets and operations; to share risk for major investments or projects; or to access skills and capabilities.

Exam Probability: **Low**

37. *Answer choices:*
(see index for correct answer)

- a. Joint venture
- b. Valuation using the Market Penetration Model
- c. Novated lease
- d. Undervalue transaction

Guidance: level 1

:: Currency ::

A _____ , in the most specific sense is money in any form when in use or circulation as a medium of exchange, especially circulating banknotes and coins. A more general definition is that a _____ is a system of money in common use, especially for people in a nation. Under this definition, US dollars, pounds sterling, Australian dollars, European euros, Russian rubles and Indian Rupees are examples of currencies. These various currencies are recognized as stores of value and are traded between nations in foreign exchange markets, which determine the relative values of the different currencies. Currencies in this sense are defined by governments, and each type has limited boundaries of acceptance.

Exam Probability: **Low**

38. *Answer choices:*

(see index for correct answer)

- a. Debasement
- b. Donationcoin
- c. Currency
- d. York rating

Guidance: level 1

:: Data collection ::

A _____ is an utterance which typically functions as a request for information. _____ s can thus be understood as a kind of illocutionary act in the field of pragmatics or as special kinds of propositions in frameworks of formal semantics such as alternative semantics or inquisitive semantics. The information requested is expected to be provided in the form of an answer. _____ s are often conflated with interrogatives, which are the grammatical forms typically used to achieve them. Rhetorical _____ s, for example, are interrogative in form but may not be considered true _____ s as they are not expected to be answered. Conversely, non-interrogative grammatical structures may be considered _____ s as in the case of the imperative sentence "tell me your name".

Exam Probability: **High**

39. *Answer choices:*

(see index for correct answer)

- a. Guardian
- b. Human-based computation game
- c. Question
- d. General Social Survey

Guidance: level 1

:: Economic globalization ::

_____ is an agreement in which one company hires another company to be responsible for a planned or existing activity that is or could be done internally, and sometimes involves transferring employees and assets from one firm to another.

Exam Probability: **Medium**

40. *Answer choices:*

(see index for correct answer)

- a. reshoring
- b. Outsourcing

Guidance: level 1

:: Contract law ::

A _____ is a legally-binding agreement which recognises and governs the rights and duties of the parties to the agreement. A _____ is legally enforceable because it meets the requirements and approval of the law. An agreement typically involves the exchange of goods, services, money, or promises of any of those. In the event of breach of _____ , the law awards the injured party access to legal remedies such as damages and cancellation.

Exam Probability: **High**

41. *Answer choices:*

(see index for correct answer)

- a. Four corners
- b. Performance Based Contracting
- c. Contract
- d. Efficient breach

Guidance: level 1

:: Management ::

_____ is the process of thinking about the activities required to achieve a desired goal. It is the first and foremost activity to achieve desired results. It involves the creation and maintenance of a plan, such as psychological aspects that require conceptual skills. There are even a couple of tests to measure someone's capability of _____ well. As such, _____ is a fundamental property of intelligent behavior. An important further meaning, often just called "_____" is the legal context of permitted building developments.

Exam Probability: **High**

42. *Answer choices:*

(see index for correct answer)

- a. Planning
- b. Peer pressure
- c. Advisory board

- d. Quality

Guidance: level 1

:: Office administration ::

An _____ is generally a room or other area where an organization's employees perform administrative work in order to support and realize objects and goals of the organization. The word "_____" may also denote a position within an organization with specific duties attached to it ; the latter is in fact an earlier usage, _____ as place originally referring to the location of one's duty. When used as an adjective, the term "_____" may refer to business-related tasks. In law, a company or organization has _____s in any place where it has an official presence, even if that presence consists of a storage silo rather than an establishment with desk-and-chair. An _____ is also an architectural and design phenomenon: ranging from a small _____ such as a bench in the corner of a small business of extremely small size , through entire floors of buildings, up to and including massive buildings dedicated entirely to one company. In modern terms an _____ is usually the location where white-collar workers carry out their functions. As per James Stephenson, "_____ is that part of business enterprise which is devoted to the direction and co-ordination of its various activities."

Exam Probability: **Medium**

43. *Answer choices:*

(see index for correct answer)

- a. Inter departmental communication
- b. Activity management

- c. Office
- d. Fish! Philosophy

Guidance: level 1

:: Stochastic processes ::

_____ in its modern meaning is a "new idea, creative thoughts, new imaginations in form of device or method". _____ is often also viewed as the application of better solutions that meet new requirements, unarticulated needs, or existing market needs. Such _____ takes place through the provision of more-effective products, processes, services, technologies, or business models that are made available to markets, governments and society. An _____ is something original and more effective and, as a consequence, new, that "breaks into" the market or society. _____ is related to, but not the same as, invention, as _____ is more apt to involve the practical implementation of an invention to make a meaningful impact in the market or society, and not all _____ s require an invention. _____ often manifests itself via the engineering process, when the problem being solved is of a technical or scientific nature. The opposite of _____ is exnovation.

Exam Probability: **Medium**

44. *Answer choices:*
(see index for correct answer)

- a. Continuous-time stochastic process
- b. Piecewise-deterministic Markov process
- c. Innovation
- d. Kinetic scheme

Guidance: level 1

:: Business models ::

A _____, _____ company or daughter company is a company that is owned or controlled by another company, which is called the parent company, parent, or holding company. The _____ can be a company, corporation, or limited liability company. In some cases it is a government or state-owned enterprise. In some cases, particularly in the music and book publishing industries, subsidiaries are referred to as imprints.

Exam Probability: **Low**

45. *Answer choices:*

(see index for correct answer)

- a. Very small business
- b. Utility computing
- c. Organizational architecture
- d. Subsidiary

Guidance: level 1

:: ::

_____ is the collection of mechanisms, processes and relations by which corporations are controlled and operated. Governance structures and principles identify the distribution of rights and responsibilities among different participants in the corporation and include the rules and procedures for making decisions in corporate affairs. _____ is necessary because of the possibility of conflicts of interests between stakeholders, primarily between shareholders and upper management or among shareholders.

Exam Probability: **High**

46. *Answer choices:*

(see index for correct answer)

- a. Corporate governance
- b. corporate values
- c. co-culture
- d. Character

Guidance: level 1

:: Analysis ::

_____ is the process of breaking a complex topic or substance into smaller parts in order to gain a better understanding of it. The technique has been applied in the study of mathematics and logic since before Aristotle, though _____ as a formal concept is a relatively recent development.

Exam Probability: **Medium**

47. *Answer choices:*

(see index for correct answer)

- a. Water pinch analysis
- b. Analysis
- c. Engineering analysis
- d. Irreducibility

Guidance: level 1

:: Generally Accepted Accounting Principles ::

An _____ or profit and loss account is one of the financial statements of a company and shows the company's revenues and expenses during a particular period.

Exam Probability: **Medium**

48. *Answer choices:*

(see index for correct answer)

- a. Fin 48
- b. net realisable value
- c. Generally Accepted Accounting Practice
- d. Income statement

Guidance: level 1

:: Supply chain management terms ::

In business and finance, _____ is a system of organizations, people, activities, information, and resources involved in moving a product or service from supplier to customer. _____ activities involve the transformation of natural resources, raw materials, and components into a finished product that is delivered to the end customer. In sophisticated _____ systems, used products may re-enter the _____ at any point where residual value is recyclable. _____ s link value chains.

Exam Probability: **High**

49. *Answer choices:*

(see index for correct answer)

- a. Consumables
- b. inventory management
- c. Direct shipment
- d. Stockout

Guidance: level 1

:: Stock market ::

A shareholder is an individual or institution that legally owns one or more shares of stock in a public or private corporation. _____ may be referred to as members of a corporation. Legally, a person is not a shareholder in a corporation until their name and other details are entered in the corporation's register of _____ or members.

Exam Probability: **Low**

50. *Answer choices:*

(see index for correct answer)

- a. Box spread
- b. Shareholders
- c. Buy side
- d. Issued shares

Guidance: level 1

:: Data management ::

_____ is a form of intellectual property that grants the creator of an original creative work an exclusive legal right to determine whether and under what conditions this original work may be copied and used by others, usually for a limited term of years. The exclusive rights are not absolute but limited by limitations and exceptions to _____ law, including fair use. A major limitation on _____ on ideas is that _____ protects only the original expression of ideas, and not the underlying ideas themselves.

Exam Probability: **Low**

51. *Answer choices:*

(see index for correct answer)

- a. Storage area network
- b. Classora
- c. Information integration
- d. Copyright

Guidance: level 1

:: Globalization-related theories ::

_____ is the process in which a nation is being improved in the sector of the economic, political, and social well-being of its people. The term has been used frequently by economists, politicians, and others in the 20th and 21st centuries. The concept, however, has been in existence in the West for centuries. "Modernization, "westernization", and especially "industrialization" are other terms often used while discussing _____ . _____ has a direct relationship with the environment and environmental issues. _____ is very often confused with industrial development, even in some academic sources.

Exam Probability: **Medium**

52. *Answer choices:*

(see index for correct answer)

- a. Capitalism
- b. postmodernism
- c. post-industrial

Guidance: level 1

:: Real estate ::

_____s serve several societal needs – primarily as shelter from weather, security, living space, privacy, to store belongings, and to comfortably live and work. A _____ as a shelter represents a physical division of the human habitat and the outside.

Exam Probability: **High**

53. *Answer choices:*
(see index for correct answer)

- a. Building
- b. 999-year lease
- c. Plantation
- d. Form-based code

Guidance: level 1

:: Management ::

The _____ is a strategy performance management tool – a semi-standard structured report, that can be used by managers to keep track of the execution of activities by the staff within their control and to monitor the consequences arising from these actions.

Exam Probability: **High**

54. *Answer choices:*

(see index for correct answer)

- a. Vasa syndrome
- b. Crisis management
- c. Goal
- d. Energy management software

Guidance: level 1

:: Management ::

In business, a _____ is the attribute that allows an organization to outperform its competitors. A _____ may include access to natural resources, such as high-grade ores or a low-cost power source, highly skilled labor, geographic location, high entry barriers, and access to new technology.

Exam Probability: **Low**

55. *Answer choices:*

(see index for correct answer)

- a. I-VMS
- b. Intopia
- c. Relational view
- d. Competitive advantage

Guidance: level 1

:: Shareholders ::

A _____ is a payment made by a corporation to its shareholders, usually as a distribution of profits. When a corporation earns a profit or surplus, the corporation is able to re-invest the profit in the business and pay a proportion of the profit as a _____ to shareholders. Distribution to shareholders may be in cash or, if the corporation has a _____ reinvestment plan, the amount can be paid by the issue of further shares or share repurchase. When _____ s are paid, shareholders typically must pay income taxes, and the corporation does not receive a corporate income tax deduction for the _____ payments.

Exam Probability: **Medium**

56. *Answer choices:*

(see index for correct answer)

- a. Shotgun clause
- b. Derivative suit
- c. UK Individual Shareholders Society

- d. Poison pill

Guidance: level 1

:: Generally Accepted Accounting Principles ::

In accounting, _____ is the income that a business have from its normal business activities, usually from the sale of goods and services to customers. _____ is also referred to as sales or turnover. Some companies receive _____ from interest, royalties, or other fees. _____ may refer to business income in general, or it may refer to the amount, in a monetary unit, earned during a period of time, as in "Last year, Company X had _____ of $42 million". Profits or net income generally imply total _____ minus total expenses in a given period. In accounting, in the balance statement it is a subsection of the Equity section and _____ increases equity, it is often referred to as the "top line" due to its position on the income statement at the very top. This is to be contrasted with the "bottom line" which denotes net income .

Exam Probability: **High**

57. *Answer choices:*
(see index for correct answer)

- a. Revenue
- b. Cost principle
- c. Provision
- d. Earnings before interest, taxes and depreciation

Guidance: level 1

:: ::

_____ is an abstract concept of management of complex systems according to a set of rules and trends. In systems theory, these types of rules exist in various fields of biology and society, but the term has slightly different meanings according to context. For example.

Exam Probability: **High**

58. *Answer choices:*

(see index for correct answer)

- a. Regulation
- b. imperative
- c. functional perspective
- d. information systems assessment

Guidance: level 1

:: Stock market ::

_____ is a form of corporate equity ownership, a type of security. The terms voting share and ordinary share are also used frequently in other parts of the world; "_____" being primarily used in the United States. They are known as Equity shares or Ordinary shares in the UK and other Commonwealth realms. This type of share gives the stockholder the right to share in the profits of the company, and to vote on matters of corporate policy and the composition of the members of the board of directors.

Exam Probability: **High**

59. *Answer choices:*

(see index for correct answer)

- a. Common stock
- b. Gross spread
- c. Mosaic theory
- d. Preferred stock

Guidance: level 1

Management

Management is the administration of an organization, whether it is a business, a not-for-profit organization, or government body. Management includes the activities of setting the strategy of an organization and coordinating the efforts of its employees (or of volunteers) to accomplish its objectives through the application of available resources, such as financial, natural, technological, and human resources.

:: Workplace ::

_____ is a systematic determination of a subject's merit, worth and significance, using criteria governed by a set of standards. It can assist an organization, program, design, project or any other intervention or initiative to assess any aim, realisable concept/proposal, or any alternative, to help in decision-making; or to ascertain the degree of achievement or value in regard to the aim and objectives and results of any such action that has been completed. The primary purpose of _____ , in addition to gaining insight into prior or existing initiatives, is to enable reflection and assist in the identification of future change.

Exam Probability: **High**

1. *Answer choices:*

(see index for correct answer)

- a. Evaluation
- b. Workplace revenge
- c. Control freak
- d. Workplace phobia

Guidance: level 1

:: Marketing ::

_____ comes from the Latin neg and otsia referring to businessmen who, unlike the patricians, had no leisure time in their industriousness; it held the meaning of business until the 17th century when it took on the diplomatic connotation as a dialogue between two or more people or parties intended to reach a beneficial outcome over one or more issues where a conflict exists with respect to at least one of these issues. Thus, _____ is a process of combining divergent positions into a joint agreement under a decision rule of unanimity.

Exam Probability: **High**

2. *Answer choices:*
(see index for correct answer)

- a. Negotiation
- b. Private label
- c. Lead generation
- d. Contribution margin-based pricing

Guidance: level 1

:: Systems thinking ::

In business management, a _____ is a company that facilitates the learning of its members and continuously transforms itself. The concept was coined through the work and research of Peter Senge and his colleagues.

Exam Probability: **Low**

3. Answer choices:

(see index for correct answer)

- a. Thought leader
- b. World Future Society
- c. Delphi method
- d. Learning organization

Guidance: level 1

:: Leadership ::

_____/Management is a part of a style of leadership that focuses on supervision, organization, and performance; it is an integral part of the Full Range Leadership Model. _____ is a style of leadership in which leaders promote compliance by followers through both rewards and punishments. Through a rewards and punishments system, transactional leaders are able to keep followers motivated for the short-term. Unlike transformational leaders, those using the transactional approach are not looking to change the future, they look to keep things the same. Leaders using _____ as a model pay attention to followers' work in order to find faults and deviations.

Exam Probability: **Low**

4. Answer choices:

(see index for correct answer)

- a. Consideration and Initiating Structure
- b. Integral leadership

- c. Transactional leadership
- d. Leadership analysis

Guidance: level 1

:: ::

The business environment is a marketing term and refers to factors and forces that affect a firm's ability to build and maintain successful customer relationships. The business environment has been defined as "the totality of physical and social factors that are taken directly into consideration in the decision-making behaviour of individuals in the organisation."

Exam Probability: **Medium**

5. *Answer choices:*

(see index for correct answer)

- a. Environmental scanning
- b. hierarchical perspective
- c. empathy
- d. Character

Guidance: level 1

:: Labor rights ::

A _____ is a wrong or hardship suffered, real or supposed, which forms legitimate grounds of complaint. In the past, the word meant the infliction or cause of hardship.

Exam Probability: **High**

6. *Answer choices:*

(see index for correct answer)

- a. Right to work
- b. The Hyatt 100
- c. Grievance
- d. Labor rights

Guidance: level 1

:: Marketing ::

_____ , in marketing, manufacturing, call centres and management, is the use of flexible computer-aided manufacturing systems to produce custom output. Such systems combine the low unit costs of mass production processes with the flexibility of individual customization.

Exam Probability: **Medium**

7. *Answer choices:*

(see index for correct answer)

- a. John Neeson
- b. Albuquerque Craft Beer Market
- c. Movement marketing
- d. Mass customization

Guidance: level 1

:: Business ::

_____ is a trade policy that does not restrict imports or exports; it can also be understood as the free market idea applied to international trade. In government, _____ is predominantly advocated by political parties that hold liberal economic positions while economically left-wing and nationalist political parties generally support protectionism, the opposite of _____ .

Exam Probability: **Low**

8. *Answer choices:*

(see index for correct answer)

- a. SONGZIO
- b. Corporate services
- c. Ametek
- d. Business analysis

Guidance: level 1

:: Product management ::

_____ s, also known as Shewhart charts or process-behavior charts, are a statistical process control tool used to determine if a manufacturing or business process is in a state of control.

Exam Probability: **Low**

9. *Answer choices:*

(see index for correct answer)

- a. Product management
- b. Product information
- c. Rapid prototyping
- d. Control chart

Guidance: level 1

:: Cognitive biases ::

The _____ is a type of immediate judgement discrepancy, or cognitive bias, where a person making an initial assessment of another person, place, or thing will assume ambiguous information based upon concrete information. A simplified example of the _____ is when an individual noticing that the person in the photograph is attractive, well groomed, and properly attired, assumes, using a mental heuristic, that the person in the photograph is a good person based upon the rules of that individual's social concept. This constant error in judgment is reflective of the individual's preferences, prejudices, ideology, aspirations, and social perception. The _____ is an evaluation by an individual and can affect the perception of a decision, action, idea, business, person, group, entity, or other whenever concrete data is generalized or influences ambiguous information.

Exam Probability: **High**

10. *Answer choices:*

(see index for correct answer)

- a. Less-is-better effect
- b. Overjustification effect
- c. Ambiguity effect
- d. Trait ascription bias

Guidance: level 1

:: Game theory ::

To _____ is to make a deal between different parties where each party gives up part of their demand. In arguments, _____ is a concept of finding agreement through communication, through a mutual acceptance of terms—often involving variations from an original goal or desires.

Exam Probability: **Low**

11. *Answer choices:*

(see index for correct answer)

- a. Congestion game
- b. Repeated game
- c. Compromise
- d. Social value orientations

Guidance: level 1

:: ::

An _____ is a contingent motivator. Traditional _____ s are extrinsic motivators which reward actions to yield a desired outcome. The effectiveness of traditional _____ s has changed as the needs of Western society have evolved. While the traditional _____ model is effective when there is a defined procedure and goal for a task, Western society started to require a higher volume of critical thinkers, so the traditional model became less effective. Institutions are now following a trend in implementing strategies that rely on intrinsic motivations rather than the extrinsic motivations that the traditional _____ s foster.

Exam Probability: **Medium**

12. *Answer choices:*

(see index for correct answer)

- a. information systems assessment
- b. empathy
- c. Incentive
- d. levels of analysis

Guidance: level 1

:: ::

> Business is the activity of making one's living or making money by producing or buying and selling products . Simply put, it is "any activity or enterprise entered into for profit. It does not mean it is a company, a corporation, partnership, or have any such formal organization, but it can range from a street peddler to General Motors."

Exam Probability: **Low**

13. *Answer choices:*

(see index for correct answer)

- a. surface-level diversity
- b. Firm

- c. levels of analysis
- d. deep-level diversity

Guidance: level 1

:: Packaging ::

In work place, _____ or job _____ means good ranking with the hypothesized conception of requirements of a role. There are two types of job _____ s: contextual and task. Task _____ is related to cognitive ability while contextual _____ is dependent upon personality. Task _____ are behavioral roles that are recognized in job descriptions and by remuneration systems, they are directly related to organizational _____ , whereas, contextual _____ are value based and additional behavioral roles that are not recognized in job descriptions and covered by compensation; they are extra roles that are indirectly related to organizational _____ . Citizenship _____ like contextual _____ means a set of individual activity/contribution that supports the organizational culture.

Exam Probability: **Low**

14. *Answer choices:*

(see index for correct answer)

- a. Permeation
- b. Shake well
- c. Phillumeny
- d. Performance

Guidance: level 1

:: Strategic management ::

_____ is a strategic planning technique used to help a person or organization identify strengths, weaknesses, opportunities, and threats related to business competition or project planning. It is intended to specify the objectives of the business venture or project and identify the internal and external factors that are favorable and unfavorable to achieving those objectives. Users of a _____ often ask and answer questions to generate meaningful information for each category to make the tool useful and identify their competitive advantage. SWOT has been described as the tried-and-true tool of strategic analysis.

Exam Probability: **Medium**

15. *Answer choices:*

(see index for correct answer)

- a. Critical success factor
- b. SWOT analysis
- c. Sales and operations planning
- d. Complementors

Guidance: level 1

:: Management ::

A _____ is someone who engages in facilitation—any activity that makes a social process easy or easier. A _____ often helps a group of people to understand their common objectives and assists them to plan how to achieve these objectives; in doing so, the _____ remains "neutral", meaning he/she does not take a particular position in the discussion. Some _____ tools will try to assist the group in achieving a consensus on any disagreements that preexist or emerge in the meeting so that it has a strong basis for future action.

Exam Probability: **Medium**

16. *Answer choices:*

(see index for correct answer)

- a. Systems analysis
- b. Facilitator
- c. Focused improvement
- d. Linear scheduling method

Guidance: level 1

:: ::

A _____ is a professional who provides expert advice in a particular area such as security , management, education, accountancy, law, human resources, marketing , finance, engineering, science or any of many other specialized fields.

Exam Probability: **Low**

17. *Answer choices:*

(see index for correct answer)

- a. empathy
- b. information systems assessment
- c. interpersonal communication
- d. Consultant

Guidance: level 1

:: ::

> Some scenarios associate "this kind of planning" with learning "life skills". Schedules are necessary, or at least useful, in situations where individuals need to know what time they must be at a specific location to receive a specific service, and where people need to accomplish a set of goals within a set time period.

Exam Probability: **Medium**

18. *Answer choices:*

(see index for correct answer)

- a. similarity-attraction theory
- b. hierarchical

- c. open system
- d. corporate values

Guidance: level 1

:: ::

_____ is the process of making predictions of the future based on past and present data and most commonly by analysis of trends. A commonplace example might be estimation of some variable of interest at some specified future date. Prediction is a similar, but more general term. Both might refer to formal statistical methods employing time series, cross-sectional or longitudinal data, or alternatively to less formal judgmental methods. Usage can differ between areas of application: for example, in hydrology the terms "forecast" and "_____" are sometimes reserved for estimates of values at certain specific future times, while the term "prediction" is used for more general estimates, such as the number of times floods will occur over a long period.

Exam Probability: **Low**

19. *Answer choices:*

(see index for correct answer)

- a. Forecasting
- b. co-culture
- c. functional perspective
- d. open system

Guidance: level 1

:: Meetings ::

A _____ is a body of one or more persons that is subordinate to a deliberative assembly. Usually, the assembly sends matters into a _____ as a way to explore them more fully than would be possible if the assembly itself were considering them. _____ s may have different functions and their type of work differ depending on the type of the organization and its needs.

Exam Probability: **High**

20. *Answer choices:*

(see index for correct answer)

- a. Coffeehouse
- b. Brown bag seminar
- c. Committee
- d. Candlelight vigil

Guidance: level 1

:: Management ::

_____ is an area of management concerned with designing and controlling the process of production and redesigning business operations in the production of goods or services. It involves the responsibility of ensuring that business operations are efficient in terms of using as few resources as needed and effective in terms of meeting customer requirements. _____ is primarily concerned with planning, organizing and supervising in the contexts of production, manufacturing or the provision of services.

Exam Probability: **Low**

21. *Answer choices:*

(see index for correct answer)

- a. Operations management
- b. Information excellence
- c. Technology scouting
- d. Authoritarian leadership style

Guidance: level 1

:: Market research ::

_____ is an organized effort to gather information about target markets or customers. It is a very important component of business strategy. The term is commonly interchanged with marketing research; however, expert practitioners may wish to draw a distinction, in that marketing research is concerned specifically about marketing processes, while _____ is concerned specifically with markets.

Exam Probability: **Medium**

22. *Answer choices:*

(see index for correct answer)

- a. Market research
- b. PreTesting Company
- c. Software Industry Survey
- d. Gerson Lehrman Group

Guidance: level 1

:: International trade ::

_____ or globalisation is the process of interaction and integration among people, companies, and governments worldwide. As a complex and multifaceted phenomenon, _____ is considered by some as a form of capitalist expansion which entails the integration of local and national economies into a global, unregulated market economy. _____ has grown due to advances in transportation and communication technology. With the increased global interactions comes the growth of international trade, ideas, and culture. _____ is primarily an economic process of interaction and integration that's associated with social and cultural aspects. However, conflicts and diplomacy are also large parts of the history of _____ , and modern _____ .

Exam Probability: **Low**

23. *Answer choices:*

(see index for correct answer)

- a. Intervention stocks
- b. Globalization
- c. Balassa index
- d. Trans-Saharan trade

Guidance: level 1

:: Socialism ::

In sociology, _____ is the process of internalizing the norms and ideologies of society. _____ encompasses both learning and teaching and is thus "the means by which social and cultural continuity are attained".

Exam Probability: **Low**

24. *Answer choices:*

(see index for correct answer)

- a. Project Cybersyn
- b. Socialization
- c. Common ownership
- d. International Working Union of Socialist Parties

Guidance: level 1

:: Project management ::

_____ and Theory Y are theories of human work motivation and management. They were created by Douglas McGregor while he was working at the MIT Sloan School of Management in the 1950s, and developed further in the 1960s. McGregor's work was rooted in motivation theory alongside the works of Abraham Maslow, who created the hierarchy of needs. The two theories proposed by McGregor describe contrasting models of workforce motivation applied by managers in human resource management, organizational behavior, organizational communication and organizational development. _____ explains the importance of heightened supervision, external rewards, and penalties, while Theory Y highlights the motivating role of job satisfaction and encourages workers to approach tasks without direct supervision. Management use of _____ and Theory Y can affect employee motivation and productivity in different ways, and managers may choose to implement strategies from both theories into their practices.

Exam Probability: **High**

25. *Answer choices:*

(see index for correct answer)

- a. Project accounting
- b. Project Management South Africa
- c. Theory X
- d. Axelos

Guidance: level 1

:: ::

_____ is the administration of an organization, whether it is a business, a not-for-profit organization, or government body. _____ includes the activities of setting the strategy of an organization and coordinating the efforts of its employees to accomplish its objectives through the application of available resources, such as financial, natural, technological, and human resources. The term "_____" may also refer to those people who manage an organization.

Exam Probability: **High**

26. *Answer choices:*

(see index for correct answer)

- a. imperative
- b. levels of analysis
- c. cultural
- d. Management

Guidance: level 1

:: ::

The _____ or just chief executive, is the most senior corporate, executive, or administrative officer in charge of managing an organization especially an independent legal entity such as a company or nonprofit institution. CEOs lead a range of organizations, including public and private corporations, non-profit organizations and even some government organizations. The CEO of a corporation or company typically reports to the board of directors and is charged with maximizing the value of the entity, which may include maximizing the share price, market share, revenues or another element. In the non-profit and government sector, CEOs typically aim at achieving outcomes related to the organization's mission, such as reducing poverty, increasing literacy, etc.

Exam Probability: **Medium**

27. *Answer choices:*

(see index for correct answer)

- a. corporate values
- b. empathy
- c. co-culture
- d. Chief executive officer

Guidance: level 1

:: Personality tests ::

The Myers–Briggs Type Indicator is an introspective self-report questionnaire with the purpose of indicating differing psychological preferences in how people perceive the world around them and make decisions. . Though the test superficially resembles some psychological theories it is commonly classified as pseudoscience, especially as pertains to its supposed predictive abilities.

Exam Probability: **High**

28. *Answer choices:*

(see index for correct answer)

- a. Johari window
- b. Keirsey Temperament Sorter
- c. personality quiz
- d. Myers-Briggs type

Guidance: level 1

:: Project management ::

_____ is a process of setting goals, planning and/or controlling the organizing and leading the execution of any type of activity, such as.

Exam Probability: **Medium**

29. *Answer choices:*

(see index for correct answer)

- a. American Society of Professional Estimators
- b. Decision table
- c. Value breakdown structure
- d. Management process

Guidance: level 1

:: ::

_____ is a means of protection from financial loss. It is a form of risk management, primarily used to hedge against the risk of a contingent or uncertain loss

Exam Probability: **Medium**

30. *Answer choices:*

(see index for correct answer)

- a. surface-level diversity
- b. levels of analysis
- c. Insurance
- d. imperative

Guidance: level 1

:: Management ::

In business, a _____ is the attribute that allows an organization to outperform its competitors. A _____ may include access to natural resources, such as high-grade ores or a low-cost power source, highly skilled labor, geographic location, high entry barriers, and access to new technology.

Exam Probability: **High**

31. *Answer choices:*
(see index for correct answer)

- a. Systems analysis
- b. Industrial forensics
- c. Competitive advantage
- d. Business chess

Guidance: level 1

:: Marketing ::

_____ is the percentage of a market accounted for by a specific entity. In a survey of nearly 200 senior marketing managers, 67% responded that they found the revenue- "dollar _____" metric very useful, while 61% found "unit _____" very useful.

Exam Probability: **Low**

32. *Answer choices:*

(see index for correct answer)

- a. Franchising
- b. Negotiation
- c. Immersion marketing
- d. Market share

Guidance: level 1

:: ::

_____ refers to the confirmation of certain characteristics of an object, person, or organization. This confirmation is often, but not always, provided by some form of external review, education, assessment, or audit. Accreditation is a specific organization's process of _____ . According to the National Council on Measurement in Education, a _____ test is a credentialing test used to determine whether individuals are knowledgeable enough in a given occupational area to be labeled "competent to practice" in that area.

Exam Probability: **Low**

33. *Answer choices:*

(see index for correct answer)

- a. Certification
- b. corporate values

- c. Character
- d. information systems assessment

Guidance: level 1

:: Business ethics ::

> _____ is a type of harassment technique that relates to a sexual nature and the unwelcome or inappropriate promise of rewards in exchange for sexual favors. _____ includes a range of actions from mild transgressions to sexual abuse or assault. Harassment can occur in many different social settings such as the workplace, the home, school, churches, etc. Harassers or victims may be of any gender.

Exam Probability: **Low**

34. *Answer choices:*

(see index for correct answer)

- a. Corporate social entrepreneurship
- b. Fair value
- c. Accounting scandals
- d. Sexual harassment

Guidance: level 1

:: Industrial agreements ::

_____ is a process of negotiation between employers and a group of employees aimed at agreements to regulate working salaries, working conditions, benefits, and other aspects of workers' compensation and rights for workers. The interests of the employees are commonly presented by representatives of a trade union to which the employees belong. The collective agreements reached by these negotiations usually set out wage scales, working hours, training, health and safety, overtime, grievance mechanisms, and rights to participate in workplace or company affairs.

Exam Probability: **High**

35. *Answer choices:*

(see index for correct answer)

- a. Collaborative bargaining
- b. Compulsory arbitration
- c. Pattern bargaining
- d. Federal Labor Relations Act

Guidance: level 1

:: Project management ::

Contemporary business and science treat as a _____ any undertaking, carried out individually or collaboratively and possibly involving research or design, that is carefully planned to achieve a particular aim.

Exam Probability: **Medium**

36. *Answer choices:*

(see index for correct answer)

- a. Rolling Wave planning
- b. Gold plating
- c. Project
- d. Life-cycle cost analysis

Guidance: level 1

:: ::

_____ is the consumption and saving opportunity gained by an entity within a specified timeframe, which is generally expressed in monetary terms. For households and individuals, " _____ is the sum of all the wages, salaries, profits, interest payments, rents, and other forms of earnings received in a given period of time."

Exam Probability: **High**

37. *Answer choices:*

(see index for correct answer)

- a. open system
- b. co-culture
- c. Income
- d. interpersonal communication

Guidance: level 1

:: Production and manufacturing ::

_____ is a set of techniques and tools for process improvement. Though as a shortened form it may be found written as 6S, it should not be confused with the methodology known as 6S.

Exam Probability: **High**

38. *Answer choices:*
(see index for correct answer)

- a. Reverse engineering
- b. Alarm fatigue
- c. Woodworking machine
- d. Six Sigma

Guidance: level 1

:: Organizational theory ::

_____ comprises the actual output or results of an organization as measured against its intended outputs.

Exam Probability: **High**

39. *Answer choices:*

(see index for correct answer)

- a. Seagull manager
- b. Organizational performance
- c. Battlefield promotion
- d. Stages of growth model

Guidance: level 1

:: Organizational theory ::

Decentralisation is the process by which the activities of an organization, particularly those regarding planning and decision making, are distributed or delegated away from a central, authoritative location or group. Concepts of _____ have been applied to group dynamics and management science in private businesses and organizations, political science, law and public administration, economics, money and technology.

Exam Probability: **Low**

40. *Answer choices:*

(see index for correct answer)

- a. Mary Parker Follett
- b. Decentralization

- c. Strategic Choice Theory
- d. Participatory organization

Guidance: level 1

:: Evaluation ::

> _____ is the practice of being honest and showing a consistent and uncompromising adherence to strong moral and ethical principles and values. In ethics, _____ is regarded as the honesty and truthfulness or accuracy of one's actions. _____ can stand in opposition to hypocrisy, in that judging with the standards of _____ involves regarding internal consistency as a virtue, and suggests that parties holding within themselves apparently conflicting values should account for the discrepancy or alter their beliefs. The word _____ evolved from the Latin adjective integer, meaning whole or complete. In this context, _____ is the inner sense of "wholeness" deriving from qualities such as honesty and consistency of character. As such, one may judge that others "have _____" to the extent that they act according to the values, beliefs and principles they claim to hold.

Exam Probability: **High**

41. *Answer choices:*

(see index for correct answer)

- a. Scale of one to ten
- b. Knowledge survey
- c. Integrity
- d. XTS-400

Guidance: level 1

:: Organizational theory ::

A _____ is an organizational theory that claims that there is no best way to organize a corporation, to lead a company, or to make decisions. Instead, the optimal course of action is contingent upon the internal and external situation. A contingent leader effectively applies their own style of leadership to the right situation.

Exam Probability: **High**

42. *Answer choices:*

(see index for correct answer)

- a. Participatory management
- b. Swift trust
- c. Contingency theory
- d. Goat rodeo

Guidance: level 1

:: Problem solving ::

A _____ is a unit or formation established to work on a single defined task or activity. Originally introduced by the United States Navy, the term has now caught on for general usage and is a standard part of NATO terminology. Many non-military organizations now create " _____ s" or task groups for temporary activities that might have once been performed by ad hoc committees.

Exam Probability: **Medium**

43. *Answer choices:*

(see index for correct answer)

- a. Unified structured inventive thinking
- b. Cornelian dilemma
- c. Divergent thinking
- d. Task force

Guidance: level 1

:: ::

_____ is a kind of action that occur as two or more objects have an effect upon one another. The idea of a two-way effect is essential in the concept of _____ , as opposed to a one-way causal effect. A closely related term is interconnectivity, which deals with the _____ s of _____ s within systems: combinations of many simple _____ s can lead to surprising emergent phenomena. _____ has different tailored meanings in various sciences. Changes can also involve _____ .

Exam Probability: **Low**

44. Answer choices:

(see index for correct answer)

- a. corporate values
- b. hierarchical
- c. similarity-attraction theory
- d. Character

Guidance: level 1

:: ::

> In sales, commerce and economics, a _____ is the recipient of a good, service, product or an idea - obtained from a seller, vendor, or supplier via a financial transaction or exchange for money or some other valuable consideration.

Exam Probability: **Low**

45. Answer choices:

(see index for correct answer)

- a. functional perspective
- b. cultural
- c. levels of analysis

- d. process perspective

Guidance: level 1

:: ::

The _____ officer or just _____ , is the most senior corporate, executive, or administrative officer in charge of managing an organization especially an independent legal entity such as a company or nonprofit institution. CEOs lead a range of organizations, including public and private corporations, non-profit organizations and even some government organizations. The CEO of a corporation or company typically reports to the board of directors and is charged with maximizing the value of the entity, which may include maximizing the share price, market share, revenues or another element. In the non-profit and government sector, CEOs typically aim at achieving outcomes related to the organization's mission, such as reducing poverty, increasing literacy, etc.

Exam Probability: **Medium**

46. *Answer choices:*

(see index for correct answer)

- a. co-culture
- b. personal values
- c. empathy
- d. Chief executive

Guidance: level 1

:: Survey methodology ::

An _____ is a conversation where questions are asked and answers are given. In common parlance, the word "_____" refers to a one-on-one conversation between an _____ er and an _____ ee. The _____ er asks questions to which the _____ ee responds, usually so information may be transferred from _____ ee to _____ er. Sometimes, information can be transferred in both directions. It is a communication, unlike a speech, which produces a one-way flow of information.

Exam Probability: **Low**

47. *Answer choices:*
(see index for correct answer)

- a. Survey research
- b. Sampling
- c. Interview
- d. Political forecasting

Guidance: level 1

:: ::

_____ involves decision making. It can include judging the merits of multiple options and selecting one or more of them. One can make a _____ between imagined options or between real options followed by the corresponding action. For example, a traveler might choose a route for a journey based on the preference of arriving at a given destination as soon as possible. The preferred route can then follow from information such as the length of each of the possible routes, traffic conditions, etc. The arrival at a _____ can include more complex motivators such as cognition, instinct, and feeling.

Exam Probability: **Medium**

48. *Answer choices:*

(see index for correct answer)

- a. functional perspective
- b. levels of analysis
- c. hierarchical
- d. Choice

Guidance: level 1

:: Decision theory ::

A _____ is a decision support tool that uses a tree-like model of decisions and their possible consequences, including chance event outcomes, resource costs, and utility. It is one way to display an algorithm that only contains conditional control statements.

Exam Probability: **Medium**

49. *Answer choices:*

(see index for correct answer)

- a. Rational Focal Point
- b. Decision tree
- c. Decisional balance sheet
- d. TOPSIS

Guidance: level 1

:: Autonomy ::

In developmental psychology and moral, political, and bioethical philosophy, _____ is the capacity to make an informed, uncoerced decision. Autonomous organizations or institutions are independent or self-governing. _____ can also be defined from a human resources perspective, where it denotes a level of discretion granted to an employee in his or her work. In such cases, _____ is known to generally increase job satisfaction. _____ is a term that is also widely used in the field of medicine — personal _____ is greatly recognized and valued in health care.

Exam Probability: **High**

50. *Answer choices:*

(see index for correct answer)

- a. Autonomy
- b. Autonomous robot
- c. Self-determination theory
- d. Stateless nation

Guidance: level 1

:: Business law ::

A _____ is a business entity created by two or more parties, generally characterized by shared ownership, shared returns and risks, and shared governance. Companies typically pursue _____ s for one of four reasons: to access a new market, particularly emerging markets; to gain scale efficiencies by combining assets and operations; to share risk for major investments or projects; or to access skills and capabilities.

Exam Probability: **High**

51. *Answer choices:*

(see index for correct answer)

- a. Joint venture
- b. Official Assignee
- c. Whitewash waiver
- d. Industrial relations

Guidance: level 1

:: Evaluation methods ::

In social psychology, _____ is the process of looking at oneself in order to assess aspects that are important to one's identity. It is one of the motives that drive self-evaluation, along with self-verification and self-enhancement. Sedikides suggests that the _____ motive will prompt people to seek information to confirm their uncertain self-concept rather than their certain self-concept and at the same time people use _____ to enhance their certainty of their own self-knowledge. However, the _____ motive could be seen as quite different from the other two self-evaluation motives. Unlike the other two motives through _____ people are interested in the accuracy of their current self view, rather than improving their self-view. This makes _____ the only self-evaluative motive that may cause a person's self-esteem to be damaged.

Exam Probability: **Low**

52. *Answer choices:*
(see index for correct answer)

- a. Proof of concept
- b. Self-assessment
- c. Rubric
- d. Logic model

Guidance: level 1

:: Human resource management ::

_____ are the people who make up the workforce of an organization, business sector, or economy. "Human capital" is sometimes used synonymously with "_____", although human capital typically refers to a narrower effect. Likewise, other terms sometimes used include manpower, talent, labor, personnel, or simply people.

Exam Probability: **High**

53. *Answer choices:*

(see index for correct answer)

- a. Induction programme
- b. Human relations movement
- c. Illness rate
- d. Employee silence

Guidance: level 1

:: ::

In a supply chain, a _____, or a seller, is an enterprise that contributes goods or services. Generally, a supply chain _____ manufactures inventory/stock items and sells them to the next link in the chain. Today, these terms refer to a supplier of any good or service.

Exam Probability: **Low**

54. *Answer choices:*

(see index for correct answer)

- a. levels of analysis
- b. open system
- c. deep-level diversity
- d. Vendor

Guidance: level 1

:: ::

The _____ or labour force is the labour pool in employment. It is generally used to describe those working for a single company or industry, but can also apply to a geographic region like a city, state, or country. Within a company, its value can be labelled as its " _____ in Place". The _____ of a country includes both the employed and the unemployed. The labour force participation rate, LFPR, is the ratio between the labour force and the overall size of their cohort. The term generally excludes the employers or management, and can imply those involved in manual labour. It may also mean all those who are available for work.

Exam Probability: **High**

55. *Answer choices:*

(see index for correct answer)

- a. functional perspective
- b. empathy

- c. co-culture
- d. Workforce

Guidance: level 1

:: Business terms ::

A _____ is a short statement of why an organization exists, what its overall goal is, identifying the goal of its operations: what kind of product or service it provides, its primary customers or market, and its geographical region of operation. It may include a short statement of such fundamental matters as the organization's values or philosophies, a business's main competitive advantages, or a desired future state—the "vision".

Exam Probability: **Low**

56. *Answer choices:*
(see index for correct answer)

- a. Mission statement
- b. organic growth
- c. noncommercial
- d. Strategic partner

Guidance: level 1

:: Grounds for termination of employment ::

_____ is a habitual pattern of absence from a duty or obligation without good reason. Generally, _____ is unplanned absences. _____ has been viewed as an indicator of poor individual performance, as well as a breach of an implicit contract between employee and employer. It is seen as a management problem, and framed in economic or quasi-economic terms. More recent scholarship seeks to understand _____ as an indicator of psychological, medical, or social adjustment to work.

Exam Probability: **Low**

57. *Answer choices:*

(see index for correct answer)

- a. Absenteeism
- b. Huffman v. Office of Personnel Management
- c. No call, no show
- d. Defense Intelligence Community Whistleblower Protection

Guidance: level 1

:: Hospitality management ::

A _____ is an establishment that provides paid lodging on a short-term basis. Facilities provided may range from a modest-quality mattress in a small room to large suites with bigger, higher-quality beds, a dresser, a refrigerator and other kitchen facilities, upholstered chairs, a flat screen television, and en-suite bathrooms. Small, lower-priced _____ s may offer only the most basic guest services and facilities. Larger, higher-priced _____ s may provide additional guest facilities such as a swimming pool, business centre, childcare, conference and event facilities, tennis or basketball courts, gymnasium, restaurants, day spa, and social function services. _____ rooms are usually numbered to allow guests to identify their room. Some boutique, high-end _____ s have custom decorated rooms. Some _____ s offer meals as part of a room and board arrangement. In the United Kingdom, a _____ is required by law to serve food and drinks to all guests within certain stated hours. In Japan, capsule _____ s provide a tiny room suitable only for sleeping and shared bathroom facilities.

Exam Probability: **Low**

58. *Answer choices:*

(see index for correct answer)

- a. Professional Development Program
- b. Group booking
- c. Hotel
- d. Hospitality Review

Guidance: level 1

:: Scientific method ::

In the social sciences and life sciences, a _____ is a research method involving an up-close, in-depth, and detailed examination of a subject of study, as well as its related contextual conditions.

Exam Probability: **High**

59. *Answer choices:*

(see index for correct answer)

- a. explanatory research
- b. pilot project
- c. Causal research
- d. Case study

Guidance: level 1

Business law

Corporate law (also known as business law) is the body of law governing the rights, relations, and conduct of persons, companies, organizations and businesses. It refers to the legal practice relating to, or the theory of corporations. Corporate law often describes the law relating to matters which derive directly from the life-cycle of a corporation. It thus encompasses the formation, funding, governance, and death of a corporation.

:: Business law ::

A _____ is a legal right granted by a debtor to a creditor over the debtor's property which enables the creditor to have recourse to the property if the debtor defaults in making payment or otherwise performing the secured obligations. One of the most common examples of a _____ is a mortgage: When person, by the action of an expressed conveyance, pledges by a promise to pay a certain sum of money, with certain conditions, on a said date or dates for a said period, that action on the page with wet ink applied on the part of the one wishing the exchange creates the original funds and negotiable Instrument. That action of pledging conveys a promise binding upon the mortgagee which creates a face value upon the Instrument of the amount of currency being asked for in exchange. It is therein in good faith offered to the Bank in exchange for local currency from the Bank to buy a house. The particular country's Bank Acts usually requires the Banks to deliver such fund bearing negotiable instruments to the Countries Main Bank such as is the case in Canada. This creates a _____ in the land the house sits on for the Bank and they file a caveat at land titles on the house as evidence of that _____ . If the mortgagee fails to pay defaulting in his promise to repay the exchange, the bank then applies to the court to for-close on your property to eventually sell the house and apply the proceeds to the outstanding exchange.

Exam Probability: **Low**

1. *Answer choices:*

(see index for correct answer)

- a. Wrongful trading
- b. WIPO Copyright Treaty
- c. Security interest
- d. Lex mercatoria

Guidance: level 1

:: Project management ::

A _____ is a source or supply from which a benefit is produced and it has some utility. _____ s can broadly be classified upon their availability—they are classified into renewable and non-renewable _____ s. Examples of non renewable _____ s are coal, crude oil natural gas nuclear energy etc. Examples of renewable _____ s are air, water, wind, solar energy etc. They can also be classified as actual and potential on the basis of level of development and use, on the basis of origin they can be classified as biotic and abiotic, and on the basis of their distribution, as ubiquitous and localized. An item becomes a _____ with time and developing technology. Typically, _____ s are materials, energy, services, staff, knowledge, or other assets that are transformed to produce benefit and in the process may be consumed or made unavailable. Benefits of _____ utilization may include increased wealth, proper functioning of a system, or enhanced well-being. From a human perspective a natural _____ is anything obtained from the environment to satisfy human needs and wants. From a broader biological or ecological perspective a _____ satisfies the needs of a living organism.

Exam Probability: **Medium**

2. *Answer choices:*

(see index for correct answer)

- a. Resource
- b. Bid manager
- c. Punch list
- d. Outcomes theory

Guidance: level 1

:: ::

A _____ is any person who contracts to acquire an asset in return for some form of consideration.

Exam Probability: **High**

3. *Answer choices:*

(see index for correct answer)

- a. Character
- b. imperative
- c. corporate values
- d. Buyer

Guidance: level 1

:: Legal procedure ::

_____ , adjective law, or rules of court comprises the rules by which a court hears and determines what happens in civil, lawsuit, criminal or administrative proceedings. The rules are designed to ensure a fair and consistent application of due process or fundamental justice to all cases that come before a court.

Exam Probability: **Medium**

4. *Answer choices:*

(see index for correct answer)

- a. Opening statement
- b. civil procedure
- c. Closing argument
- d. appellate

Guidance: level 1

:: Legal doctrines and principles ::

> In some common law jurisdictions, _____ is a defense to a tort claim based on negligence. If it is available, the defense completely bars plaintiffs from any recovery if they contribute to their own injury through their own negligence.

Exam Probability: **High**

5. *Answer choices:*

(see index for correct answer)

- a. Mutual mistake
- b. Contributory negligence
- c. unconscionable contract
- d. Duty to rescue

Guidance: level 1

:: ::

An _____ is a contingent motivator. Traditional _____ s are extrinsic motivators which reward actions to yield a desired outcome. The effectiveness of traditional _____ s has changed as the needs of Western society have evolved. While the traditional _____ model is effective when there is a defined procedure and goal for a task, Western society started to require a higher volume of critical thinkers, so the traditional model became less effective. Institutions are now following a trend in implementing strategies that rely on intrinsic motivations rather than the extrinsic motivations that the traditional _____ s foster.

Exam Probability: **High**

6. *Answer choices:*

(see index for correct answer)

- a. co-culture
- b. levels of analysis
- c. hierarchical
- d. Incentive

Guidance: level 1

:: Fraud ::

_____ is the deliberate use of someone else's identity, usually as a method to gain a financial advantage or obtain credit and other benefits in the other person's name, and perhaps to the other person's disadvantage or loss. The person whose identity has been assumed may suffer adverse consequences, especially if they are held responsible for the perpetrator's actions.
_____ occurs when someone uses another's personally identifying information, like their name, identifying number, or credit card number, without their permission, to commit fraud or other crimes. The term _____ was coined in 1964. Since that time, the definition of _____ has been statutorily prescribed throughout both the U.K. and the United States as the theft of personally identifying information, generally including a person's name, date of birth, social security number, driver's license number, bank account or credit card numbers, PIN numbers, electronic signatures, fingerprints, passwords, or any other information that can be used to access a person's financial resources.

Exam Probability: **High**

7. *Answer choices:*

(see index for correct answer)

- a. Identity theft
- b. Shell corporation
- c. Lip sync
- d. Employment fraud

Guidance: level 1

:: Legal doctrines and principles ::

In the United States, the _____ is a legal rule, based on constitutional law, that prevents evidence collected or analyzed in violation of the defendant's constitutional rights from being used in a court of law. This may be considered an example of a prophylactic rule formulated by the judiciary in order to protect a constitutional right. The _____ may also, in some circumstances at least, be considered to follow directly from the constitutional language, such as the Fifth Amendment's command that no person "shall be compelled in any criminal case to be a witness against himself" and that no person "shall be deprived of life, liberty or property without due process of law".

Exam Probability: **High**

8. *Answer choices:*

(see index for correct answer)

- a. Exclusionary rule
- b. Attractive nuisance
- c. Proximate cause
- d. Attractive nuisance doctrine

Guidance: level 1

:: Parental leave ::

_____ is a type of employment discrimination that occurs when expectant women are fired, not hired, or otherwise discriminated against due to their pregnancy or intention to become pregnant. Common forms of _____ include not being hired due to visible pregnancy or likelihood of becoming pregnant, being fired after informing an employer of one's pregnancy, being fired after maternity leave, and receiving a pay dock due to pregnancy. Convention on the Elimination of All Forms of Discrimination against Women prohibits dismissal on the grounds of maternity or pregnancy and ensures right to maternity leave or comparable social benefits. The Maternity Protection Convention C 183 proclaims adequate protection for pregnancy as well. Though women have some protection in the United States because of the _____ Act of 1978, it has not completely curbed the incidence of _____ . The Equal Rights Amendment could ensure more robust sex equality ensuring that women and men could both work and have children at the same time.

Exam Probability: **High**

9. *Answer choices:*

(see index for correct answer)

- a. Pregnancy discrimination
- b. Parental leave economics
- c. Geduldig v. Aiello
- d. Additional Paternity Leave Regulations 2010

Guidance: level 1

:: Business law ::

A _____ is a document guaranteeing the payment of a specific amount of money, either on demand, or at a set time, with the payer usually named on the document. More specifically, it is a document contemplated by or consisting of a contract, which promises the payment of money without condition, which may be paid either on demand or at a future date. The term can have different meanings, depending on what law is being applied and what country and context it is used in.

Exam Probability: **Low**

10. *Answer choices:*

(see index for correct answer)

- a. Undervalue transaction
- b. Negotiable instrument
- c. Unfair competition
- d. Complex structured finance transactions

Guidance: level 1

:: Insurance terms ::

_____ is the assumption by a third party of another party's legal right to collect a debt or damages. It is a legal doctrine whereby one person is entitled to enforce the subsisting or revived rights of another for one's own benefit. A right of _____ typically arises by operation of law, but can also arise by statute or by agreement. _____ is an equitable remedy, having first developed in the English Court of Chancery. It is a familiar feature of common law systems. Analogous doctrines exist in civil law jurisdictions.

Exam Probability: **Low**

11. *Answer choices:*

(see index for correct answer)

- a. Accident management
- b. Subrogation
- c. Beneficiary
- d. Aggression insurance

Guidance: level 1

:: Anti-competitive behaviour ::

Restraints of trade is a common law doctrine relating to the enforceability of contractual restrictions on freedom to conduct business. It is a precursor of modern competition law. In an old leading case of Mitchel v Reynolds Lord Smith LC said,

Exam Probability: **Low**

12. *Answer choices:*

(see index for correct answer)

- a. Tying
- b. Restraint of trade
- c. Pacman conjecture
- d. Ernest Varacalli

Guidance: level 1

:: ::

A contract is a legally-binding agreement which recognises and governs the rights and duties of the parties to the agreement. A contract is legally enforceable because it meets the requirements and approval of the law. An agreement typically involves the exchange of goods, services, money, or promises of any of those. In the event of breach of contract, the law awards the injured party access to legal remedies such as damages and cancellation.

Exam Probability: **Low**

13. *Answer choices:*

(see index for correct answer)

- a. Contract law
- b. empathy

- c. imperative
- d. levels of analysis

Guidance: level 1

:: Debt ::

A _____ is a party that has a claim on the services of a second party. It is a person or institution to whom money is owed. The first party, in general, has provided some property or service to the second party under the assumption that the second party will return an equivalent property and service. The second party is frequently called a debtor or borrower. The first party is called the _____ , which is the lender of property, service, or money.

Exam Probability: **High**

14. *Answer choices:*

(see index for correct answer)

- a. Museum of Foreign Debt
- b. Troubled Debt Restructuring
- c. Consumer debt
- d. Creditor

Guidance: level 1

_____s and acquisitions are transactions in which the ownership of companies, other business organizations, or their operating units are transferred or consolidated with other entities. As an aspect of strategic management, M&A can allow enterprises to grow or downsize, and change the nature of their business or competitive position.

Exam Probability: **Medium**

15. *Answer choices:*

(see index for correct answer)

- a. empathy
- b. interpersonal communication
- c. hierarchical perspective
- d. open system

Guidance: level 1

Employment is a relationship between two parties, usually based on a contract where work is paid for, where one party, which may be a corporation, for profit, not-for-profit organization, co-operative or other entity is the employer and the other is the employee. Employees work in return for payment, which may be in the form of an hourly wage, by piecework or an annual salary, depending on the type of work an employee does or which sector she or he is working in. Employees in some fields or sectors may receive gratuities, bonus payment or stock options. In some types of employment, employees may receive benefits in addition to payment. Benefits can include health insurance, housing, disability insurance or use of a gym. Employment is typically governed by employment laws, regulations or legal contracts.

Exam Probability: **High**

16. *Answer choices:*

(see index for correct answer)

- a. open system
- b. hierarchical perspective
- c. deep-level diversity
- d. Personnel

Guidance: level 1

:: Commercial crimes ::

In law, _____ is the unauthorized use of another's name, likeness, or identity without that person's permission, resulting in harm to that person.

Exam Probability: **Medium**

17. *Answer choices:*

(see index for correct answer)

- a. Skimming
- b. Anti-money laundering software
- c. Fraudulent conveyance
- d. Late trading

Guidance: level 1

:: ::

Business is the activity of making one's living or making money by producing or buying and selling products . Simply put, it is "any activity or enterprise entered into for profit. It does not mean it is a company, a corporation, partnership, or have any such formal organization, but it can range from a street peddler to General Motors."

Exam Probability: **Low**

18. *Answer choices:*

(see index for correct answer)

- a. hierarchical
- b. Firm

- c. similarity-attraction theory
- d. cultural

Guidance: level 1

:: Intention ::

> _____ is the mental element of a person's intention to commit a crime; or knowledge that one's action or lack of action would cause a crime to be committed. It is a necessary element of many crimes.

Exam Probability: **Low**

19. *Answer choices:*

(see index for correct answer)

- a. Mens rea
- b. Letter of Intent

Guidance: level 1

:: Contract law ::

Offer and acceptance analysis is a traditional approach in contract law. The offer and acceptance formula, developed in the 19th century, identifies a moment of formation when the parties are of one mind. This classical approach to contract formation has been modified by developments in the law of estoppel, misleading conduct, misrepresentation and unjust enrichment.

Exam Probability: **Low**

20. *Answer choices:*

(see index for correct answer)

- a. Offeror
- b. French contract law
- c. Exceptio non adimpleti contractus
- d. Fixed-price contract

Guidance: level 1

:: Commercial crimes ::

_____ is the process of concealing the origins of money obtained illegally by passing it through a complex sequence of banking transfers or commercial transactions. The overall scheme of this process returns the money to the launderer in an obscure and indirect way.

Exam Probability: **Medium**

21. *Answer choices:*

(see index for correct answer)

- a. Financial intelligence
- b. Chiasso financial smuggling case
- c. Cartel
- d. Money laundering

Guidance: level 1

:: Fair use ::

> _____ is a doctrine in the law of the United States that permits limited use of copyrighted material without having to first acquire permission from the copyright holder. _____ is one of the limitations to copyright intended to balance the interests of copyright holders with the public interest in the wider distribution and use of creative works by allowing as a defense to copyright infringement claims certain limited uses that might otherwise be considered infringement.

Exam Probability: **Low**

22. *Answer choices:*

(see index for correct answer)

- a. Fair use
- b. Toward a Fair Use Standard
- c. Derivative work

- d. Nominative use

Guidance: level 1

:: Business law ::

_____ is where a person's financial liability is limited to a fixed sum, most commonly the value of a person's investment in a company or partnership. If a company with _____ is sued, then the claimants are suing the company, not its owners or investors. A shareholder in a limited company is not personally liable for any of the debts of the company, other than for the amount already invested in the company and for any unpaid amount on the shares in the company, if any. The same is true for the members of a _____ partnership and the limited partners in a limited partnership. By contrast, sole proprietors and partners in general partnerships are each liable for all the debts of the business.

Exam Probability: **High**

23. *Answer choices:*

(see index for correct answer)

- a. Stick licensing
- b. Trading while insolvent
- c. Power harassment
- d. Limited liability

Guidance: level 1

:: Marketing ::

_____ comes from the Latin neg and otsia referring to businessmen who, unlike the patricians, had no leisure time in their industriousness; it held the meaning of business until the 17th century when it took on the diplomatic connotation as a dialogue between two or more people or parties intended to reach a beneficial outcome over one or more issues where a conflict exists with respect to at least one of these issues. Thus, _____ is a process of combining divergent positions into a joint agreement under a decision rule of unanimity.

Exam Probability: **Low**

24. *Answer choices:*

(see index for correct answer)

- a. Negotiation
- b. Inventory
- c. Corporate capabilities package
- d. Davie-Brown Index

Guidance: level 1

:: Labour relations ::

_____ is a field of study that can have different meanings depending on the context in which it is used. In an international context, it is a subfield of labor history that studies the human relations with regard to work – in its broadest sense – and how this connects to questions of social inequality. It explicitly encompasses unregulated, historical, and non-Western forms of labor. Here, _____ define "for or with whom one works and under what rules. These rules determine the type of work, type and amount of remuneration, working hours, degrees of physical and psychological strain, as well as the degree of freedom and autonomy associated with the work."

Exam Probability: **Low**

25. *Answer choices:*

(see index for correct answer)

- a. Comprehensive campaign
- b. Labor relations
- c. Inflatable rat
- d. Association of German Chambers of Industry and Commerce

Guidance: level 1

:: ::

> Punishment is the imposition of an undesirable or unpleasant outcome upon a group or individual, meted out by an authority—in contexts ranging from child discipline to criminal law—as a response and deterrent to a particular action or behaviour that is deemed undesirable or unacceptable. The reasoning may be to condition a child to avoid self-endangerment, to impose social conformity, to defend norms, to protect against future harms, and to maintain the law—and respect for rule of law—under which the social group is governed. Punishment may be self-inflicted as with self-flagellation and mortification of the flesh in the religious setting, but is most often a form of social coercion.

Exam Probability: **High**

26. *Answer choices:*

(see index for correct answer)

- a. functional perspective
- b. deep-level diversity
- c. process perspective
- d. Punitive

Guidance: level 1

:: ::

A lawsuit is a proceeding by a party or parties against another in the civil court of law. The archaic term "suit in law" is found in only a small number of laws still in effect today. The term "lawsuit" is used in reference to a civil action brought in a court of law in which a plaintiff, a party who claims to have incurred loss as a result of a defendant's actions, demands a legal or equitable remedy. The defendant is required to respond to the plaintiff's complaint. If the plaintiff is successful, judgment is in the plaintiff's favor, and a variety of court orders may be issued to enforce a right, award damages, or impose a temporary or permanent injunction to prevent an act or compel an act. A declaratory judgment may be issued to prevent future legal disputes.

Exam Probability: **Low**

27. *Answer choices:*
(see index for correct answer)

- a. process perspective
- b. Litigation
- c. interpersonal communication
- d. deep-level diversity

Guidance: level 1

:: ::

In legal terminology, a _____ is any formal legal document that sets out the facts and legal reasons that the filing party or parties believes are sufficient to support a claim against the party or parties against whom the claim is brought that entitles the plaintiff to a remedy. For example, the Federal Rules of Civil Procedure that govern civil litigation in United States courts provide that a civil action is commenced with the filing or service of a pleading called a _____. Civil court rules in states that have incorporated the Federal Rules of Civil Procedure use the same term for the same pleading.

Exam Probability: **Low**

28. *Answer choices:*

(see index for correct answer)

- a. cultural
- b. Complaint
- c. imperative
- d. open system

Guidance: level 1

:: ::

In common law legal systems, _____ is a principle or rule established in a previous legal case that is either binding on or persuasive for a court or other tribunal when deciding subsequent cases with similar issues or facts. Common-law legal systems place great value on deciding cases according to consistent principled rules, so that similar facts will yield similar and predictable outcomes, and observance of _____ is the mechanism by which that goal is attained. The principle by which judges are bound to _____ s is known as stare decisis. Common-law _____ is a third kind of law, on equal footing with statutory law and delegated legislation or regulatory law.

Exam Probability: **High**

29. *Answer choices:*

(see index for correct answer)

- a. functional perspective
- b. Precedent
- c. open system
- d. surface-level diversity

Guidance: level 1

:: ::

The _____ of 1973, , is a federal law, codified as 29 U.S.C. § 701 et seq. The principal sponsor of the bill was Rep. John Brademas [IN-3]. The _____ of 1973 replaces the Vocational _____ of 1973, to extend and revise the authorization of grants to States for vocational rehabilitation services, with special emphasis on services to those with the most severe disabilities, to expand special Federal responsibilities and research and training programs with respect to individuals with disabilities, to establish special responsibilities in the Secretary of Health, Education, and Welfare for coordination of all programs with respect to individuals with disabilities within the Department of Health, Education, and Welfare, and for other purposes.

Exam Probability: **High**

30. *Answer choices:*

(see index for correct answer)

- a. interpersonal communication
- b. information systems assessment
- c. empathy
- d. Rehabilitation Act

Guidance: level 1

:: Legal doctrines and principles ::

In law, a _____ is an event sufficiently related to an injury that the courts deem the event to be the cause of that injury. There are two types of causation in the law: cause-in-fact, and proximate cause. Cause-in-fact is determined by the "but for" test: But for the action, the result would not have happened. The action is a necessary condition, but may not be a sufficient condition, for the resulting injury. A few circumstances exist where the but for test is ineffective. Since but-for causation is very easy to show, a second test is used to determine if an action is close enough to a harm in a "chain of events" to be legally valid. This test is called _____.
_____ is a key principle of Insurance and is concerned with how the loss or damage actually occurred. There are several competing theories of _____. For an act to be deemed to cause a harm, both tests must be met; _____ is a legal limitation on cause-in-fact.

Exam Probability: **High**

31. *Answer choices:*

(see index for correct answer)

- a. Acquiescence
- b. Abstention doctrine
- c. Proximate cause
- d. Caveat emptor

Guidance: level 1

_____ is widespread, interconnected digital technology. The term entered the popular culture from science fiction and the arts but is now used by technology strategists, security professionals, government, military and industry leaders and entrepreneurs to describe the domain of the global technology environment. Others consider _____ to be just a notional environment in which communication over computer networks occurs. The word became popular in the 1990s when the uses of the Internet, networking, and digital communication were all growing dramatically and the term "_____" was able to represent the many new ideas and phenomena that were emerging. It has been called the largest unregulated and uncontrolled domain in the history of mankind, and is also unique because it is a domain created by people vice the traditional physical domains.

Exam Probability: **Medium**

32. *Answer choices:*

(see index for correct answer)

- a. interpersonal communication
- b. deep-level diversity
- c. similarity-attraction theory
- d. hierarchical

Guidance: level 1

:: Sureties ::

In finance, a _____, _____ bond or guaranty involves a promise by one party to assume responsibility for the debt obligation of a borrower if that borrower defaults. The person or company providing the promise is also known as a "_____" or as a "guarantor".

Exam Probability: **Medium**

33. *Answer choices:*

(see index for correct answer)

- a. Surety
- b. Parole bond
- c. Little Miller Act
- d. Estreature

Guidance: level 1

:: ::

A _____, or trial by jury, is a lawful proceeding in which a jury makes a decision or findings of fact. It is distinguished from a bench trial in which a judge or panel of judges makes all decisions.

Exam Probability: **Medium**

34. *Answer choices:*

(see index for correct answer)

- a. deep-level diversity
- b. cultural
- c. co-culture
- d. Jury Trial

Guidance: level 1

:: ::

An _____ is an area of the production, distribution, or trade, and consumption of goods and services by different agents. Understood in its broadest sense, `The _____ is defined as a social domain that emphasize the practices, discourses, and material expressions associated with the production, use, and management of resources`. Economic agents can be individuals, businesses, organizations, or governments. Economic transactions occur when two parties agree to the value or price of the transacted good or service, commonly expressed in a certain currency. However, monetary transactions only account for a small part of the economic domain.

Exam Probability: **Medium**

35. *Answer choices:*
(see index for correct answer)

- a. Economy
- b. levels of analysis
- c. Sarbanes-Oxley act of 2002
- d. process perspective

Guidance: level 1

:: Auctioneering ::

An _____ is a process of buying and selling goods or services by offering them up for bid, taking bids, and then selling the item to the highest bidder. The open ascending price _____ is arguably the most common form of _____ in use today. Participants bid openly against one another, with each subsequent bid required to be higher than the previous bid. An _____ eer may announce prices, bidders may call out their bids themselves, or bids may be submitted electronically with the highest current bid publicly displayed. In a Dutch _____ , the _____ eer begins with a high asking price for some quantity of like items; the price is lowered until a participant is willing to accept the _____ eer's price for some quantity of the goods in the lot or until the seller's reserve price is met. While _____ s are most associated in the public imagination with the sale of antiques, paintings, rare collectibles and expensive wines, _____ s are also used for commodities, livestock, radio spectrum and used cars. In economic theory, an _____ may refer to any mechanism or set of trading rules for exchange.

Exam Probability: **Low**

36. *Answer choices:*

(see index for correct answer)

- a. Auction catalog
- b. Forward auction
- c. Vehicle impoundment
- d. Auction

Guidance: level 1

:: ::

A federation is a political entity characterized by a union of partially self-governing provinces, states, or other regions under a central _____ . In a federation, the self-governing status of the component states, as well as the division of power between them and the central government, is typically constitutionally entrenched and may not be altered by a unilateral decision of either party, the states or the federal political body. Alternatively, federation is a form of government in which sovereign power is formally divided between a central authority and a number of constituent regions so that each region retains some degree of control over its internal affairs. It is often argued that federal states where the central government has the constitutional authority to suspend a constituent state's government by invoking gross mismanagement or civil unrest, or to adopt national legislation that overrides or infringe on the constituent states' powers by invoking the central government's constitutional authority to ensure "peace and good government" or to implement obligations contracted under an international treaty, are not truly federal states.

Exam Probability: **Low**

37. *Answer choices:*

(see index for correct answer)

- a. surface-level diversity
- b. information systems assessment
- c. interpersonal communication
- d. Federal government

Guidance: level 1

:: Commercial crimes ::

_____ is the act of withholding assets for the purpose of conversion of such assets, by one or more persons to whom the assets were entrusted, either to be held or to be used for specific purposes. _____ is a type of financial fraud. For example, a lawyer might embezzle funds from the trust accounts of their clients; a financial advisor might embezzle the funds of investors; and a husband or a wife might embezzle funds from a bank account jointly held with the spouse.

Exam Probability: **Medium**

38. *Answer choices:*

(see index for correct answer)

- a. pilferage
- b. Offshore leaks
- c. Price gouging
- d. False advertising

Guidance: level 1

:: ::

A concept of English law, a _____ is an untrue or misleading statement of fact made during negotiations by one party to another, the statement then inducing that other party into the contract. The misled party may normally rescind the contract, and sometimes may be awarded damages as well.

Exam Probability: **High**

39. *Answer choices:*

(see index for correct answer)

- a. open system
- b. imperative
- c. Misrepresentation
- d. deep-level diversity

Guidance: level 1

:: ::

_____ is a process under which executive or legislative actions are subject to review by the judiciary. A court with authority for _____ may invalidate laws, acts and governmental actions that are incompatible with a higher authority: an executive decision may be invalidated for being unlawful or a statute may be invalidated for violating the terms of a constitution. _____ is one of the checks and balances in the separation of powers: the power of the judiciary to supervise the legislative and executive branches when the latter exceed their authority. The doctrine varies between jurisdictions, so the procedure and scope of _____ may differ between and within countries.

Exam Probability: **Low**

40. *Answer choices:*

(see index for correct answer)

- a. Judicial review
- b. similarity-attraction theory
- c. open system
- d. surface-level diversity

Guidance: level 1

:: Legal terms ::

_____, a form of alternative dispute resolution, is a way to resolve disputes outside the courts. The dispute will be decided by one or more persons, which renders the " _____ award". An _____ award is legally binding on both sides and enforceable in the courts.

Exam Probability: **High**

41. *Answer choices:*

(see index for correct answer)

- a. Ex demissione
- b. McKenzie friend
- c. Arbitration
- d. Harmonisation of law

Guidance: level 1

:: ::

> In international relations, _____ is – from the perspective of governments – a voluntary transfer of resources from one country to another.

Exam Probability: **High**

42. *Answer choices:*

(see index for correct answer)

- a. deep-level diversity
- b. Aid
- c. hierarchical perspective
- d. surface-level diversity

Guidance: level 1

:: ::

_____ is that part of a civil law legal system which is part of the jus commune that involves relationships between individuals, such as the law of contracts or torts , and the law of obligations . It is to be distinguished from public law, which deals with relationships between both natural and artificial persons and the state, including regulatory statutes, penal law and other law that affects the public order. In general terms, _____ involves interactions between private citizens, whereas public law involves interrelations between the state and the general population.

Exam Probability: **High**

43. *Answer choices:*

(see index for correct answer)

- a. personal values
- b. Private law
- c. Sarbanes-Oxley act of 2002
- d. functional perspective

Guidance: level 1

:: Contract law ::

_____, in human interactions, is a sincere intention to be fair, open, and honest, regardless of the outcome of the interaction. While some Latin phrases lose their literal meaning over centuries, this is not the case with bona fides; it is still widely used and interchangeable with its generally accepted modern-day English translation of _____. It is an important concept within law and business. The opposed concepts are bad faith, mala fides and perfidy. In contemporary English, the usage of bona fides is synonymous with credentials and identity. The phrase is sometimes used in job advertisements, and should not be confused with the bona fide occupational qualifications or the employer's _____ effort, as described below.

Exam Probability: **Medium**

44. *Answer choices:*

(see index for correct answer)

- a. Community Benefits Agreement
- b. Terms of service
- c. Publishing contract
- d. Good faith

Guidance: level 1

:: Generally Accepted Accounting Principles ::

Expenditure is an outflow of money to another person or group to pay for an item or service, or for a category of costs. For a tenant, rent is an _____. For students or parents, tuition is an _____. Buying food, clothing, furniture or an automobile is often referred to as an _____. An _____ is a cost that is "paid" or "remitted", usually in exchange for something of value. Something that seems to cost a great deal is "expensive". Something that seems to cost little is "inexpensive". "_____ s of the table" are _____ s of dining, refreshments, a feast, etc.

Exam Probability: **Low**

45. *Answer choices:*

(see index for correct answer)

- a. Indian Accounting Standards
- b. Expense
- c. AICPA Statements of Position
- d. Consolidation

Guidance: level 1

:: ::

In logic and philosophy, an _____ is a series of statements, called the premises or premisses, intended to determine the degree of truth of another statement, the conclusion. The logical form of an _____ in a natural language can be represented in a symbolic formal language, and independently of natural language formally defined "_____ s" can be made in math and computer science.

Exam Probability: **High**

46. *Answer choices:*

(see index for correct answer)

- a. Argument
- b. surface-level diversity
- c. hierarchical perspective
- d. Character

Guidance: level 1

:: Stock market ::

The _____ of a corporation is all of the shares into which ownership of the corporation is divided. In American English, the shares are commonly known as " _____ s". A single share of the _____ represents fractional ownership of the corporation in proportion to the total number of shares. This typically entitles the _____ holder to that fraction of the company's earnings, proceeds from liquidation of assets, or voting power, often dividing these up in proportion to the amount of money each _____ holder has invested. Not all _____ is necessarily equal, as certain classes of _____ may be issued for example without voting rights, with enhanced voting rights, or with a certain priority to receive profits or liquidation proceeds before or after other classes of shareholders.

Exam Probability: **Medium**

47. *Answer choices:*

(see index for correct answer)

- a. Clientele effect
- b. Initial public offering
- c. Block premium
- d. Stock

Guidance: level 1

:: Real property law ::

> _____, sometimes colloquially described as 'squatter's rights', is a legal principle under which a person who does not have legal title to a piece of property—usually land —acquires legal ownership based on continuous possession or occupation of the land without the permission of its legal owner.

Exam Probability: **High**

48. *Answer choices:*

(see index for correct answer)

- a. Deed
- b. Servient estate
- c. Half-foot
- d. Adverse possession

Guidance: level 1

:: ::

_____ or accountancy is the measurement, processing, and communication of financial information about economic entities such as businesses and corporations. The modern field was established by the Italian mathematician Luca Pacioli in 1494. _____, which has been called the "language of business", measures the results of an organization's economic activities and conveys this information to a variety of users, including investors, creditors, management, and regulators. Practitioners of _____ are known as accountants. The terms "_____" and "financial reporting" are often used as synonyms.

Exam Probability: **Medium**

49. *Answer choices:*

(see index for correct answer)

- a. personal values
- b. similarity-attraction theory
- c. deep-level diversity
- d. Accounting

Guidance: level 1

:: Criminal procedure ::

In law, a verdict is the formal finding of fact made by a jury on matters or questions submitted to the jury by a judge. In a bench trial, the judge's decision near the end of the trial is simply referred to as a finding. In England and Wales, a coroner's findings are called verdicts.

Exam Probability: **Medium**

50. *Answer choices:*

(see index for correct answer)

- a. criminal procedure
- b. Directed verdict

Guidance: level 1

:: ::

The U.S. _____ is an independent agency of the United States federal government. The SEC holds primary responsibility for enforcing the federal securities laws, proposing securities rules, and regulating the securities industry, the nation's stock and options exchanges, and other activities and organizations, including the electronic securities markets in the United States.

Exam Probability: **Low**

51. *Answer choices:*

(see index for correct answer)

- a. Character
- b. information systems assessment
- c. Securities and Exchange Commission
- d. similarity-attraction theory

Guidance: level 1

:: ::

In financial markets, a share is a unit used as mutual funds, limited partnerships, and real estate investment trusts. The owner of _____ in the corporation/company is a shareholder of the corporation. A share is an indivisible unit of capital, expressing the ownership relationship between the company and the shareholder. The denominated value of a share is its face value, and the total of the face value of issued _____ represent the capital of a company, which may not reflect the market value of those _____ .

Exam Probability: **High**

52. *Answer choices:*

(see index for correct answer)

- a. empathy
- b. Shares
- c. corporate values

- d. Sarbanes-Oxley act of 2002

Guidance: level 1

:: Business models ::

A _____ is "an autonomous association of persons united voluntarily to meet their common economic, social, and cultural needs and aspirations through a jointly-owned and democratically-controlled enterprise". _____ s may include.

Exam Probability: **Medium**

53. *Answer choices:*
(see index for correct answer)

- a. Organizational architecture
- b. Data as a service
- c. Defensive patent aggregation
- d. Cooperative

Guidance: level 1

:: ::

The _____ Act of 1890 was a United States antitrust law that regulates competition among enterprises, which was passed by Congress under the presidency of Benjamin Harrison.

Exam Probability: **Low**

54. *Answer choices:*

(see index for correct answer)

- a. hierarchical
- b. Sherman Antitrust
- c. empathy
- d. functional perspective

Guidance: level 1

:: ::

_____ is a judicial device in common law legal systems whereby a court may prevent, or "estop" a person from making assertions or from going back on his or her word; the person being sanctioned is "estopped". _____ may prevent someone from bringing a particular claim. Legal doctrines of _____ are based in both common law and equity.

Exam Probability: **High**

55. *Answer choices:*

(see index for correct answer)

- a. deep-level diversity
- b. hierarchical
- c. Estoppel
- d. functional perspective

Guidance: level 1

:: ::

In regulatory jurisdictions that provide for it , _____ is a group of laws and organizations designed to ensure the rights of consumers as well as fair trade, competition and accurate information in the marketplace. The laws are designed to prevent the businesses that engage in fraud or specified unfair practices from gaining an advantage over competitors. They may also provides additional protection for those most vulnerable in society. _____ laws are a form of government regulation that aim to protect the rights of consumers. For example, a government may require businesses to disclose detailed information about products—particularly in areas where safety or public health is an issue, such as food.

Exam Probability: **Low**

56. *Answer choices:*
(see index for correct answer)

- a. similarity-attraction theory
- b. Consumer protection

- c. information systems assessment
- d. functional perspective

Guidance: level 1

:: Contract law ::

In the United States, the _____ rule refers to the legal right for a buyer of goods to insist upon " _____ " by the seller. In a contract for the sale of goods, if the goods fail to conform exactly to the description in the contract the buyer may nonetheless accept the goods, or reject the goods, or reject the nonconforming part of the tender and accept the conforming part. The buyer does not have an unfettered ability to reject tender.

Exam Probability: **High**

57. *Answer choices:*

(see index for correct answer)

- a. Offeree
- b. Per minas
- c. Seaworthiness
- d. Duress

Guidance: level 1

:: ::

_____ is the consumption and saving opportunity gained by an entity within a specified timeframe, which is generally expressed in monetary terms. For households and individuals, "_____ is the sum of all the wages, salaries, profits, interest payments, rents, and other forms of earnings received in a given period of time."

Exam Probability: **High**

58. *Answer choices:*

(see index for correct answer)

- a. surface-level diversity
- b. interpersonal communication
- c. corporate values
- d. Income

Guidance: level 1

:: ::

A _____ is the party who initiates a lawsuit before a court. By doing so, the _____ seeks a legal remedy; if this search is successful, the court will issue judgment in favor of the _____ and make the appropriate court order . "_____" is the term used in civil cases in most English-speaking jurisdictions, the notable exception being England and Wales, where a _____ has, since the introduction of the Civil Procedure Rules in 1999, been known as a "claimant", but that term also has other meanings. In criminal cases, the prosecutor brings the case against the defendant, but the key complaining party is often called the "complainant".

Exam Probability: **Low**

59. *Answer choices:*

(see index for correct answer)

- a. surface-level diversity
- b. Plaintiff
- c. cultural
- d. empathy

Guidance: level 1

Finance

Finance is a field that is concerned with the allocation (investment) of assets and liabilities over space and time, often under conditions of risk or uncertainty. Finance can also be defined as the science of money management. Participants in the market aim to price assets based on their risk level, fundamental value, and their expected rate of return. Finance can be split into three sub-categories: public finance, corporate finance and personal finance.

:: Project management ::

Some scenarios associate "this kind of planning" with learning "life skills". _____ s are necessary, or at least useful, in situations where individuals need to know what time they must be at a specific location to receive a specific service, and where people need to accomplish a set of goals within a set time period.

Exam Probability: **Medium**

1. *Answer choices:*

(see index for correct answer)

- a. System anatomy
- b. Schedule
- c. Life-cycle cost analysis
- d. Cone of Uncertainty

Guidance: level 1

:: Basic financial concepts ::

In finance, maturity or _____ refers to the final payment date of a loan or other financial instrument, at which point the principal is due to be paid.

Exam Probability: **Medium**

2. *Answer choices:*

(see index for correct answer)

- a. Maturity date
- b. Lodgement
- c. Base effect
- d. Eurodollar

Guidance: level 1

:: Options (finance) ::

A _____, often simply labeled a "call", is a financial contract between two parties, the buyer and the seller of this type of option. The buyer of the _____ has the right, but not the obligation, to buy an agreed quantity of a particular commodity or financial instrument from the seller of the option at a certain time for a certain price. The seller is obligated to sell the commodity or financial instrument to the buyer if the buyer so decides. The buyer pays a fee for this right. The term "call" comes from the fact that the owner has the right to "call the stock away" from the seller.

Exam Probability: **Medium**

3. *Answer choices:*

(see index for correct answer)

- a. Credit default option
- b. LEAPS
- c. Chicago Options Associates

- d. Call option

Guidance: level 1

:: ::

_____ is a marketing communication that employs an openly sponsored, non-personal message to promote or sell a product, service or idea. Sponsors of _____ are typically businesses wishing to promote their products or services. _____ is differentiated from public relations in that an advertiser pays for and has control over the message. It differs from personal selling in that the message is non-personal, i.e., not directed to a particular individual. _____ is communicated through various mass media, including traditional media such as newspapers, magazines, television, radio, outdoor _____ or direct mail; and new media such as search results, blogs, social media, websites or text messages. The actual presentation of the message in a medium is referred to as an advertisement, or "ad" or advert for short.

Exam Probability: **Low**

4. *Answer choices:*

(see index for correct answer)

- a. interpersonal communication
- b. process perspective
- c. Advertising
- d. functional perspective

Guidance: level 1

:: Financial accounting ::

_____ is a financial metric which represents operating liquidity available to a business, organisation or other entity, including governmental entities. Along with fixed assets such as plant and equipment, _____ is considered a part of operating capital. Gross _____ is equal to current assets. _____ is calculated as current assets minus current liabilities. If current assets are less than current liabilities, an entity has a _____ deficiency, also called a _____ deficit.

Exam Probability: **Low**

5. *Answer choices:*

(see index for correct answer)

- a. Advance payment
- b. Working capital
- c. Fixed asset register
- d. Hidden asset

Guidance: level 1

:: Finance ::

The _____ of a corporation is the accumulated net income of the corporation that is retained by the corporation at a particular point of time, such as at the end of the reporting period. At the end of that period, the net income at that point is transferred from the Profit and Loss Account to the _____ account. If the balance of the _____ account is negative it may be called accumulated losses, retained losses or accumulated deficit, or similar terminology.

Exam Probability: **High**

6. *Answer choices:*

(see index for correct answer)

- a. Property income
- b. SUGAM ITR-4S
- c. Retained earnings
- d. Standard budget

Guidance: level 1

:: Bonds (finance) ::

A _____ is a type of bond that allows the issuer of the bond to retain the privilege of redeeming the bond at some point before the bond reaches its date of maturity. In other words, on the call date, the issuer has the right, but not the obligation, to buy back the bonds from the bond holders at a defined call price. Technically speaking, the bonds are not really bought and held by the issuer but are instead cancelled immediately.

Exam Probability: **Low**

7. *Answer choices:*

(see index for correct answer)

- a. Auction rate security
- b. Adjusted current yield
- c. Bond Rider
- d. Callable bond

Guidance: level 1

:: Financial markets ::

A _____ is a financial market in which long-term debt or equity-backed securities are bought and sold. _____ s channel the wealth of savers to those who can put it to long-term productive use, such as companies or governments making long-term investments. Financial regulators like the Bank of England and the U.S. Securities and Exchange Commission oversee _____ s to protect investors against fraud, among other duties.

Exam Probability: **High**

8. *Answer choices:*

(see index for correct answer)

- a. Round lot
- b. Financial instrument

- c. Capital market
- d. Virtual bidding

Guidance: level 1

:: Accounting terminology ::

Accounts are typically defined by an identifier and a caption or header and are coded by account type. In computerized accounting systems with computable quantity accounting, the accounts can have a quantity measure definition.

Exam Probability: **Low**

9. *Answer choices:*

(see index for correct answer)

- a. Accrual
- b. managerial accounting
- c. Enterprise liquidity
- d. Statement of financial position

Guidance: level 1

:: Elementary geometry ::

The _____ is the front of an animal's head that features three of the head's sense organs, the eyes, nose, and mouth, and through which animals express many of their emotions. The _____ is crucial for human identity, and damage such as scarring or developmental deformities affects the psyche adversely.

Exam Probability: **High**

10. *Answer choices:*

(see index for correct answer)

- a. Angle bisector theorem
- b. Face
- c. Base
- d. Multilateration

Guidance: level 1

:: Interest ::

In finance, _____ is the interest on a bond or loan that has accumulated since the principal investment, or since the previous coupon payment if there has been one already.

Exam Probability: **Medium**

11. *Answer choices:*

(see index for correct answer)

- a. Riba
- b. Accrued interest
- c. Interest sensitivity gap
- d. Fisher hypothesis

Guidance: level 1

:: ::

_____ is the study and management of exchange relationships. _____ is the business process of creating relationships with and satisfying customers. With its focus on the customer, _____ is one of the premier components of business management.

Exam Probability: **High**

12. *Answer choices:*

(see index for correct answer)

- a. hierarchical perspective
- b. interpersonal communication
- c. Marketing
- d. personal values

Guidance: level 1

:: Actuarial science ::

The _____ is the greater benefit of receiving money now rather than an identical sum later. It is founded on time preference.

Exam Probability: **Medium**

13. *Answer choices:*

(see index for correct answer)

- a. Fictional actuaries
- b. Time value of money
- c. Anders Lindstedt
- d. Risk aversion

Guidance: level 1

:: Accounting terminology ::

_____ are liabilities that reflect expenses that have not yet been paid or logged under accounts payable during an accounting period; in other words, a company's obligation to pay for goods and services that have been provided for which invoices have not yet been received. Examples would include accrued wages payable, accrued sales tax payable, and accrued rent payable.

Exam Probability: **Medium**

14. *Answer choices:*

(see index for correct answer)

- a. Accrued liabilities
- b. Checkoff
- c. outstanding balance
- d. Internal auditing

Guidance: level 1

:: Business ::

The seller, or the provider of the goods or services, completes a sale in response to an acquisition, appropriation, requisition or a direct interaction with the buyer at the point of sale. There is a passing of title of the item, and the settlement of a price, in which agreement is reached on a price for which transfer of ownership of the item will occur. The seller, not the purchaser typically executes the sale and it may be completed prior to the obligation of payment. In the case of indirect interaction, a person who sells goods or service on behalf of the owner is known as a _____ man or _____ woman or _____ person, but this often refers to someone selling goods in a store/shop, in which case other terms are also common, including _____ clerk, shop assistant, and retail clerk.

Exam Probability: **High**

15. *Answer choices:*

(see index for correct answer)

- a. Street marketing
- b. Attribution
- c. Joint employment
- d. Business service management

Guidance: level 1

:: Marketing ::

A _____ is an overall experience of a customer that distinguishes an organization or product from its rivals in the eyes of the customer. _____ s are used in business, marketing, and advertising. Name _____ s are sometimes distinguished from generic or store _____ s.

Exam Probability: **Medium**

16. *Answer choices:*

(see index for correct answer)

- a. LGBT marketing
- b. Field research
- c. Outsourcing relationship management
- d. Brand

Guidance: level 1

:: Accounting ::

_____ is a process of providing relief to shared service organization's cost centers that provide a product or service. In turn, the associated expense is assigned to internal clients' cost centers that consume the products and services. For example, the CIO may provide all IT services within the company and assign the costs back to the business units that consume each offering.

Exam Probability: **High**

17. *Answer choices:*

(see index for correct answer)

- a. Accountant General
- b. Financing cost
- c. Merdiban
- d. Cost allocation

Guidance: level 1

:: Asset ::

_____ s, also known as tangible assets or property, plant and equipment , is a term used in accounting for assets and property that cannot easily be converted into cash. This can be compared with current assets such as cash or bank accounts, described as liquid assets. In most cases, only tangible assets are referred to as fixed. IAS 16 defines _____ s as assets whose future economic benefit is probable to flow into the entity, whose cost can be measured reliably. _____ s belong to one of 2 types:"Freehold Assets" – assets which are purchased with legal right of ownership and used,and "Leasehold Assets" – assets used by owner without legal right for a particular period of time.

Exam Probability: **High**

18. *Answer choices:*

(see index for correct answer)

- a. Asset
- b. Fixed asset

Guidance: level 1

:: Marketing ::

A _____ is the quantity of payment or compensation given by one party to another in return for one unit of goods or services.. A _____ is influenced by both production costs and demand for the product. A _____ may be determined by a monopolist or may be imposed on the firm by market conditions.

Exam Probability: **Medium**

19. *Answer choices:*

(see index for correct answer)

- a. Price
- b. National brand
- c. Prommercial
- d. Product naming convention

Guidance: level 1

:: International Financial Reporting Standards ::

_____, usually called IFRS, are standards issued by the IFRS Foundation and the International Accounting Standards Board to provide a common global language for business affairs so that company accounts are understandable and comparable across international boundaries. They are a consequence of growing international shareholding and trade and are particularly important for companies that have dealings in several countries. They are progressively replacing the many different national accounting standards. They are the rules to be followed by accountants to maintain books of accounts which are comparable, understandable, reliable and relevant as per the users internal or external. IFRS, with the exception of IAS 29 Financial Reporting in Hyperinflationary Economies and IFRIC 7 Applying the Restatement Approach under IAS 29, are authorized in terms of the historical cost paradigm. IAS 29 and IFRIC 7 are authorized in terms of the units of constant purchasing power paradigm.IAS 2 is related to inventories in this standard we talk about the stock its production process etcIFRS began as an attempt to harmonize accounting across the European Union but the value of harmonization quickly made the concept attractive around the world. However, it has been debated whether or not de facto harmonization has occurred. Standards that were issued by IASC are still within use today and go by the name International Accounting Standards , while standards issued by IASB are called IFRS. IAS were issued between 1973 and 2001 by the Board of the International Accounting Standards Committee . On 1 April 2001, the new International Accounting Standards Board took over from the IASC the responsibility for setting International Accounting Standards. During its first meeting the new Board adopted existing IAS and Standing Interpretations Committee standards . The IASB has continued to develop standards calling the new standards " _____ ".

Exam Probability: **Medium**

20. *Answer choices:*

(see index for correct answer)

- a. International Financial Reporting Standards
- b. IFRS 1
- c. IAS 37

- d. IAS 10

Guidance: level 1

:: Financial accounting ::

_____ is the value of all the non-financial and financial assets owned by an institutional unit or sector minus the value of all its outstanding liabilities. Since financial assets minus outstanding liabilities equal net financial assets, _____ can also be conveniently expressed as non-financial assets plus net financial assets. _____ can apply to companies, individuals, governments or economic sectors such as the sector of financial corporations or to entire countries.

Exam Probability: **High**

21. *Answer choices:*

(see index for correct answer)

- a. Net worth
- b. Intellectual capital
- c. Equity method
- d. SEC filing

Guidance: level 1

:: Financial ratios ::

_____ or asset turns is a financial ratio that measures the efficiency of a company's use of its assets in generating sales revenue or sales income to the company.

Exam Probability: **Medium**

22. *Answer choices:*

(see index for correct answer)

- a. Beta
- b. Asset turnover
- c. Debt-to-income ratio
- d. interest margin

Guidance: level 1

:: Global systemically important banks ::

The _____ Corporation is an American multinational investment bank and financial services company based in Charlotte, North Carolina with central hubs in New York City, London, Hong Kong, Minneapolis, and Toronto. _____ was formed through NationsBank's acquisition of BankAmerica in 1998. It is the second largest banking institution in the United States, after JP Morgan Chase. As a part of the Big Four, it services approximately 10.73% of all American bank deposits, in direct competition with Citigroup, Wells Fargo, and JPMorgan Chase. Its primary financial services revolve around commercial banking, wealth management, and investment banking.

Exam Probability: **Medium**

23. *Answer choices:*

(see index for correct answer)

- a. BNP Paribas
- b. Bank of America
- c. Groupe BPCE
- d. Nordea

Guidance: level 1

:: Materials ::

A _____ , also known as a feedstock, unprocessed material, or primary commodity, is a basic material that is used to produce goods, finished products, energy, or intermediate materials which are feedstock for future finished products. As feedstock, the term connotes these materials are bottleneck assets and are highly important with regard to producing other products. An example of this is crude oil, which is a _____ and a feedstock used in the production of industrial chemicals, fuels, plastics, and pharmaceutical goods; lumber is a _____ used to produce a variety of products including all types of furniture. The term " _____ " denotes materials in minimally processed or unprocessed in states; e.g., raw latex, crude oil, cotton, coal, raw biomass, iron ore, air, logs, or water i.e. "...any product of agriculture, forestry, fishing and any other mineral that is in its natural form or which has undergone the transformation required to prepare it for internationally marketing in substantial volumes."

Exam Probability: **High**

24. *Answer choices:*

(see index for correct answer)

- a. Raw material
- b. Coal tar
- c. Plastic bottle
- d. Noil

Guidance: level 1

:: Banking ::

A _____ is a financial account maintained by a bank for a customer. A _____ can be a deposit account, a credit card account, a current account, or any other type of account offered by a financial institution, and represents the funds that a customer has entrusted to the financial institution and from which the customer can make withdrawals. Alternatively, accounts may be loan accounts in which case the customer owes money to the financial institution.

Exam Probability: **High**

25. *Answer choices:*

(see index for correct answer)

- a. Bank account
- b. Europeans for Financial Reform
- c. Bank examiner
- d. Joint account

Guidance: level 1

:: Subprime mortgage crisis ::

> The _____ Group, Inc., is an American multinational investment bank and financial services company headquartered in New York City. It offers services in investment management, securities, asset management, prime brokerage, and securities underwriting.

Exam Probability: **Low**

26. *Answer choices:*

(see index for correct answer)

- a. Hope Now Alliance
- b. Goldman Sachs
- c. National City acquisition by PNC
- d. Cramdown

Guidance: level 1

:: Scheduling (computing) ::

Ageing or _____ is the process of becoming older. The term refers especially to human beings, many animals, and fungi, whereas for example bacteria, perennial plants and some simple animals are potentially biologically immortal. In the broader sense, ageing can refer to single cells within an organism which have ceased dividing or to the population of a species.

Exam Probability: **Low**

27. *Answer choices:*

(see index for correct answer)

- a. Kernel preemption
- b. Idle
- c. Run queue
- d. Random boosting

Guidance: level 1

_____ is the process of making predictions of the future based on past and present data and most commonly by analysis of trends. A commonplace example might be estimation of some variable of interest at some specified future date. Prediction is a similar, but more general term. Both might refer to formal statistical methods employing time series, cross-sectional or longitudinal data, or alternatively to less formal judgmental methods. Usage can differ between areas of application: for example, in hydrology the terms "forecast" and "_____" are sometimes reserved for estimates of values at certain specific future times, while the term "prediction" is used for more general estimates, such as the number of times floods will occur over a long period.

Exam Probability: **Low**

28. *Answer choices:*

(see index for correct answer)

- a. Forecasting
- b. levels of analysis
- c. Character
- d. corporate values

Guidance: level 1

:: Income taxes ::

An _____ is a tax imposed on individuals or entities that varies with respective income or profits . _____ generally is computed as the product of a tax rate times taxable income. Taxation rates may vary by type or characteristics of the taxpayer.

Exam Probability: **Low**

29. *Answer choices:*

(see index for correct answer)

- a. Income Tax Assessment Act 1936
- b. Tax refund interception
- c. Income tax
- d. Income and Corporation Taxes Act 1988

Guidance: level 1

:: Accounting terminology ::

_____ is money owed by a business to its suppliers shown as a liability on a company's balance sheet. It is distinct from notes payable liabilities, which are debts created by formal legal instrument documents.

Exam Probability: **Medium**

30. *Answer choices:*

(see index for correct answer)

- a. outstanding balance
- b. Accounts payable
- c. Accrual
- d. Fair value accounting

Guidance: level 1

:: Business economics ::

_____ is one of the constituents of a leasing calculus or operation. It describes the future value of a good in terms of absolute value in monetary terms and it is sometimes abbreviated into a percentage of the initial price when the item was new.

Exam Probability: **High**

31. *Answer choices:*

(see index for correct answer)

- a. Residual value
- b. Vendor finance
- c. Tradespace
- d. Staple financing

Guidance: level 1

:: Financial regulatory authorities of the United States ::

The _____ is the revenue service of the United States federal government. The government agency is a bureau of the Department of the Treasury, and is under the immediate direction of the Commissioner of Internal Revenue, who is appointed to a five-year term by the President of the United States. The IRS is responsible for collecting taxes and administering the Internal Revenue Code, the main body of federal statutory tax law of the United States. The duties of the IRS include providing tax assistance to taxpayers and pursuing and resolving instances of erroneous or fraudulent tax filings. The IRS has also overseen various benefits programs, and enforces portions of the Affordable Care Act.

Exam Probability: **Medium**

32. *Answer choices:*

(see index for correct answer)

- a. Office of Thrift Supervision
- b. Internal Revenue Service
- c. U.S. Securities and Exchange Commission
- d. National Credit Union Administration

Guidance: level 1

:: Marketing ::

_____ or stock is the goods and materials that a business holds for the ultimate goal of resale.

Exam Probability: **Medium**

33. *Answer choices:*

(see index for correct answer)

- a. Digital billboard
- b. Branding national myths and symbols
- c. Buyer decision process
- d. Inventory

Guidance: level 1

:: ::

_____ is the production of products for use or sale using labour and machines, tools, chemical and biological processing, or formulation. The term may refer to a range of human activity, from handicraft to high tech, but is most commonly applied to industrial design, in which raw materials are transformed into finished goods on a large scale. Such finished goods may be sold to other manufacturers for the production of other, more complex products, such as aircraft, household appliances, furniture, sports equipment or automobiles, or sold to wholesalers, who in turn sell them to retailers, who then sell them to end users and consumers.

Exam Probability: **Low**

34. *Answer choices:*

(see index for correct answer)

- a. Manufacturing
- b. open system
- c. interpersonal communication
- d. imperative

Guidance: level 1

:: Marketing ::

_____ is a financial mechanism in which a debtor obtains the right to delay payments to a creditor, for a defined period of time, in exchange for a charge or fee. Essentially, the party that owes money in the present purchases the right to delay the payment until some future date. The discount, or charge, is the difference between the original amount owed in the present and the amount that has to be paid in the future to settle the debt.

Exam Probability: **Low**

35. *Answer choices:*
(see index for correct answer)

- a. Counteradvertising
- b. Pharmaceutical marketing
- c. Discounting
- d. Jobbing house

Guidance: level 1

:: ::

_____ focuses on ratios, equities and debts. It is useful for portfolio management,distribution of dividend,capital raising,hedging and looking after fluctuations in foreign currency and product cycles.Financial managers are the people who will do research and based on the research, decide what sort of capital to obtain in order to fund the company's assets as well as maximizing the value of the firm for all the stakeholders. It also refers to the efficient and effective management of money in such a manner as to accomplish the objectives of the organization. It is the specialized function directly associated with the top management. The significance of this function is not seen in the `Line` but also in the capacity of the `Staff` in overall of a company. It has been defined differently by different experts in the field.

Exam Probability: **Medium**

36. *Answer choices:*

(see index for correct answer)

- a. surface-level diversity
- b. deep-level diversity
- c. open system
- d. levels of analysis

Guidance: level 1

:: Money ::

Cash and _____s are the most liquid current assets found on a business's balance sheet. _____s are short-term commitments "with temporarily idle cash and easily convertible into a known cash amount". An investment normally counts to be a _____ when it has a short maturity period of 90 days or less, and can be included in the cash and _____s balance from the date of acquisition when it carries an insignificant risk of changes in the asset value; with more than 90 days maturity, the asset is not considered as cash and _____s. Equity investments mostly are excluded from _____s, unless they are essentially _____s, for instance, if the preferred shares acquired within a short maturity period and with specified recovery date.

Exam Probability: **High**

37. *Answer choices:*

(see index for correct answer)

- a. Metallism
- b. Cash equivalent
- c. Green money
- d. Key money

Guidance: level 1

:: Commerce ::

Continuation of an entity as a _____ is presumed as the basis for financial reporting unless and until the entity's liquidation becomes imminent. Preparation of financial statements under this presumption is commonly referred to as the _____ basis of accounting. If and when an entity's liquidation becomes imminent, financial statements are prepared under the liquidation basis of accounting.

Exam Probability: **High**

38. *Answer choices:*

(see index for correct answer)

- a. Staple right
- b. White Elephant Sale
- c. Sell-side analyst
- d. Going concern

Guidance: level 1

:: Corporate finance ::

_____ in corporate finance is the way a corporation finances its assets through some combination of equity, debt, or hybrid securities.

Exam Probability: **Low**

39. *Answer choices:*

(see index for correct answer)

- a. Demutualization
- b. Avellum Partners
- c. Bankmail
- d. Equity issuance

Guidance: level 1

:: ::

An _____ is a systematic and independent examination of books, accounts, statutory records, documents and vouchers of an organization to ascertain how far the financial statements as well as non-financial disclosures present a true and fair view of the concern. It also attempts to ensure that the books of accounts are properly maintained by the concern as required by law. _____ ing has become such a ubiquitous phenomenon in the corporate and the public sector that academics started identifying an " _____ Society". The _____ or perceives and recognises the propositions before them for examination, obtains evidence, evaluates the same and formulates an opinion on the basis of his judgement which is communicated through their _____ ing report.

Exam Probability: **Low**

40. *Answer choices:*

(see index for correct answer)

- a. hierarchical perspective

- b. corporate values
- c. Audit
- d. imperative

Guidance: level 1

:: ::

_____ involves decision making. It can include judging the merits of multiple options and selecting one or more of them. One can make a _____ between imagined options or between real options followed by the corresponding action. For example, a traveler might choose a route for a journey based on the preference of arriving at a given destination as soon as possible. The preferred route can then follow from information such as the length of each of the possible routes, traffic conditions, etc. The arrival at a _____ can include more complex motivators such as cognition, instinct, and feeling.

Exam Probability: **High**

41. *Answer choices:*

(see index for correct answer)

- a. information systems assessment
- b. similarity-attraction theory
- c. Character
- d. Choice

Guidance: level 1

:: ::

_____ is the administration of an organization, whether it is a business, a not-for-profit organization, or government body. _____ includes the activities of setting the strategy of an organization and coordinating the efforts of its employees to accomplish its objectives through the application of available resources, such as financial, natural, technological, and human resources. The term " _____ " may also refer to those people who manage an organization.

Exam Probability: **Low**

42. *Answer choices:*

(see index for correct answer)

- a. open system
- b. co-culture
- c. cultural
- d. Management

Guidance: level 1

:: Contract law ::

A _____ is a legally-binding agreement which recognises and governs the rights and duties of the parties to the agreement. A _____ is legally enforceable because it meets the requirements and approval of the law. An agreement typically involves the exchange of goods, services, money, or promises of any of those. In the event of breach of _____ , the law awards the injured party access to legal remedies such as damages and cancellation.

Exam Probability: **High**

43. *Answer choices:*

(see index for correct answer)

- a. Indian contract law
- b. Contract
- c. Capacity
- d. History of contract law

Guidance: level 1

:: Insolvency ::

_____ is the process in accounting by which a company is brought to an end in the United Kingdom, Republic of Ireland and United States. The assets and property of the company are redistributed. _____ is also sometimes referred to as winding-up or dissolution, although dissolution technically refers to the last stage of _____ . The process of _____ also arises when customs, an authority or agency in a country responsible for collecting and safeguarding customs duties, determines the final computation or ascertainment of the duties or drawback accruing on an entry.

Exam Probability: **Low**

44. *Answer choices:*

(see index for correct answer)

- a. United Kingdom insolvency law
- b. Debt consolidation
- c. Official Committee of Equity Security Holders
- d. Liquidation

Guidance: level 1

:: Accounting journals and ledgers ::

The subledger, or _____ , provides details behind entries in the general ledger used in accounting. The subledger shows detail for part of the accounting records such as property and equipment, prepaid expenses, etc. The detail would include such items as date the item was purchased or expense incurred, a description of the item, the original balance, and the net book value. The total of the subledger would match the line item amount on the general ledger. This corresponding line item in the general ledger is referred to as the controlling account. The _____ balance is compared with its controlling account balance as part of the process of preparing a trial balance.

Exam Probability: **Low**

45. *Answer choices:*

(see index for correct answer)

- a. Subledger
- b. Subsidiary ledger
- c. Cash receipts journal
- d. General journal

Guidance: level 1

:: Financial ratios ::

> The _____ is a liquidity ratio that measures whether a firm has enough resources to meet its short-term obligations. It compares a firm's current assets to its current liabilities, and is expressed as follows.

Exam Probability: **Medium**

46. *Answer choices:*

(see index for correct answer)

- a. Infection ratio
- b. Statutory liquidity ratio
- c. Implied multiple
- d. Price-to-book ratio

Guidance: level 1

:: Management accounting ::

"_____ s are the structural determinants of the cost of an activity, reflecting any linkages or interrelationships that affect it". Therefore we could assume that the _____ s determine the cost behavior within the activities, reflecting the links that these have with other activities and relationships that affect them.

Exam Probability: **Low**

47. *Answer choices:*

(see index for correct answer)

- a. Construction accounting
- b. Pre-determined overhead rate
- c. Owner earnings
- d. Cost driver

Guidance: level 1

:: Fixed income market ::

In finance, the _____ is a curve showing several yields or interest rates across different contract lengths for a similar debt contract. The curve shows the relation between the interest rate and the time to maturity, known as the "term", of the debt for a given borrower in a given currency. For example, the U.S. dollar interest rates paid on U.S. Treasury securities for various maturities are closely watched by many traders, and are commonly plotted on a graph such as the one on the right which is informally called "the _____ ". More formal mathematical descriptions of this relation are often called the term structure of interest rates.

Exam Probability: **Medium**

48. *Answer choices:*

(see index for correct answer)

- a. Bond market
- b. Bond Exchange of South Africa
- c. Yield curve
- d. credit market

Guidance: level 1

:: Consumer theory ::

_____ is the quantity of a good that consumers are willing and able to purchase at various prices during a given period of time.

Exam Probability: **Low**

49. *Answer choices:*

(see index for correct answer)

- a. Consumer service
- b. Bliss point
- c. Demand
- d. Consumption

Guidance: level 1

:: Fundamental analysis ::

_____ is the monetary value of earnings per outstanding share of common stock for a company.

Exam Probability: **Medium**

50. *Answer choices:*

(see index for correct answer)

- a. economic Value Added
- b. Market value added
- c. Fundamental analysis
- d. Earnings per share

Guidance: level 1

:: Generally Accepted Accounting Principles ::

Financial statements prepared and presented by a company typically follow an external standard that specifically guides their preparation. These standards vary across the globe and are typically overseen by some combination of the private accounting profession in that specific nation and the various government regulators. Variations across countries may be considerable, making cross-country evaluation of financial data challenging.

Exam Probability: **Low**

51. *Answer choices:*

(see index for correct answer)

- a. Operating income
- b. Reserve
- c. Generally accepted accounting principles
- d. Financial position of the United States

Guidance: level 1

:: Portfolio theories ::

In finance, the _____ is a model used to determine a theoretically appropriate required rate of return of an asset, to make decisions about adding assets to a well-diversified portfolio.

Exam Probability: **High**

52. *Answer choices:*

(see index for correct answer)

- a. Capital asset pricing model
- b. Behavioral portfolio theory
- c. Returns-based style analysis
- d. Post-modern portfolio theory

Guidance: level 1

:: Business law ::

> A _____ , also known as the sole trader, individual entrepreneurship or proprietorship, is a type of enterprise that is owned and run by one person and in which there is no legal distinction between the owner and the business entity. A sole trader does not necessarily work `alone`—it is possible for the sole trader to employ other people.

Exam Probability: **Medium**

53. *Answer choices:*

(see index for correct answer)

- a. Doing business as
- b. Copyright transfer agreement
- c. Tacit relocation
- d. Sole proprietorship

Guidance: level 1

:: Fraud ::

In law, _____ is intentional deception to secure unfair or unlawful gain, or to deprive a victim of a legal right. _____ can violate civil law, a criminal law, or it may cause no loss of money, property or legal right but still be an element of another civil or criminal wrong. The purpose of _____ may be monetary gain or other benefits, for example by obtaining a passport, travel document, or driver's license, or mortgage _____, where the perpetrator may attempt to qualify for a mortgage by way of false statements.

Exam Probability: **Low**

54. *Answer choices:*

(see index for correct answer)

- a. misleading advertising
- b. Extrinsic fraud
- c. Fraud
- d. World Luxury Association

Guidance: level 1

:: Banking ::

A _____ is a financial institution that accepts deposits from the public and creates credit. Lending activities can be performed either directly or indirectly through capital markets. Due to their importance in the financial stability of a country, _____ s are highly regulated in most countries. Most nations have institutionalized a system known as fractional reserve _____ ing under which _____ s hold liquid assets equal to only a portion of their current liabilities. In addition to other regulations intended to ensure liquidity, _____ s are generally subject to minimum capital requirements based on an international set of capital standards, known as the Basel Accords.

Exam Probability: **High**

55. *Answer choices:*

(see index for correct answer)

- a. Savings account
- b. Bank
- c. Overnight market
- d. Transactional account

Guidance: level 1

:: Mathematical finance ::

_____ is the value of an asset at a specific date. It measures the nominal future sum of money that a given sum of money is "worth" at a specified time in the future assuming a certain interest rate, or more generally, rate of return; it is the present value multiplied by the accumulation function. The value does not include corrections for inflation or other factors that affect the true value of money in the future. This is used in time value of money calculations.

Exam Probability: **High**

56. *Answer choices:*

(see index for correct answer)

- a. Earnings response coefficient
- b. Holding period return
- c. Future value
- d. Implied volatility

Guidance: level 1

:: Payments ::

A _____ is the trade of value from one party to another for goods, or services, or to fulfill a legal obligation.

Exam Probability: **Medium**

57. *Answer choices:*

(see index for correct answer)

- a. Payment
- b. Direct Payments
- c. Deficiency payments
- d. Tuition payments

Guidance: level 1

:: Business law ::

_____ is where a person's financial liability is limited to a fixed sum, most commonly the value of a person's investment in a company or partnership. If a company with _____ is sued, then the claimants are suing the company, not its owners or investors. A shareholder in a limited company is not personally liable for any of the debts of the company, other than for the amount already invested in the company and for any unpaid amount on the shares in the company, if any. The same is true for the members of a _____ partnership and the limited partners in a limited partnership. By contrast, sole proprietors and partners in general partnerships are each liable for all the debts of the business .

Exam Probability: **Medium**

58. *Answer choices:*

(see index for correct answer)

- a. Lease

- b. Limited liability
- c. Personal Property Security Act
- d. Extraordinary resolution

Guidance: level 1

:: Financial ratios ::

A _____ or accounting ratio is a relative magnitude of two selected numerical values taken from an enterprise's financial statements. Often used in accounting, there are many standard ratios used to try to evaluate the overall financial condition of a corporation or other organization. _____ s may be used by managers within a firm, by current and potential shareholders of a firm, and by a firm's creditors. Financial analysts use _____ s to compare the strengths and weaknesses in various companies. If shares in a company are traded in a financial market, the market price of the shares is used in certain _____ s.

Exam Probability: **Medium**

59. *Answer choices:*

(see index for correct answer)

- a. Incremental capital-output ratio
- b. Sharpe ratio
- c. PE ratio
- d. Financial ratio

Guidance: level 1

Human resource management

Human resource (HR) management is the strategic approach to the effective management of organization workers so that they help the business gain a competitive advantage. It is designed to maximize employee performance in service of an employer's strategic objectives. HR is primarily concerned with the management of people within organizations, focusing on policies and on systems. HR departments are responsible for overseeing employee-benefits design, employee recruitment, training and development, performance appraisal, and rewarding (e.g., managing pay and benefit systems). HR also concerns itself with organizational change and industrial relations, that is, the balancing of organizational practices with requirements arising from collective bargaining and from governmental laws.

:: Validity (statistics) ::

In psychometrics, _____ is the extent to which a score on a scale or test predicts scores on some criterion measure.

Exam Probability: **Low**

1. *Answer choices:*

(see index for correct answer)

- a. Ecological validity
- b. Face validity
- c. Statistical conclusion validity
- d. Predictive validity

Guidance: level 1

:: Behaviorism ::

In behavioral psychology, _____ is a consequence applied that will strengthen an organism's future behavior whenever that behavior is preceded by a specific antecedent stimulus. This strengthening effect may be measured as a higher frequency of behavior, longer duration, greater magnitude, or shorter latency. There are two types of _____, known as positive _____ and negative _____; positive is where by a reward is offered on expression of the wanted behaviour and negative is taking away an undesirable element in the persons environment whenever the desired behaviour is achieved.

Exam Probability: **Low**

2. *Answer choices:*

(see index for correct answer)

- a. Reinforcement
- b. chaining
- c. Systematic desensitization
- d. Matching Law

Guidance: level 1

:: ::

The _____ of 1938 29 U.S.C. § 203 is a United States labor law that creates the right to a minimum wage, and "time-and-a-half" overtime pay when people work over forty hours a week. It also prohibits most employment of minors in "oppressive child labor". It applies to employees engaged in interstate commerce or employed by an enterprise engaged in commerce or in the production of goods for commerce, unless the employer can claim an exemption from coverage.

Exam Probability: **Medium**

3. *Answer choices:*

(see index for correct answer)

- a. corporate values
- b. deep-level diversity
- c. Fair Labor Standards Act

- d. information systems assessment

Guidance: level 1

:: Employee relations ::

_____ is a fundamental concept in the effort to understand and describe, both qualitatively and quantitatively, the nature of the relationship between an organization and its employees. An "engaged employee" is defined as one who is fully absorbed by and enthusiastic about their work and so takes positive action to further the organization's reputation and interests. An engaged employee has a positive attitude towards the organization and its values. In contrast, a disengaged employee may range from someone doing the bare minimum at work , up to an employee who is actively damaging the company's work output and reputation.

Exam Probability: **High**

4. *Answer choices:*

(see index for correct answer)

- a. Employee motivation
- b. Employee morale
- c. Employee engagement
- d. Employee surveys

Guidance: level 1

:: ::

_____ is an experience a person may have when one moves to a cultural environment which is different from one's own; it is also the personal disorientation a person may feel when experiencing an unfamiliar way of life due to immigration or a visit to a new country, a move between social environments, or simply transition to another type of life. One of the most common causes of _____ involves individuals in a foreign environment. _____ can be described as consisting of at least one of four distinct phases: honeymoon, negotiation, adjustment, and adaptation.

Exam Probability: **Medium**

5. *Answer choices:*

(see index for correct answer)

- a. Culture shock
- b. cultural
- c. hierarchical
- d. open system

Guidance: level 1

:: Human resource management ::

_____ is a method of job analysis that was developed by the Employment and Training Administration of the United States Department of Labor. FJA produces standardized occupational information specific to the performance of the work and the performer.

Exam Probability: **Medium**

6. *Answer choices:*

(see index for correct answer)

- a. Training and development
- b. Job enrichment
- c. Functional job analysis
- d. Human resource accounting

Guidance: level 1

:: Validity (statistics) ::

In psychometrics, criterion or concrete validity is the extent to which a measure is related to an outcome. _____ is often divided into concurrent and predictive validity. Concurrent validity refers to a comparison between the measure in question and an outcome assessed at the same time. In Standards for Educational & Psychological Tests, it states, "concurrent validity reflects only the status quo at a particular time." Predictive validity, on the other hand, compares the measure in question with an outcome assessed at a later time. Although concurrent and predictive validity are similar, it is cautioned to keep the terms and findings separated. "Concurrent validity should not be used as a substitute for predictive validity without an appropriate supporting rationale."

Exam Probability: **High**

7. *Answer choices:*

(see index for correct answer)

- a. Construct validity
- b. Nomological network
- c. Statistical conclusion validity
- d. Concurrent validity

Guidance: level 1

:: Training ::

_____ is action or inaction that is regulated to be in accordance with a particular system of governance. _____ is commonly applied to regulating human and animal behavior, and furthermore, it is applied to each activity-branch in all branches of organized activity, knowledge, and other fields of study and observation. _____ can be a set of expectations that are required by any governing entity including the self, groups, classes, fields, industries, or societies.

Exam Probability: **Medium**

8. *Answer choices:*

(see index for correct answer)

- a. Confidence-based learning
- b. G-learning
- c. Enforcement
- d. Fartlek

Guidance: level 1

:: Meetings ::

A _____ is a formal meeting of the representatives of different countries, constituent states, organizations, trade unions, political parties or other groups. The term, originally denoting a parley during battle in the Late Middle Ages, is derived from the Latin _____ us.

Exam Probability: **Medium**

9. *Answer choices:*

(see index for correct answer)

- a. Popular assembly
- b. Congress
- c. Program book
- d. Open town meeting

Guidance: level 1

:: Recruitment ::

Recruitment refers to the overall process of attracting, shortlisting, selecting and appointing suitable candidates for jobs within an organization. Recruitment can also refer to processes involved in choosing individuals for unpaid roles. Managers, human resource generalists and recruitment specialists may be tasked with carrying out recruitment, but in some cases public-sector employment agencies, commercial recruitment agencies, or specialist search consultancies are used to undertake parts of the process. Internet-based technologies which support all aspects of recruitment have become widespread.

Exam Probability: **High**

10. *Answer choices:*

(see index for correct answer)

- a. Probation
- b. Riviera Partners

- c. Sourcing
- d. The Talent Myth

Guidance: level 1

:: Multiple choice ::

The _____ is a standardized psychometric test of adult personality and psychopathology. Psychologists and other mental health professionals use various versions of the MMPI to help develop treatment plans; assist with differential diagnosis; help answer legal questions ; screen job candidates during the personnel selection process; or as part of a therapeutic assessment procedure.

Exam Probability: **Low**

11. *Answer choices:*
(see index for correct answer)

- a. Minnesota Multiphasic Personality Inventory
- b. Multiple choice
- c. Millon Clinical Multiaxial Inventory
- d. Eddy Test

Guidance: level 1

:: Human resource management ::

An _____ is a software application that enables the electronic handling of recruitment needs. An ATS can be implemented or accessed online on an enterprise or small business level, depending on the needs of the company and there is also free and open source ATS software available. An ATS is very similar to customer relationship management systems, but are designed for recruitment tracking purposes. In many cases they filter applications automatically based on given criteria such as keywords, skills, former employers, years of experience and schools attended. This has caused many to adapt resume optimization techniques similar to those used in search engine optimization when creating and formatting their résumé.

Exam Probability: **High**

12. *Answer choices:*

(see index for correct answer)

- a. Organizational culture
- b. Applicant tracking system
- c. Human resource management in public administration
- d. Person specification

Guidance: level 1

:: Occupational safety and health ::

_____ is a set of six naturally occurring silicate minerals, which all have in common their asbestiform habit: i.e., long, thin fibrous crystals, with each visible fiber composed of millions of microscopic "fibrils" that can be released by abrasion and other processes. The minerals are chrysotile, amosite, crocidolite, tremolite, anthophyllite, and actinolite.

Exam Probability: **Low**

13. *Answer choices:*

(see index for correct answer)

- a. Ethylene oxide
- b. Asbestos
- c. Risk Information Exchange
- d. Work improvement in small enterprises

Guidance: level 1

:: Trade unions ::

A _____, in North America, or union branch, in the United Kingdom and other countries, is a local branch of a usually national trade union. The terms used for sub-branches of _____ s vary from country to country and include "shop committee", "shop floor committee", "board of control", "chapel", and others.

Exam Probability: **High**

14. *Answer choices:*

(see index for correct answer)

- a. Local union
- b. TU
- c. General union
- d. Independent union

Guidance: level 1

:: Labor ::

_____ s are workers whose main capital is knowledge. Examples include programmers, physicians, pharmacists, architects, engineers, scientists, design thinkers, public accountants, lawyers, and academics, and any other white-collar workers, whose line of work requires the one to "think for a living".

Exam Probability: **Medium**

15. *Answer choices:*

(see index for correct answer)

- a. Surplus labour
- b. Lump of labour fallacy
- c. Roughneck
- d. Side letter

Guidance: level 1

:: Human resource management ::

_____, Inc. is an American office staffing company that operates globally. The company places employees at all levels in various sectors including financial services, information technology, and law. Also, its professional services include human resource and management consulting, outsourcing, recruitment, career transition, and vendor management. _____ was founded by William Russell Kelly in 1946 and is headquartered in Troy, Michigan. In 2015, the company reported 8,100 employees, $5.5 billion in revenue, and placed 550,000 employees to work in positions in various sectors, making it one of the world's largest staffing firms.

Exam Probability: **High**

16. *Answer choices:*
(see index for correct answer)

- a. human resource
- b. CEO succession
- c. Kelly Services
- d. Human resource management in public administration

Guidance: level 1

:: Employment ::

A _____, a concept developed in contemporary research by organizational scholar Denise Rousseau, represents the mutual beliefs, perceptions and informal obligations between an employer and an employee. It sets the dynamics for the relationship and defines the detailed practicality of the work to be done. It is distinguishable from the formal written contract of employment which, for the most part, only identifies mutual duties and responsibilities in a generalized form.

Exam Probability: **High**

17. *Answer choices:*
(see index for correct answer)

- a. Customized employment
- b. Liaison job
- c. Psychological contract
- d. Work-in

Guidance: level 1

:: Human resource management ::

_____ is athletic training in sports other than the athlete's usual sport. The goal is improving overall performance. It takes advantage of the particular effectiveness of one training method to negate the shortcomings of another.

Exam Probability: **Low**

18. *Answer choices:*

(see index for correct answer)

- a. Talent management system
- b. Cross-training
- c. Competency-based recruitment
- d. Talascend

Guidance: level 1

:: Leadership ::

_____ is a theory of leadership where a leader works with teams to identify needed change, creating a vision to guide the change through inspiration, and executing the change in tandem with committed members of a group; it is an integral part of the Full Range Leadership Model. _____ serves to enhance the motivation, morale, and job performance of followers through a variety of mechanisms; these include connecting the follower's sense of identity and self to a project and to the collective identity of the organization; being a role model for followers in order to inspire them and to raise their interest in the project; challenging followers to take greater ownership for their work, and understanding the strengths and weaknesses of followers, allowing the leader to align followers with tasks that enhance their performance.

Exam Probability: **Low**

19. *Answer choices:*

(see index for correct answer)

- a. Authentic leadership
- b. Transformational leadership
- c. Transactional leadership
- d. Trait leadership

Guidance: level 1

:: Learning methods ::

> _____ is an approach to problem solving. It involves taking action and reflecting upon the results. This helps improve the problem-solving process as well as simplify the solutions developed by the team.

Exam Probability: **Low**

20. *Answer choices:*

(see index for correct answer)

- a. double loop learning
- b. Action learning
- c. Audience response system
- d. Double-loop learning

Guidance: level 1

:: Sexual harassment in the United States ::

In law, a _____, reasonable man, or the man on the Clapham omnibus is a hypothetical person of legal fiction crafted by the courts and communicated through case law and jury instructions.

Exam Probability: **High**

21. *Answer choices:*

(see index for correct answer)

- a. Alexander v. Yale
- b. Sandy Gallin
- c. Reasonable person
- d. Hostile Advances

Guidance: level 1

:: Outsourcing ::

_____ is the practice of sourcing from the global market for goods and services across geopolitical boundaries. _____ often aims to exploit global efficiencies in the delivery of a product or service. These efficiencies include low cost skilled labor, low cost raw material and other economic factors like tax breaks and low trade tariffs. A large number of Information Technology projects and Services, including IS Applications and Mobile Apps and database services are outsourced globally to countries like Pakistan and India for more economical pricing.

Exam Probability: **Medium**

22. Answer choices:

(see index for correct answer)

- a. Pillsbury Winthrop Shaw Pittman
- b. Farmshoring
- c. Global sourcing
- d. LEO

Guidance: level 1

:: Human resource management ::

_____ involves improving the effectiveness of organizations and the individuals and teams within them. Training may be viewed as related to immediate changes in organizational effectiveness via organized instruction, while development is related to the progress of longer-term organizational and employee goals. While _____ technically have differing definitions, the two are oftentimes used interchangeably and/or together. _____ has historically been a topic within applied psychology but has within the last two decades become closely associated with human resources management, talent management, human resources development, instructional design, human factors, and knowledge management.

Exam Probability: **Medium**

23. Answer choices:

(see index for correct answer)

- a. Induction programme

- b. Training and development
- c. ABC Consultants
- d. Illness rate

Guidance: level 1

:: Management ::

_____ is a set of activities that ensure goals are met in an effective and efficient manner. _____ can focus on the performance of an organization, a department, an employee, or the processes in place to manage particular tasks. _____ standards are generally organized and disseminated by senior leadership at an organization, and by task owners.

Exam Probability: **High**

24. *Answer choices:*

(see index for correct answer)

- a. Association management company
- b. Responsible autonomy
- c. Performance management
- d. Vasa syndrome

Guidance: level 1

:: Power (social and political) ::

_____ is a form of reverence gained by a leader who has strong interpersonal relationship skills. _____, as an aspect of personal power, becomes particularly important as organizational leadership becomes increasingly about collaboration and influence, rather than command and control.

Exam Probability: **Low**

25. *Answer choices:*

(see index for correct answer)

- a. Hard power
- b. need for power
- c. Referent power

Guidance: level 1

:: Offshoring ::

A _____ is the temporary suspension or permanent termination of employment of an employee or, more commonly, a group of employees for business reasons, such as personnel management or downsizing an organization. Originally, _____ referred exclusively to a temporary interruption in work, or employment but this has evolved to a permanent elimination of a position in both British and US English, requiring the addition of "temporary" to specify the original meaning of the word. A _____ is not to be confused with wrongful termination. Laid off workers or displaced workers are workers who have lost or left their jobs because their employer has closed or moved, there was insufficient work for them to do, or their position or shift was abolished . Downsizing in a company is defined to involve the reduction of employees in a workforce. Downsizing in companies became a popular practice in the 1980s and early 1990s as it was seen as a way to deliver better shareholder value as it helps to reduce the costs of employers . Indeed, recent research on downsizing in the U.S., UK, and Japan suggests that downsizing is being regarded by management as one of the preferred routes to help declining organizations, cutting unnecessary costs, and improve organizational performance. Usually a _____ occurs as a cost cutting measure.

Exam Probability: **Low**

26. *Answer choices:*

(see index for correct answer)

- a. Layoff
- b. Offshore company
- c. TeleTech
- d. Antex

Guidance: level 1

:: ::

_____ involves the development of an action plan designed to motivate and guide a person or group toward a goal. _____ can be guided by goal-setting criteria such as SMART criteria. _____ is a major component of personal-development and management literature.

Exam Probability: **Low**

27. *Answer choices:*

(see index for correct answer)

- a. functional perspective
- b. corporate values
- c. Goal setting
- d. open system

Guidance: level 1

:: Occupational safety and health law ::

The _____ of 1970 is a US labor law governing the federal law of occupational health and safety in the private sector and federal government in the United States. It was enacted by Congress in 1970 and was signed by President Richard Nixon on December 29, 1970. Its main goal is to ensure that employers provide employees with an environment free from recognized hazards, such as exposure to toxic chemicals, excessive noise levels, mechanical dangers, heat or cold stress, or unsanitary conditions. The Act created the Occupational Safety and Health Administration and the National Institute for Occupational Safety and Health .

Exam Probability: **High**

28. *Answer choices:*

(see index for correct answer)

- a. Employment Standards Act
- b. Health and Morals of Apprentices Act 1802
- c. Health and Safety at Work etc. Act 1974
- d. Employment Standards Act of British Columbia

Guidance: level 1

:: Human resource management ::

_____ is the strategic approach to the effective management of people in an organization so that they help the business to gain a competitive advantage. It is designed to maximize employee performance in service of an employer's strategic objectives. HR is primarily concerned with the management of people within organizations, focusing on policies and on systems. HR departments are responsible for overseeing employee-benefits design, employee recruitment, training and development, performance appraisal, and Reward management . HR also concerns itself with organizational change and industrial relations, that is, the balancing of organizational practices with requirements arising from collective bargaining and from governmental laws.

Exam Probability: **Medium**

29. *Answer choices:*

(see index for correct answer)

- a. Flextime
- b. Organizational behavior and human resources
- c. Human resource management
- d. Internal communications

Guidance: level 1

:: ::

Domestic violence is violence or other abuse by one person against another in a domestic setting, such as in marriage or cohabitation. It may be termed intimate partner violence when committed by a spouse or partner in an intimate relationship against the other spouse or partner, and can take place in heterosexual or same-sex relationships, or between former spouses or partners. Domestic violence can also involve violence against children, parents, or the elderly. It takes a number of forms, including physical, verbal, emotional, economic, religious, reproductive, and sexual abuse, which can range from subtle, coercive forms to marital rape and to violent physical abuse such as choking, beating, female genital mutilation, and acid throwing that results in disfigurement or death. Domestic murders include stoning, bride burning, honor killings, and dowry deaths.

Exam Probability: **High**

30. *Answer choices:*

(see index for correct answer)

- a. Sarbanes-Oxley act of 2002
- b. surface-level diversity
- c. Family violence
- d. cultural

Guidance: level 1

:: Employment ::

_____ s are experiential learning opportunities, similar to internships but generally shorter, provided by partnerships between educational institutions and employers to give students short practical experiences in their field of study. In medicine it may refer to a visiting physician who is not part of the regular staff. In law, it usually refers to rigorous legal work opportunities undertaken by law students for law school credit and pay, similar to that of a junior attorney. It is derived from Latin externus and from English -ship.

Exam Probability: **Low**

31. *Answer choices:*

(see index for correct answer)

- a. Gold-collar worker
- b. Working holiday visa
- c. Customized employment
- d. Careers advisory service

Guidance: level 1

:: Management ::

In organizational studies, _____ is the efficient and effective development of an organization's resources when they are needed. Such resources may include financial resources, inventory, human skills, production resources, or information technology and natural resources.

Exam Probability: **High**

32. *Answer choices:*

(see index for correct answer)

- a. Resource management
- b. Perth leadership outcome model
- c. Mobile sales enablement
- d. Leadership Series

Guidance: level 1

:: Stochastic processes ::

_____ in its modern meaning is a "new idea, creative thoughts, new imaginations in form of device or method". _____ is often also viewed as the application of better solutions that meet new requirements, unarticulated needs, or existing market needs. Such _____ takes place through the provision of more-effective products, processes, services, technologies, or business models that are made available to markets, governments and society. An _____ is something original and more effective and, as a consequence, new, that "breaks into" the market or society. _____ is related to, but not the same as, invention, as _____ is more apt to involve the practical implementation of an invention to make a meaningful impact in the market or society, and not all _____ s require an invention. _____ often manifests itself via the engineering process, when the problem being solved is of a technical or scientific nature. The opposite of _____ is exnovation.

Exam Probability: **High**

33. *Answer choices:*

(see index for correct answer)

- a. Innovation
- b. Fractional Brownian motion
- c. Local time
- d. Hitting time

Guidance: level 1

:: Recruitment ::

_____ , also known as Recruitment communications and Recruitment agency, includes all communications used by an organization to attract talent to work within it. Recruitment advertisements may be the first impression of a company for many job seekers. In turn, the strength of employer branding in job postings can directly impact interest in job openings.

Exam Probability: **High**

34. *Answer choices:*

(see index for correct answer)

- a. Recruitment advertising
- b. S.I.R. Method of Recruiting
- c. Screening resumes
- d. Job fraud

Guidance: level 1

:: Trade unions ::

An _____ is a form of union security agreement where the employer may hire union or non-union workers, and employees need not join the union in order to remain employed. However, the non-union worker must pay a fee to cover collective bargaining costs. The fee paid by non-union members under the _____ is known as the "agency fee".

Exam Probability: **Low**

35. *Answer choices:*

(see index for correct answer)

- a. Trade union
- b. Agency shop
- c. Union democracy
- d. Unfair list

Guidance: level 1

:: Employment compensation ::

_____ is time off from work that workers can use to stay home to address their health and safety needs without losing pay. Paid _____ is a statutory requirement in many nations. Most European, many Latin American, a few African and a few Asian countries have legal requirements for paid _____ .

Exam Probability: **Low**

36. *Answer choices:*

(see index for correct answer)

- a. Lockstep compensation
- b. Sick leave
- c. Workers Compensation Act 1987
- d. Real wage

Guidance: level 1

:: Human resource management ::

_____ , also known as organizational socialization, is management jargon first created in 1988 that refers to the mechanism through which new employees acquire the necessary knowledge, skills, and behaviors in order to become effective organizational members and insiders.

Exam Probability: **Low**

37. *Answer choices:*

(see index for correct answer)

- a. Organizational ethics
- b. Onboarding
- c. Cross-training
- d. On-ramping

Guidance: level 1

:: Income ::

A _____ is a unit in systems of monetary compensation for employment. It is commonly used in public service, both civil and military, but also for companies of the private sector. _____ s facilitate the employment process by providing a fixed framework of salary ranges, as opposed to a free negotiation. Typically, _____ s encompass two dimensions: a "vertical" range where each level corresponds to the responsibility of, and requirements needed for a certain position; and a "horizontal" range within this scale to allow for monetary incentives rewarding the employee's quality of performance or length of service. Thus, an employee progresses within the horizontal and vertical ranges upon achieving positive appraisal on a regular basis. In most cases, evaluation is done annually and encompasses more than one method.

Exam Probability: **Low**

38. *Answer choices:*

(see index for correct answer)

- a. Income Per User
- b. Pay grade
- c. Trinity study
- d. Mandatory tipping

Guidance: level 1

:: Employment ::

The _____ is an individual's metaphorical "journey" through learning, work and other aspects of life. There are a number of ways to define _____ and the term is used in a variety of ways.

Exam Probability: **High**

39. *Answer choices:*

(see index for correct answer)

- a. Workhaven
- b. Taleo
- c. Skilled worker
- d. Career

Guidance: level 1

:: Human resource management ::

_____ is a family of procedures to identify the content of a job in terms of activities involved and attributes or job requirements needed to perform the activities. _____ provides information of organizations which helps to determine which employees are best fit for specific jobs. Through _____, the analyst needs to understand what the important tasks of the job are, how they are carried out, and the necessary human qualities needed to complete the job successfully.

Exam Probability: **Low**

40. *Answer choices:*

(see index for correct answer)

- a. Internal communications
- b. Aspiring Minds
- c. Job analysis
- d. Skills management

Guidance: level 1

:: Organizational structure ::

An _____ defines how activities such as task allocation, coordination, and supervision are directed toward the achievement of organizational aims.

Exam Probability: **Medium**

41. *Answer choices:*

(see index for correct answer)

- a. Unorganisation
- b. Followership
- c. Blessed Unrest
- d. Automated Bureaucracy

Guidance: level 1

:: ::

A _____ service is an online platform which people use to build social networks or social relationship with other people who share similar personal or career interests, activities, backgrounds or real-life connections.

Exam Probability: **Low**

42. *Answer choices:*

(see index for correct answer)

- a. personal values
- b. Social networking
- c. hierarchical perspective
- d. process perspective

Guidance: level 1

:: Business law ::

_____ or employment relations is the multidisciplinary academic field that studies the employment relationship; that is, the complex interrelations between employers and employees, labor/trade unions, employer organizations and the state.

Exam Probability: **Medium**

43. *Answer choices:*

(see index for correct answer)

- a. Unfair competition
- b. Hundi
- c. Contract A
- d. Industrial relations

Guidance: level 1

:: ::

Educational technology is "the study and ethical practice of facilitating learning and improving performance by creating, using, and managing appropriate technological processes and resources".

Exam Probability: **Medium**

44. *Answer choices:*

(see index for correct answer)

- a. surface-level diversity
- b. E-learning
- c. deep-level diversity
- d. cultural

Guidance: level 1

:: United States federal labor legislation ::

The _____ of 1988 is a United States federal law that generally prevents employers from using polygraph tests, either for pre-employment screening or during the course of employment, with certain exemptions.

Exam Probability: **High**

45. *Answer choices:*

(see index for correct answer)

- a. Adamson Act
- b. Pension Protection Act of 2006
- c. Employee Polygraph Protection Act
- d. Reliable Home Heating Act

Guidance: level 1

:: Business law ::

> An _____ is a natural person, business, or corporation that provides goods or services to another entity under terms specified in a contract or within a verbal agreement. Unlike an employee, an _____ does not work regularly for an employer but works as and when required, during which time they may be subject to law of agency. _____ s are usually paid on a freelance basis. Contractors often work through a limited company or franchise, which they themselves own, or may work through an umbrella company.

Exam Probability: **Low**

46. *Answer choices:*

(see index for correct answer)

- a. Independent contractor
- b. Novation
- c. Holder
- d. Uniform Partnership Act

Guidance: level 1

:: Employment ::

_____ is the probability that an individual will keep his/her job; a job with a high level of _____ is such that a person with the job would have a small chance of losing it.

Exam Probability: **High**

47. *Answer choices:*

(see index for correct answer)

- a. Job security
- b. Working holiday visa
- c. Skilled worker
- d. Extreme Blue

Guidance: level 1

:: Production and manufacturing ::

_____ consists of organization-wide efforts to "install and make permanent climate where employees continuously improve their ability to provide on demand products and services that customers will find of particular value." "Total" emphasizes that departments in addition to production are obligated to improve their operations; "management" emphasizes that executives are obligated to actively manage quality through funding, training, staffing, and goal setting. While there is no widely agreed-upon approach, TQM efforts typically draw heavily on the previously developed tools and techniques of quality control. TQM enjoyed widespread attention during the late 1980s and early 1990s before being overshadowed by ISO 9000, Lean manufacturing, and Six Sigma.

Exam Probability: **Medium**

48. *Answer choices:*

(see index for correct answer)

- a. Production part approval process
- b. ERPNEXT
- c. production control
- d. Total Quality Management

Guidance: level 1

:: Labour relations ::

_____ is the practice of hiring more workers than are needed to perform a given job, or to adopt work procedures which appear pointless, complex and time-consuming merely to employ additional workers. The term "make-work" is sometimes used as a synonym for _____ .

Exam Probability: **Low**

49. *Answer choices:*

(see index for correct answer)

- a. Boulwarism
- b. Inflatable rat
- c. Featherbedding

- d. Broad left

Guidance: level 1

:: Human resource management ::

_____ refers to the ratio of the number of job positions to the number of job applicants and is used in the context of selection and recruitment.

Exam Probability: **Medium**

50. *Answer choices:*

(see index for correct answer)

- a. Continuing professional development
- b. Induction training
- c. Selection ratio
- d. Compensation and benefits

Guidance: level 1

:: Behavior ::

_____ refers to behavior-change procedures that were employed during the 1970s and early 1980s. Based on methodological behaviorism, overt behavior was modified with presumed consequences, including artificial positive and negative reinforcement contingencies to increase desirable behavior, or administering positive and negative punishment and/or extinction to reduce problematic behavior. For the treatment of phobias, habituation and punishment were the basic principles used in flooding, a subcategory of desensitization.

Exam Probability: **High**

51. *Answer choices:*

(see index for correct answer)

- a. Behavior modification
- b. theory of planned behavior

Guidance: level 1

_____, also known as alcohol use disorder, is a broad term for any drinking of alcohol that results in mental or physical health problems. The disorder was previously divided into two types: alcohol abuse and alcohol dependence. In a medical context, _____ is said to exist when two or more of the following conditions are present: a person drinks large amounts of alcohol over a long time period, has difficulty cutting down, acquiring and drinking alcohol takes up a great deal of time, alcohol is strongly desired, usage results in not fulfilling responsibilities, usage results in social problems, usage results in health problems, usage results in risky situations, withdrawal occurs when stopping, and alcohol tolerance has occurred with use. Risky situations include drinking and driving or having unsafe sex, among other things. Alcohol use can affect all parts of the body, but it particularly affects the brain, heart, liver, pancreas and immune system. This can result in mental illness, Wernicke–Korsakoff syndrome, irregular heartbeat, an impaired immune response, liver cirrhosis and increased cancer risk, among other diseases. Drinking during pregnancy can cause damage to the baby resulting in fetal alcohol spectrum disorders. Women are generally more sensitive than men to the harmful physical and mental effects of alcohol.

Exam Probability: **High**

52. *Answer choices:*
(see index for correct answer)

- a. levels of analysis
- b. open system
- c. hierarchical perspective
- d. corporate values

Guidance: level 1

The causes of _____ are heavily debated. Classical economics, new classical economics, and the Austrian School of economics argued that market mechanisms are reliable means of resolving _____. These theories argue against interventions imposed on the labor market from the outside, such as unionization, bureaucratic work rules, minimum wage laws, taxes, and other regulations that they claim discourage the hiring of workers. Keynesian economics emphasizes the cyclical nature of _____ and recommends government interventions in the economy that it claims will reduce _____ during recessions. This theory focuses on recurrent shocks that suddenly reduce aggregate demand for goods and services and thus reduce demand for workers. Keynesian models recommend government interventions designed to increase demand for workers; these can include financial stimuli, publicly funded job creation, and expansionist monetary policies. Its namesake economist, John Maynard Keynes, believed that the root cause of _____ is the desire of investors to receive more money rather than produce more products, which is not possible without public bodies producing new money. A third group of theories emphasize the need for a stable supply of capital and investment to maintain full employment. On this view, government should guarantee full employment through fiscal policy, monetary policy and trade policy as stated, for example, in the US Employment Act of 1946, by counteracting private sector or trade investment volatility, and reducing inequality.

Exam Probability: **Medium**

53. *Answer choices:*

(see index for correct answer)

- a. Unemployment
- b. cultural
- c. empathy
- d. corporate values

Guidance: level 1

:: Management education ::

> _____ is the implementation of government policy and also an academic discipline that studies this implementation and prepares civil servants for working in the public service. As a "field of inquiry with a diverse scope" whose fundamental goal is to "advance management and policies so that government can function". Some of the various definitions which have been offered for the term are: "the management of public programs"; the "translation of politics into the reality that citizens see every day"; and "the study of government decision making, the analysis of the policies themselves, the various inputs that have produced them, and the inputs necessary to produce alternative policies."

Exam Probability: **Low**

54. *Answer choices:*

(see index for correct answer)

- a. Master of Science in Management
- b. Entrepreneur in residence
- c. Asian Business Case Competition @ Nanyang
- d. Academy of Management

Guidance: level 1

:: Human resource management ::

A _____ is a group of people with different functional expertise working toward a common goal. It may include people from finance, marketing, operations, and human resources departments. Typically, it includes employees from all levels of an organization. Members may also come from outside an organization .

Exam Probability: **High**

55. *Answer choices:*

(see index for correct answer)

- a. Cross-functional team
- b. Joint Personnel Administration
- c. Adaptive performance
- d. SLT Human Capital Solutions

Guidance: level 1

:: Employment compensation ::

_____ refers to various incentive plans introduced by businesses that provide direct or indirect payments to employees that depend on company's profitability in addition to employees' regular salary and bonuses. In publicly traded companies these plans typically amount to allocation of shares to employees. One of the earliest pioneers of _____ was Englishman Theodore Cooke Taylor, who is known to have introduced the practice in his woollen mills during the late 1800s .

Exam Probability: **High**

56. *Answer choices:*

(see index for correct answer)

- a. Crowell v. Benson
- b. Severance package
- c. Profit sharing
- d. Performance-related pay

Guidance: level 1

:: Recruitment ::

_____ is a specialized recruitment service which organizations pay to seek out and recruit highly qualified candidates for senior-level and executive jobs . Headhunters may also seek out and recruit other highly specialized and/or skilled positions in organizations for which there is strong competition in the job market for the top talent, such as senior data analysts or computer programmers. The method usually involves commissioning a third-party organization, typically an _____ firm, but possibly a standalone consultant or consulting firm, to research the availability of suitable qualified candidates working for competitors or related businesses or organizations. Having identified a shortlist of qualified candidates who match the client's requirements, the _____ firm may act as an intermediary to contact the individual and see if they might be interested in moving to a new employer. The _____ firm may also carry out initial screening of the candidate, negotiations on remuneration and benefits, and preparing the employment contract. In some markets there has been a move towards using _____ for lower positions driven by the fact that there are less candidates for some positions even on lower levels than executive.

Exam Probability: **Medium**

57. *Answer choices:*

(see index for correct answer)

- a. S.I.R. Method of Recruiting
- b. Peak earning years
- c. Global Career Development Facilitator
- d. Association of Graduate Recruiters

Guidance: level 1

:: Industrial engineering ::

_____ is the formal process that sits alongside Requirements analysis and focuses on the human elements of the requirements.

Exam Probability: **Medium**

58. *Answer choices:*

(see index for correct answer)

- a. Industrial ecology
- b. Material flow
- c. Industrial engineering and operations research
- d. Indian Institution of Industrial Engineering

Guidance: level 1

:: Power (social and political) ::

> In a notable study of power conducted by social psychologists John R. P. French and Bertram Raven in 1959, power is divided into five separate and distinct forms. In 1965 Raven revised this model to include a sixth form by separating the informational power base as distinct from the _____ base.

Exam Probability: **Low**

59. *Answer choices:*

(see index for correct answer)

- a. need for power
- b. Referent power
- c. Expert power

Guidance: level 1

Information systems

Information systems (IS) are formal, sociotechnical, organizational systems designed to collect, process, store, and distribute information. In a sociotechnical perspective Information Systems are composed by four components: technology, process, people and organizational structure.

:: Network management ::

_____ is the process of administering and managing computer networks. Services provided by this discipline include fault analysis, performance management, provisioning of networks and maintaining the quality of service. Software that enables network administrators to perform their functions is called _____ software.

Exam Probability: **Low**

1. *Answer choices:*

(see index for correct answer)

- a. Network management
- b. Jumpnode
- c. Cisco Prime
- d. Operations support system

Guidance: level 1

:: Data security ::

_____ are safeguards or countermeasures to avoid, detect, counteract, or minimize security risks to physical property, information, computer systems, or other assets.

Exam Probability: **Low**

2. *Answer choices:*

(see index for correct answer)

- a. Security controls
- b. Paper key
- c. Certified Information Systems Auditor
- d. Backup validation

Guidance: level 1

:: World Wide Web Consortium standards ::

> _____ is a markup language that defines a set of rules for encoding documents in a format that is both human-readable and machine-readable. The W3C's XML 1.0 Specification and several other related specifications—all of them free open standards—define XML.

Exam Probability: **Low**

3. *Answer choices:*

(see index for correct answer)

- a. Extensible Markup Language
- b. Hypertext markup language

Guidance: level 1

:: Data security ::

> In information technology, a _____ , or data _____ , or the process of backing up, refers to the copying into an archive file of computer data that is already in secondary storage—so that it may be used to restore the original after a data loss event. The verb form is "back up" , whereas the noun and adjective form is " _____ ".

Exam Probability: **Medium**

4. *Answer choices:*

(see index for correct answer)

- a. Doxing
- b. Virtual private database
- c. Air gap
- d. Backup

Guidance: level 1

:: ::

A _____ , sometimes called a passcode, is a memorized secret used to confirm the identity of a user. Using the terminology of the NIST Digital Identity Guidelines, the secret is memorized by a party called the claimant while the party verifying the identity of the claimant is called the verifier. When the claimant successfully demonstrates knowledge of the _____ to the verifier through an established authentication protocol, the verifier is able to infer the claimant's identity.

Exam Probability: **High**

5. *Answer choices:*

(see index for correct answer)

- a. deep-level diversity

- b. Sarbanes-Oxley act of 2002
- c. open system
- d. empathy

Guidance: level 1

:: ::

A _____ is an organized collection of data, generally stored and accessed electronically from a computer system. Where _____ s are more complex they are often developed using formal design and modeling techniques.

Exam Probability: **Low**

6. *Answer choices:*

(see index for correct answer)

- a. Database
- b. interpersonal communication
- c. hierarchical perspective
- d. information systems assessment

Guidance: level 1

:: Google services ::

A blog is a discussion or informational website published on the World Wide Web consisting of discrete, often informal diary-style text entries. Posts are typically displayed in reverse chronological order, so that the most recent post appears first, at the top of the web page. Until 2009, blogs were usually the work of a single individual, occasionally of a small group, and often covered a single subject or topic. In the 2010s, "multi-author blogs" emerged, featuring the writing of multiple authors and sometimes professionally edited. MABs from newspapers, other media outlets, universities, think tanks, advocacy groups, and similar institutions account for an increasing quantity of blog traffic. The rise of Twitter and other "microblogging" systems helps integrate MABs and single-author blogs into the news media. Blog can also be used as a verb, meaning to maintain or add content to a blog.

Exam Probability: **Low**

7. *Answer choices:*

(see index for correct answer)

- a. AdSense
- b. WDYL
- c. Blogger
- d. Google Cultural Institute

Guidance: level 1

:: ::

_____ rate is the ratio of users who click on a specific link to the number of total users who view a page, email, or advertisement. It is commonly used to measure the success of an online advertising campaign for a particular website as well as the effectiveness of email campaigns.

Exam Probability: **Medium**

8. *Answer choices:*

(see index for correct answer)

- a. hierarchical
- b. levels of analysis
- c. Click-through
- d. functional perspective

Guidance: level 1

:: Computer security standards ::

The _____ for Information Technology Security Evaluation is an international standard for computer security certification. It is currently in version 3.1 revision 5.

Exam Probability: **High**

9. *Answer choices:*

(see index for correct answer)

- a. Common Criteria
- b. Trusted Computer System Evaluation Criteria
- c. ISO 15292
- d. IEC 60870-6

Guidance: level 1

:: ::

> The _____ of 1996 was enacted by the 104th United States Congress and signed by President Bill Clinton in 1996. It was created primarily to modernize the flow of healthcare information, stipulate how Personally Identifiable Information maintained by the healthcare and healthcare insurance industries should be protected from fraud and theft, and address limitations on healthcare insurance coverage.

Exam Probability: **High**

10. *Answer choices:*
(see index for correct answer)

- a. hierarchical
- b. hierarchical perspective
- c. surface-level diversity
- d. Health Insurance Portability and Accountability Act

Guidance: level 1

:: Online companies ::

_____ is a business directory service and crowd-sourced review forum, and a public company of the same name that is headquartered in San Francisco, California. The company develops, hosts and markets the _____ .com website and the _____ mobile app, which publish crowd-sourced reviews about businesses. It also operates an online reservation service called _____ Reservations.

Exam Probability: **Medium**

11. *Answer choices:*

(see index for correct answer)

- a. Cyworld
- b. Yelp
- c. Justdial
- d. Whotrades

Guidance: level 1

:: Data interchange standards ::

_____ is the concept of businesses electronically communicating information that was traditionally communicated on paper, such as purchase orders and invoices. Technical standards for EDI exist to facilitate parties transacting such instruments without having to make special arrangements.

Exam Probability: **Low**

12. *Answer choices:*

(see index for correct answer)

- a. Interaction protocol
- b. Domain Application Protocol
- c. Data Interchange Standards Association
- d. Electronic data interchange

Guidance: level 1

:: Marketing ::

_____ is the percentage of a market accounted for by a specific entity. In a survey of nearly 200 senior marketing managers, 67% responded that they found the revenue- "dollar _____ " metric very useful, while 61% found "unit _____ " very useful.

Exam Probability: **Medium**

13. *Answer choices:*

(see index for correct answer)

- a. Market overhang
- b. Franchise fee
- c. Macromarketing
- d. Market share

Guidance: level 1

:: Strategic management ::

In marketing strategy, first-mover advantage is the advantage gained by the initial significant occupant of a market segment. First-mover advantage may be gained by technological leadership, or early purchase of resources.

Exam Probability: **High**

14. *Answer choices:*

(see index for correct answer)

- a. First mover advantage
- b. Business system planning
- c. customer lock-in
- d. E-learning Maturity Model

Guidance: level 1

:: History of human–computer interaction ::

A _____ , plural mice, is a small rodent characteristically having a pointed snout, small rounded ears, a body-length scaly tail and a high breeding rate. The best known _____ species is the common house _____ . It is also a popular pet. In some places, certain kinds of field mice are locally common. They are known to invade homes for food and shelter.

Exam Probability: **Low**

15. *Answer choices:*

(see index for correct answer)

- a. Trackball
- b. Mousepad
- c. Block-oriented terminal
- d. History of the graphical user interface

Guidance: level 1

:: Computer access control protocols ::

An _____ is a type of computer communications protocol or cryptographic protocol specifically designed for transfer of authentication data between two entities. It allows the receiving entity to authenticate the connecting entity as well as authenticate itself to the connecting entity by declaring the type of information needed for authentication as well as syntax. It is the most important layer of protection needed for secure communication within computer networks.

Exam Probability: **Medium**

16. *Answer choices:*

(see index for correct answer)

- a. Protected Extensible Authentication Protocol
- b. Authentication protocol
- c. POP before SMTP
- d. ID-MM7

Guidance: level 1

:: Information technology management ::

_____ s or pop-ups are forms of online advertising on the World Wide Web. A pop-up is a graphical user interface display area, usually a small window, that suddenly appears in the foreground of the visual interface. The pop-up window containing an advertisement is usually generated by JavaScript that uses cross-site scripting, sometimes with a secondary payload that uses Adobe Flash. They can also be generated by other vulnerabilities/security holes in browser security.

Exam Probability: **Medium**

17. *Answer choices:*

(see index for correct answer)

- a. Digital asset management
- b. IFPUG
- c. Data warehouse appliance
- d. Pop-up ad

Guidance: level 1

:: Data management ::

Data aggregation is the compiling of information from databases with intent to prepare combined datasets for data processing.

Exam Probability: **Low**

18. *Answer choices:*

(see index for correct answer)

- a. single sourcing
- b. Content inventory
- c. Data conditioning
- d. Data aggregator

Guidance: level 1

:: Data management ::

_____ means protecting digital data, such as those in a database, from destructive forces and from the unwanted actions of unauthorized users, such as a cyberattack or a data breach.

Exam Probability: **Medium**

19. *Answer choices:*
(see index for correct answer)

- a. Government Performance Management
- b. Very large database
- c. Scriptella
- d. Enterprise Data Planning

Guidance: level 1

:: Management ::

A _____ defines or constrains some aspect of business and always resolves to either true or false. _____ s are intended to assert business structure or to control or influence the behavior of the business. _____ s describe the operations, definitions and constraints that apply to an organization. _____ s can apply to people, processes, corporate behavior and computing systems in an organization, and are put in place to help the organization achieve its goals.

Exam Probability: **High**

20. *Answer choices:*

(see index for correct answer)

- a. Main Street Manager
- b. Balanced scorecard
- c. Swarm Development Group
- d. Marketing science

Guidance: level 1

:: Infographics ::

A _____ is a graphical representation of data, in which "the data is represented by symbols, such as bars in a bar _____, lines in a line _____, or slices in a pie _____". A _____ can represent tabular numeric data, functions or some kinds of qualitative structure and provides different info.

Exam Probability: **Low**

21. *Answer choices:*

(see index for correct answer)

- a. Check sheet
- b. Nameplate
- c. Patent visualisation
- d. State diagram

Guidance: level 1

:: Production economics ::

In microeconomics, _____ are the cost advantages that enterprises obtain due to their scale of operation, with cost per unit of output decreasing with increasing scale.

Exam Probability: **Low**

22. *Answer choices:*

(see index for correct answer)

- a. The labor problem
- b. Hicks-neutral technical change
- c. Sharing
- d. Economies of scale

Guidance: level 1

:: Geographic information systems ::

_____ is the computational process of transforming a physical address description to a location on the Earth's surface. Reverse _____, on the other hand, converts geographic coordinates to a description of a location, usually the name of a place or an addressable location. _____ relies on a computer representation of address points, the street / road network, together with postal and administrative boundaries.

Exam Probability: **Medium**

23. *Answer choices:*

(see index for correct answer)

- a. Distributed GIS
- b. Geoportal
- c. Geocoding
- d. Aerodrome mapping database

Guidance: level 1

:: Strategic management ::

_____ is a management term for an element that is necessary for an organization or project to achieve its mission. Alternative terms are key result area and key success factor .

Exam Probability: **High**

24. *Answer choices:*

(see index for correct answer)

- a. SWOT analysis
- b. Operational responsiveness
- c. Critical success factor
- d. Talent portfolio management

Guidance: level 1

:: Payment systems ::

_____ s are part of a payment system issued by financial institutions, such as a bank, to a customer that enables its owner to access the funds in the customer's designated bank accounts, or through a credit account and make payments by electronic funds transfer and access automated teller machines . Such cards are known by a variety of names including bank cards, ATM cards, MAC , client cards, key cards or cash cards.

Exam Probability: **Low**

25. *Answer choices:*

(see index for correct answer)

- a. Payment card
- b. Currence
- c. Boleto
- d. Concord EFS, Inc.

Guidance: level 1

:: Identity management ::

_____ is the ability of an individual or group to seclude themselves, or information about themselves, and thereby express themselves selectively. The boundaries and content of what is considered private differ among cultures and individuals, but share common themes. When something is private to a person, it usually means that something is inherently special or sensitive to them. The domain of _____ partially overlaps with security, which can include the concepts of appropriate use, as well as protection of information. _____ may also take the form of bodily integrity.

Exam Probability: **Medium**

26. *Answer choices:*

(see index for correct answer)

- a. Identity 3.0
- b. Service Provisioning Markup Language

- c. Privacy
- d. Password manager

Guidance: level 1

:: Knowledge engineering ::

The _____ is an extension of the World Wide Web through standards by the World Wide Web Consortium. The standards promote common data formats and exchange protocols on the Web, most fundamentally the Resource Description Framework. According to the W3C, "The _____ provides a common framework that allows data to be shared and reused across application, enterprise, and community boundaries". The _____ is therefore regarded as an integrator across different content, information applications and systems.

Exam Probability: **Medium**

27. *Answer choices:*
(see index for correct answer)

- a. Information Routing Group
- b. International Journal of Software Engineering and Knowledge Engineering
- c. Knowledge Collection from Volunteer Contributors
- d. Semantic Web

Guidance: level 1

:: Internet marketing ::

_____ is the measurement, collection, analysis and reporting of web data for purposes of understanding and optimizing web usage. However, _____ is not just a process for measuring web traffic but can be used as a tool for business and market research, and to assess and improve the effectiveness of a website. _____ applications can also help companies measure the results of traditional print or broadcast advertising campaigns. It helps one to estimate how traffic to a website changes after the launch of a new advertising campaign. _____ provides information about the number of visitors to a website and the number of page views. It helps gauge traffic and popularity trends which is useful for market research.

Exam Probability: **High**

28. *Answer choices:*

(see index for correct answer)

- a. Web analytics
- b. Search engine optimization
- c. Guided selling
- d. Get into Bed with Google

Guidance: level 1

:: Metadata ::

_____ s usage can be discovered by inspection of software applications or application data files through a process of manual or automated Application Discovery and Understanding. Once _____ s are discovered they can be registered in a metadata registry.

Exam Probability: **Medium**

29. *Answer choices:*

(see index for correct answer)

- a. N-Triples
- b. Rights Expression Language
- c. File association
- d. Metacrap

Guidance: level 1

:: ::

A web _____ or Internet _____ is a software system that is designed to carry out web search , which means to search the World Wide Web in a systematic way for particular information specified in a web search query. The search results are generally presented in a line of results, often referred to as _____ results pages . The information may be a mix of web pages, images, videos, infographics, articles, research papers and other types of files. Some _____ s also mine data available in databases or open directories. Unlike web directories, which are maintained only by human editors, _____ s also maintain real-time information by running an algorithm on a web crawler.Internet content that is not capable of being searched by a web _____ is generally described as the deep web.

Exam Probability: **High**

30. *Answer choices:*

(see index for correct answer)

- a. levels of analysis
- b. Search engine
- c. hierarchical perspective
- d. surface-level diversity

Guidance: level 1

:: Teams ::

A _____ usually refers to a group of individuals who work together from different geographic locations and rely on communication technology such as email, FAX, and video or voice conferencing services in order to collaborate. The term can also refer to groups or teams that work together asynchronously or across organizational levels. Powell, Piccoli and Ives define _____ s as "groups of geographically, organizationally and/or time dispersed workers brought together by information and telecommunication technologies to accomplish one or more organizational tasks." According to Ale Ebrahim et. al. , _____ s can also be defined as "small temporary groups of geographically, organizationally and/or time dispersed knowledge workers who coordinate their work predominantly with electronic information and communication technologies in order to accomplish one or more organization tasks."

Exam Probability: **Medium**

31. *Answer choices:*

(see index for correct answer)

- a. team composition
- b. Team-building

Guidance: level 1

:: Data management ::

Given organizations' increasing dependency on information technology to run their operations, Business continuity planning covers the entire organization, and Disaster recovery focuses on IT.

Exam Probability: **Medium**

32. *Answer choices:*

(see index for correct answer)

- a. Database transaction
- b. Modular serializability
- c. Data access
- d. Machine-readable data

Guidance: level 1

:: IT risk management ::

_____ involves a set of policies, tools and procedures to enable the recovery or continuation of vital technology infrastructure and systems following a natural or human-induced disaster. _____ focuses on the IT or technology systems supporting critical business functions, as opposed to business continuity, which involves keeping all essential aspects of a business functioning despite significant disruptive events. _____ can therefore be considered as a subset of business continuity.

Exam Probability: **Low**

33. *Answer choices:*

(see index for correct answer)

- a. Incident response team

- b. Information assurance
- c. Business continuity

Guidance: level 1

:: Telecommunication theory ::

In reliability theory and reliability engineering, the term _____ has the following meanings.

Exam Probability: **Low**

34. *Answer choices:*

(see index for correct answer)

- a. Availability
- b. Bias distortion
- c. Harmonic mixer
- d. Trellis

Guidance: level 1

:: Management ::

In business, a _____ is the attribute that allows an organization to outperform its competitors. A _____ may include access to natural resources, such as high-grade ores or a low-cost power source, highly skilled labor, geographic location, high entry barriers, and access to new technology.

Exam Probability: **High**

35. *Answer choices:*

(see index for correct answer)

- a. Facilitator
- b. Competitive advantage
- c. Productive efficiency
- d. Mushroom management

Guidance: level 1

:: Commercial item transport and distribution ::

In commerce, supply-chain management, the management of the flow of goods and services, involves the movement and storage of raw materials, of work-in-process inventory, and of finished goods from point of origin to point of consumption. Interconnected or interlinked networks, channels and node businesses combine in the provision of products and services required by end customers in a supply chain. Supply-chain management has been defined as the "design, planning, execution, control, and monitoring of supply-chain activities with the objective of creating net value, building a competitive infrastructure, leveraging worldwide logistics, synchronizing supply with demand and measuring performance globally."SCM practice draws heavily from the areas of industrial engineering, systems engineering, operations management, logistics, procurement, information technology, and marketing and strives for an integrated approach. Marketing channels play an important role in supply-chain management. Current research in supply-chain management is concerned with topics related to sustainability and risk management, among others. Some suggest that the "people dimension" of SCM, ethical issues, internal integration, transparency/visibility, and human capital/talent management are topics that have, so far, been underrepresented on the research agenda.

Exam Probability: **Medium**

36. *Answer choices:*

(see index for correct answer)

- a. Surface Freight Forwarder Deregulation Act of 1986
- b. MC Freight Systems
- c. Australia standard pallets
- d. Fuel cell forklift

Guidance: level 1

:: Outsourcing ::

A service-level agreement is a commitment between a service provider and a client. Particular aspects of the service – quality, availability, responsibilities – are agreed between the service provider and the service user. The most common component of SLA is that the services should be provided to the customer as agreed upon in the contract. As an example, Internet service providers and telcos will commonly include _____ s within the terms of their contracts with customers to define the level of service being sold in plain language terms. In this case the SLA will typically have a technical definition in mean time between failures , mean time to repair or mean time to recovery ; identifying which party is responsible for reporting faults or paying fees; responsibility for various data rates; throughput; jitter; or similar measurable details.

Exam Probability: **High**

37. *Answer choices:*
(see index for correct answer)

- a. Telarus
- b. Service level agreement
- c. Managed security service
- d. Website Management Outsourcing

Guidance: level 1

:: User interfaces ::

_____, keystroke biometrics, typing dynamics and lately typing biometrics, is the detailed timing information which describes exactly when each key was pressed and when it was released as a person is typing at a computer keyboard.

Exam Probability: **Medium**

38. *Answer choices:*

(see index for correct answer)

- a. Sparsh
- b. Light-on-dark color scheme
- c. Dasher
- d. Keystroke dynamics

Guidance: level 1

:: Internet advertising ::

_____ is software that aims to gather information about a person or organization, sometimes without their knowledge, that may send such information to another entity without the consumer's consent, that asserts control over a device without the consumer's knowledge, or it may send such information to another entity with the consumer's consent, through cookies.

Exam Probability: **Low**

39. Answer choices:

(see index for correct answer)

- a. Spyware
- b. Boltblue
- c. Value Per Action
- d. Jason Harris

Guidance: level 1

:: Enterprise modelling ::

> _____ are large-scale application software packages that support business processes, information flows, reporting, and data analytics in complex organizations. While ES are generally packaged enterprise application software systems they can also be bespoke, custom developed systems created to support a specific organization's needs.

Exam Probability: **Low**

40. Answer choices:

(see index for correct answer)

- a. Generalised Enterprise Reference Architecture and Methodology
- b. Avolution
- c. Enterprise systems
- d. Behavior Trees

Guidance: level 1

:: Business process ::

A _____ or business method is a collection of related, structured activities or tasks by people or equipment which in a specific sequence produce a service or product for a particular customer or customers. _____ es occur at all organizational levels and may or may not be visible to the customers. A _____ may often be visualized as a flowchart of a sequence of activities with interleaving decision points or as a process matrix of a sequence of activities with relevance rules based on data in the process. The benefits of using _____ es include improved customer satisfaction and improved agility for reacting to rapid market change. Process-oriented organizations break down the barriers of structural departments and try to avoid functional silos.

Exam Probability: **Medium**

41. *Answer choices:*

(see index for correct answer)

- a. Business process outsourcing
- b. Order processing
- c. Business process
- d. Signavio

Guidance: level 1

:: Survey methodology ::

An _____ is a conversation where questions are asked and answers are given. In common parlance, the word " _____ " refers to a one-on-one conversation between an _____ er and an _____ ee. The _____ er asks questions to which the _____ ee responds, usually so information may be transferred from _____ ee to _____ er. Sometimes, information can be transferred in both directions. It is a communication, unlike a speech, which produces a one-way flow of information.

Exam Probability: **Medium**

42. *Answer choices:*

(see index for correct answer)

- a. Coverage error
- b. Interview
- c. Self-report
- d. World Association for Public Opinion Research

Guidance: level 1

:: E-commerce ::

Electronic governance or e-governance is the application of information and communication technology for delivering government services, exchange of information, communication transactions, integration of various stand-alone systems and services between _____ , government-to-business , government-to-government , government-to-employees as well as back-office processes and interactions within the entire government framework. Through e-governance, government services are made available to citizens in a convenient, efficient, and transparent manner. The three main target groups that can be distinguished in governance concepts are government, citizens, andbusinesses/interest groups. In e-governance, there are no distinct boundaries.

Exam Probability: **Low**

43. *Answer choices:*

(see index for correct answer)

- a. Coinye
- b. Confinity
- c. Government-to-citizen
- d. Digital certificate

Guidance: level 1

:: E-commerce ::

_____ is a subset of electronic commerce that involves social media, online media that supports social interaction, and user contributions to assist online buying and selling of products and services.

Exam Probability: **High**

44. *Answer choices:*

(see index for correct answer)

- a. Sears Israel
- b. FastSpring
- c. TRADACOMS
- d. Social commerce

Guidance: level 1

:: ::

_____ is a free email service developed by Google. Users can access _____ on the web and using third-party programs that synchronize email content through POP or IMAP protocols. _____ started as a limited beta release on April 1, 2004 and ended its testing phase on July 7, 2009.

Exam Probability: **High**

45. *Answer choices:*

(see index for correct answer)

- a. Gmail
- b. functional perspective
- c. co-culture

- d. Sarbanes-Oxley act of 2002

Guidance: level 1

:: Business ::

_____ is a sourcing model in which individuals or organizations obtain goods and services, including ideas and finances, from a large, relatively open and often rapidly-evolving group of internet users; it divides work between participants to achieve a cumulative result. The word _____ itself is a portmanteau of crowd and outsourcing, and was coined in 2005. As a mode of sourcing, _____ existed prior to the digital age .

Exam Probability: **Low**

46. *Answer choices:*
(see index for correct answer)

- a. Absentee business owner
- b. Counter trade
- c. Gray ceiling
- d. Business

Guidance: level 1

:: Data transmission ::

In telecommunication a _____ is the means of connecting one location to another for the purpose of transmitting and receiving digital information. It can also refer to a set of electronics assemblies, consisting of a transmitter and a receiver and the interconnecting data telecommunication circuit. These are governed by a link protocol enabling digital data to be transferred from a data source to a data sink.

Exam Probability: **Medium**

47. *Answer choices:*

(see index for correct answer)

- a. Data link
- b. SENT
- c. Viterbi decoder
- d. CSIX

Guidance: level 1

:: Database theory ::

_____ is the organisation of data according to a database model. The designer determines what data must be stored and how the data elements interrelate. With this information, they can begin to fit the data to the database model.

Exam Probability: **Medium**

48. *Answer choices:*

(see index for correct answer)

- a. Database design
- b. Range searching
- c. Universal relation assumption
- d. Exclusive relationship

Guidance: level 1

:: Google services ::

_____ is a time-management and scheduling calendar service developed by Google. It became available in beta release April 13, 2006, and in general release in July 2009, on the web and as mobile apps for the Android and iOS platforms.

Exam Probability: **Low**

49. *Answer choices:*

(see index for correct answer)

- a. Google IME
- b. Google Classroom
- c. Google Person Finder
- d. Google Calendar

Guidance: level 1

:: Data privacy ::

_____ is the relationship between the collection and dissemination of data, technology, the public expectation of privacy, legal and political issues surrounding them. It is also known as data privacy or data protection.

Exam Probability: **High**

50. *Answer choices:*

(see index for correct answer)

- a. Information privacy
- b. Habeas data
- c. Information Commissioner
- d. Payment Card Industry Data Security Standard

Guidance: level 1

:: Computer networking ::

_____ is a method of grouping data that is transmitted over a digital network into packets. Packets are made of a header and a payload. Data in the header are used by networking hardware to direct the packet to its destination where the payload is extracted and used by application software. _____ is the primary basis for data communications in computer networks worldwide.

Exam Probability: **High**

51. *Answer choices:*

(see index for correct answer)

- a. Security domain
- b. SMDS
- c. Packet switching
- d. Hostname

Guidance: level 1

:: World Wide Web ::

A _____ is a document that is suitable to act as a web resource on the World Wide Web. In order to graphically display a _____ , a web browser is needed. This is a type of software that can retrieve _____ s from the Internet. When accessed by a web browser it may be displayed as a _____ on a monitor or mobile device. Typical _____ s are hypertext documents which contain hyperlinks, often referred to as links, for browsing to other _____ s.

Exam Probability: **High**

52. *Answer choices:*

(see index for correct answer)

- a. Ovi
- b. Server Side Includes
- c. Digital Concert Hall
- d. Web page

Guidance: level 1

:: ::

_____ are interactive computer-mediated technologies that facilitate the creation and sharing of information, ideas, career interests and other forms of expression via virtual communities and networks. The variety of stand-alone and built-in _____ services currently available introduces challenges of definition; however, there are some common features.

Exam Probability: **Medium**

53. *Answer choices:*

(see index for correct answer)

- a. Social media
- b. cultural

- c. functional perspective
- d. Sarbanes-Oxley act of 2002

Guidance: level 1

:: Domain name system ::

The _____ is a hierarchical and decentralized naming system for computers, services, or other resources connected to the Internet or a private network. It associates various information with domain names assigned to each of the participating entities. Most prominently, it translates more readily memorized domain names to the numerical IP addresses needed for locating and identifying computer services and devices with the underlying network protocols. By providing a worldwide, distributed directory service, the _____ has been an essential component of the functionality of the Internet since 1985.

Exam Probability: **Medium**

54. *Answer choices:*

(see index for correct answer)

- a. Fully qualified domain name
- b. Dynamic Delegation Discovery System
- c. Dig
- d. Domain Name System

Guidance: level 1

:: Ethically disputed business practices ::

_____ is the use of messaging systems to send an unsolicited message, especially advertising, as well as sending messages repeatedly on the same site. While the most widely recognized form of spam is email spam, the term is applied to similar abuses in other media: instant messaging spam, Usenet newsgroup spam, Web search engine spam, spam in blogs, wiki spam, online classified ads spam, mobile phone messaging spam, Internet forum spam, junk fax transmissions, social spam, spam mobile apps, television advertising and file sharing spam. It is named after Spam, a luncheon meat, by way of a Monty Python sketch about a restaurant that has Spam in every dish and where patrons annoyingly chant "Spam!" over and over again.

Exam Probability: **High**

55. *Answer choices:*

(see index for correct answer)

- a. Earnings management
- b. Spiv
- c. Anti-competitive practices
- d. Spamming

Guidance: level 1

:: Market structure and pricing ::

_____ is a term denoting that a product includes permission to use its source code, design documents, or content. It most commonly refers to the open-source model, in which open-source software or other products are released under an open-source license as part of the open-source-software movement. Use of the term originated with software, but has expanded beyond the software sector to cover other open content and forms of open collaboration.

Exam Probability: **Medium**

56. *Answer choices:*

(see index for correct answer)

- a. Market structure
- b. Open-source economics
- c. industry concentration
- d. Liberalization

Guidance: level 1

:: Industrial design ::

Across the many fields concerned with _____, including information science, computer science, human-computer interaction, communication, and industrial design, there is little agreement over the meaning of the term "_____", although all are related to interaction with computers and other machines with a user interface.

Exam Probability: **Low**

57. *Answer choices:*

(see index for correct answer)

- a. Projection augmented model
- b. Sky-Sailor
- c. Slow design
- d. Danish design

Guidance: level 1

:: Telecommunications engineering ::

A _____ is a computer processor that incorporates the functions of a central processing unit on a single integrated circuit, or at most a few integrated circuits. The _____ is a multipurpose, clock driven, register based, digital integrated circuit that accepts binary data as input, processes it according to instructions stored in its memory and provides results as output. _____ s contain both combinational logic and sequential digital logic. _____ s operate on numbers and symbols represented in the binary number system.

Exam Probability: **High**

58. *Answer choices:*

(see index for correct answer)

- a. network architecture
- b. Microprocessor

Guidance: level 1

:: Network performance ::

_____ is a distributed computing paradigm which brings computer data storage closer to the location where it is needed. Computation is largely or completely performed on distributed device nodes. _____ pushes applications, data and computing power away from centralized points to locations closer to the user. The target of _____ is any application or general functionality needing to be closer to the source of the action where distributed systems technology interacts with the physical world. _____ does not need contact with any centralized cloud, although it may interact with one. In contrast to cloud computing, _____ refers to decentralized data processing at the edge of the network.

Exam Probability: **Medium**

59. *Answer choices:*

(see index for correct answer)

- a. Traffic shaping
- b. Service assurance
- c. Rate limiting
- d. Goodput

Guidance: level 1

Marketing

Marketing is the study and management of exchange relationships. Marketing is the business process of creating relationships with and satisfying customers. With its focus on the customer, marketing is one of the premier components of business management.

Marketing is defined by the American Marketing Association as "the activity, set of institutions, and processes for creating, communicating, delivering, and exchanging offerings that have value for customers, clients, partners, and society at large."

:: Stochastic processes ::

_____ in its modern meaning is a "new idea, creative thoughts, new imaginations in form of device or method". _____ is often also viewed as the application of better solutions that meet new requirements, unarticulated needs, or existing market needs. Such _____ takes place through the provision of more-effective products, processes, services, technologies, or business models that are made available to markets, governments and society. An _____ is something original and more effective and, as a consequence, new, that "breaks into" the market or society. _____ is related to, but not the same as, invention, as _____ is more apt to involve the practical implementation of an invention to make a meaningful impact in the market or society, and not all _____ s require an invention. _____ often manifests itself via the engineering process, when the problem being solved is of a technical or scientific nature. The opposite of _____ is exnovation.

Exam Probability: **High**

1. *Answer choices:*

(see index for correct answer)

- a. Traffic equations
- b. Gibbs state
- c. Dirichlet process
- d. Innovation

Guidance: level 1

:: Pricing ::

_____ is unwanted sound judged to be unpleasant, loud or disruptive to hearing. From a physics standpoint, _____ is indistinguishable from sound, as both are vibrations through a medium, such as air or water. The difference arises when the brain receives and perceives a sound.

Exam Probability: **High**

2. *Answer choices:*

(see index for correct answer)

- a. Registration fee
- b. Capital loss
- c. Noise
- d. Big ticket item

Guidance: level 1

:: Cognitive dissonance ::

In the field of psychology, _____ is the mental discomfort experienced by a person who holds two or more contradictory beliefs, ideas, or values. This discomfort is triggered by a situation in which a person's belief clashes with new evidence perceived by the person. When confronted with facts that contradict beliefs, ideals, and values, people will try to find a way to resolve the contradiction to reduce their discomfort.

Exam Probability: **High**

3. *Answer choices:*

(see index for correct answer)

- a. Emotional conflict
- b. Hypocrisy
- c. Cognitive dissonance
- d. Self-refuting idea

Guidance: level 1

:: Direct marketing ::

_____ is a method of direct marketing in which a salesperson solicits prospective customers to buy products or services, either over the phone or through a subsequent face to face or Web conferencing appointment scheduled during the call. _____ can also include recorded sales pitches programmed to be played over the phone via automatic dialing.

Exam Probability: **High**

4. *Answer choices:*

(see index for correct answer)

- a. Telemarketing
- b. Telebrands
- c. Caging
- d. Harriet Carter

Guidance: level 1

:: Project management ::

A _____ is a source or supply from which a benefit is produced and it has some utility. _____ s can broadly be classified upon their availability—they are classified into renewable and non-renewable _____ s. Examples of non renewable _____ s are coal ,crude oil natural gas nuclear energy etc. Examples of renewable _____ s are air,water,wind,solar energy etc. They can also be classified as actual and potential on the basis of level of development and use, on the basis of origin they can be classified as biotic and abiotic, and on the basis of their distribution, as ubiquitous and localized . An item becomes a _____ with time and developing technology. Typically, _____ s are materials, energy, services, staff, knowledge, or other assets that are transformed to produce benefit and in the process may be consumed or made unavailable. Benefits of _____ utilization may include increased wealth, proper functioning of a system, or enhanced well-being. From a human perspective a natural _____ is anything obtained from the environment to satisfy human needs and wants. From a broader biological or ecological perspective a _____ satisfies the needs of a living organism .

Exam Probability: **High**

5. *Answer choices:*

(see index for correct answer)

- a. Project plan
- b. Requirements traceability
- c. Theory X and Theory Y
- d. Resource

Guidance: level 1

:: Commercial item transport and distribution ::

> Wholesaling or distributing is the sale of goods or merchandise to retailers; to industrial, commercial, institutional, or other professional business users; or to other _____ rs and related subordinated services. In general, it is the sale of goods to anyone other than a standard consumer.

Exam Probability: **High**

6. *Answer choices:*

(see index for correct answer)

- a. Wholesale
- b. Freight forwarder
- c. Land bridge
- d. Drop shipping

Guidance: level 1

:: ::

According to the philosopher Piyush Mathur, "Tangibility is the property that a phenomenon exhibits if it has and/or transports mass and/or energy and/or momentum".

Exam Probability: **High**

7. *Answer choices:*

(see index for correct answer)

- a. deep-level diversity
- b. personal values
- c. hierarchical
- d. Tangible

Guidance: level 1

:: ::

_____ is the study and management of exchange relationships. _____ is the business process of creating relationships with and satisfying customers. With its focus on the customer, _____ is one of the premier components of business management.

Exam Probability: **Low**

8. *Answer choices:*

(see index for correct answer)

- a. Character
- b. process perspective
- c. open system
- d. Sarbanes-Oxley act of 2002

Guidance: level 1

:: ::

> Distribution is one of the four elements of the marketing mix. Distribution is the process of making a product or service available for the consumer or business user who needs it. This can be done directly by the producer or service provider, or using indirect channels with distributors or intermediaries. The other three elements of the marketing mix are product, pricing, and promotion.

Exam Probability: **High**

9. *Answer choices:*

(see index for correct answer)

- a. hierarchical perspective
- b. Character
- c. Distribution channel
- d. open system

Guidance: level 1

:: ::

A _____ consists of one people who live in the same dwelling and share meals. It may also consist of a single family or another group of people. A dwelling is considered to contain multiple _____ s if meals or living spaces are not shared. The _____ is the basic unit of analysis in many social, microeconomic and government models, and is important to economics and inheritance.

Exam Probability: **Low**

10. *Answer choices:*

(see index for correct answer)

- a. Household
- b. similarity-attraction theory
- c. co-culture
- d. imperative

Guidance: level 1

:: Financial economics ::

In management, business value is an informal term that includes all forms of value that determine the health and well-being of the firm in the long run. Business value expands concept of value of the firm beyond economic value to include other forms of value such as employee value, _____ , supplier value, channel partner value, alliance partner value, managerial value, and societal value. Many of these forms of value are not directly measured in monetary terms.

Exam Probability: **Low**

11. *Answer choices:*

(see index for correct answer)

- a. Single-index model
- b. Customer value
- c. Portfolio insurance
- d. Triangular arbitrage

Guidance: level 1

:: Marketing ::

_____ is a marketing practice of individuals or organizations. It allows them to sell products or services to other companies or organizations that resell them, use them in their products or services or use them to support their works.

Exam Probability: **High**

12. Answer choices:

(see index for correct answer)

- a. Affective design
- b. Discoverability
- c. Albuquerque Craft Beer Market
- d. Personalized marketing

Guidance: level 1

:: Advertising ::

A _____ is a document used by creative professionals and agencies to develop creative deliverables: visual design, copy, advertising, web sites, etc. The document is usually developed by the requestor and approved by the creative team of designers, writers, and project managers. In some cases, the project's _____ may need creative director approval before work will commence.

Exam Probability: **High**

13. Answer choices:

(see index for correct answer)

- a. Visualizer
- b. Advertising column
- c. Creative brief
- d. Advertising education

Guidance: level 1

:: Investment ::

In finance, the benefit from an _____ is called a return. The return may consist of a gain realised from the sale of property or an _____, unrealised capital appreciation, or _____ income such as dividends, interest, rental income etc., or a combination of capital gain and income. The return may also include currency gains or losses due to changes in foreign currency exchange rates.

Exam Probability: **Low**

14. *Answer choices:*

(see index for correct answer)

- a. Indo Premier Investment Management
- b. Investment
- c. Tontine
- d. Investor awareness

Guidance: level 1

:: ::

The _____ is an agreement signed by Canada, Mexico, and the United States, creating a trilateral trade bloc in North America. The agreement came into force on January 1, 1994, and superseded the 1988 Canada–United States Free Trade Agreement between the United States and Canada. The NAFTA trade bloc is one of the largest trade blocs in the world by gross domestic product.

Exam Probability: **Low**

15. *Answer choices:*

(see index for correct answer)

- a. surface-level diversity
- b. North American Free Trade Agreement
- c. deep-level diversity
- d. personal values

Guidance: level 1

:: ::

_____ involves decision making. It can include judging the merits of multiple options and selecting one or more of them. One can make a _____ between imagined options or between real options followed by the corresponding action. For example, a traveler might choose a route for a journey based on the preference of arriving at a given destination as soon as possible. The preferred route can then follow from information such as the length of each of the possible routes, traffic conditions, etc. The arrival at a _____ can include more complex motivators such as cognition, instinct, and feeling.

Exam Probability: **High**

16. *Answer choices:*

(see index for correct answer)

- a. imperative
- b. hierarchical
- c. open system
- d. Choice

Guidance: level 1

:: Product development ::

_____ is the understanding of the dynamics of the product in order to showcase the best qualities and maximum features of the product. Marketers spend a lot of time and research in order to target their attended audience. Marketers will look into a _____ before marketing a product towards their customers.

Exam Probability: **Medium**

17. *Answer choices:*

(see index for correct answer)

- a. Product concept
- b. Design brief

- c. Front end innovation
- d. DFMA

Guidance: level 1

:: ::

_____ is the process of gathering and measuring information on targeted variables in an established system, which then enables one to answer relevant questions and evaluate outcomes. _____ is a component of research in all fields of study including physical and social sciences, humanities, and business. While methods vary by discipline, the emphasis on ensuring accurate and honest collection remains the same. The goal for all _____ is to capture quality evidence that allows analysis to lead to the formulation of convincing and credible answers to the questions that have been posed.

Exam Probability: **High**

18. *Answer choices:*

(see index for correct answer)

- a. cultural
- b. Data collection
- c. corporate values
- d. open system

Guidance: level 1

:: Strategic alliances ::

A _____ is an agreement between two or more parties to pursue a set of agreed upon objectives needed while remaining independent organizations. A _____ will usually fall short of a legal partnership entity, agency, or corporate affiliate relationship. Typically, two companies form a _____ when each possesses one or more business assets or have expertise that will help the other by enhancing their businesses. _____s can develop in outsourcing relationships where the parties desire to achieve long-term win-win benefits and innovation based on mutually desired outcomes.

Exam Probability: **Medium**

19. *Answer choices:*

(see index for correct answer)

- a. Strategic alliance
- b. International joint venture
- c. Cross-licensing
- d. Bridge Alliance

Guidance: level 1

:: Consumer theory ::

A _____ is a technical term in psychology, economics and philosophy usually used in relation to choosing between alternatives. For example, someone prefers A over B if they would rather choose A than B.

Exam Probability: **High**

20. *Answer choices:*

(see index for correct answer)

- a. Quality bias
- b. Permanent income hypothesis
- c. Preference
- d. Demand set

Guidance: level 1

:: Supply chain management ::

_____ is the removal of intermediaries in economics from a supply chain, or cutting out the middlemen in connection with a transaction or a series of transactions. Instead of going through traditional distribution channels, which had some type of intermediary, companies may now deal with customers directly, for example via the Internet. Hence, the use of factory direct and direct from the factory to mean the same thing.

Exam Probability: **High**

21. *Answer choices:*

(see index for correct answer)

- a. Enterprise carbon accounting
- b. Keith Oliver

- c. Disintermediation
- d. Yield management

Guidance: level 1

:: Marketing ::

_____ is the marketing of products that are presumed to be environmentally safe. It incorporates a broad range of activities, including product modification, changes to the production process, sustainable packaging, as well as modifying advertising. Yet defining _____ is not a simple task where several meanings intersect and contradict each other; an example of this will be the existence of varying social, environmental and retail definitions attached to this term. Other similar terms used are environmental marketing and ecological marketing.

Exam Probability: **High**

22. *Answer choices:*

(see index for correct answer)

- a. Adobe Target
- b. Green marketing
- c. Kronos Effect
- d. Processing fluency theory of aesthetic pleasure

Guidance: level 1

:: Legal terms ::

A _____ is a person who is called upon to issue a response to a communication made by another. The term is used in legal contexts, in survey methodology, and in psychological conditioning.

Exam Probability: **High**

23. *Answer choices:*

(see index for correct answer)

- a. Foral
- b. Law of the land
- c. Respondent
- d. Contravention

Guidance: level 1

:: Product management ::

`_____` is a phrase used in the marketing industry which describes the value of having a well-known brand name, based on the idea that the owner of a well-known brand name can generate more revenue simply from brand recognition; that is from products with that brand name than from products with a less well known name, as consumers believe that a product with a well-known name is better than products with less well-known names.

Exam Probability: **High**

24. *Answer choices:*

(see index for correct answer)

- a. Tipping point
- b. Diffusion of innovations
- c. Service life
- d. Product cost management

Guidance: level 1

:: Logistics ::

_____ is generally the detailed organization and implementation of a complex operation. In a general business sense, _____ is the management of the flow of things between the point of origin and the point of consumption in order to meet requirements of customers or corporations. The resources managed in _____ may include tangible goods such as materials, equipment, and supplies, as well as food and other consumable items. The _____ of physical items usually involves the integration of information flow, materials handling, production, packaging, inventory, transportation, warehousing, and often security.

Exam Probability: **High**

25. *Answer choices:*

(see index for correct answer)

- a. Design for availability
- b. Logistics
- c. Ground Parachute Extraction System
- d. Tracking number

Guidance: level 1

:: Advertising by type ::

> _____ or advertising war is an advertisement in which a particular product, or service, specifically mentions a competitor by name for the express purpose of showing why the competitor is inferior to the product naming it. Also referred to as "knocking copy", it is loosely defined as advertising where "the advertised brand is explicitly compared with one or more competing brands and the comparison is obvious to the audience."

Exam Probability: **Medium**

26. *Answer choices:*

(see index for correct answer)

- a. Comparative advertising
- b. Non-commercial advertising
- c. In-flight advertising
- d. Parody advertisement

Guidance: level 1

:: ::

_____ refers to a diverse array of media technologies that reach a large audience via mass communication. The technologies through which this communication takes place include a variety of outlets.

Exam Probability: **High**

27. *Answer choices:*

(see index for correct answer)

- a. empathy
- b. Mass media
- c. cultural
- d. personal values

Guidance: level 1

:: ::

_____ s are formal, sociotechnical, organizational systems designed to collect, process, store, and distribute information. In a sociotechnical perspective, _____ s are composed by four components: task, people, structure, and technology.

Exam Probability: **Medium**

28. *Answer choices:*

(see index for correct answer)

- a. Information system
- b. empathy
- c. imperative
- d. levels of analysis

Guidance: level 1

:: Meetings ::

A _____ is a body of one or more persons that is subordinate to a deliberative assembly. Usually, the assembly sends matters into a _____ as a way to explore them more fully than would be possible if the assembly itself were considering them. _____ s may have different functions and their type of work differ depending on the type of the organization and its needs.

Exam Probability: **High**

29. *Answer choices:*

(see index for correct answer)

- a. Convocation
- b. Audience
- c. Over the Air
- d. Brown bag seminar

Guidance: level 1

_____ Corporation is an American multinational technology company with headquarters in Redmond, Washington. It develops, manufactures, licenses, supports and sells computer software, consumer electronics, personal computers, and related services. Its best known software products are the _____ Windows line of operating systems, the _____ Office suite, and the Internet Explorer and Edge Web browsers. Its flagship hardware products are the Xbox video game consoles and the _____ Surface lineup of touchscreen personal computers. As of 2016, it is the world's largest software maker by revenue, and one of the world's most valuable companies. The word "_____" is a portmanteau of "microcomputer" and "software". _____ is ranked No. 30 in the 2018 Fortune 500 rankings of the largest United States corporations by total revenue.

Exam Probability: **Medium**

30. *Answer choices:*

(see index for correct answer)

- a. Microsoft
- b. deep-level diversity
- c. information systems assessment
- d. levels of analysis

Guidance: level 1

:: Costs ::

In economics, _____ is the total economic cost of production and is made up of variable cost, which varies according to the quantity of a good produced and includes inputs such as labour and raw materials, plus fixed cost, which is independent of the quantity of a good produced and includes inputs that cannot be varied in the short term: fixed costs such as buildings and machinery, including sunk costs if any. Since cost is measured per unit of time, it is a flow variable.

Exam Probability: **High**

31. *Answer choices:*

(see index for correct answer)

- a. Direct materials cost
- b. Travel and subsistence
- c. Further processing cost
- d. Direct labor cost

Guidance: level 1

:: ::

Advertising is a marketing communication that employs an openly sponsored, non-personal message to promote or sell a product, service or idea. Sponsors of advertising are typically businesses wishing to promote their products or services. Advertising is differentiated from public relations in that an advertiser pays for and has control over the message. It differs from personal selling in that the message is non-personal, i.e., not directed to a particular individual. Advertising is communicated through various mass media, including traditional media such as newspapers, magazines, television, radio, outdoor advertising or direct mail; and new media such as search results, blogs, social media, websites or text messages. The actual presentation of the message in a medium is referred to as an _____ , or "ad" or advert for short.

Exam Probability: **High**

32. *Answer choices:*

(see index for correct answer)

- a. hierarchical perspective
- b. interpersonal communication
- c. corporate values
- d. similarity-attraction theory

Guidance: level 1

:: Advertising ::

_____ is the behavioral and cognitive process of selectively concentrating on a discrete aspect of information, whether deemed subjective or objective, while ignoring other perceivable information. It is a state of arousal. It is the taking possession by the mind in clear and vivid form of one out of what seem several simultaneous objects or trains of thought. Focalization, the concentration of consciousness, is of its essence. _____ has also been described as the allocation of limited cognitive processing resources.

Exam Probability: **Medium**

33. *Answer choices:*

(see index for correct answer)

- a. Flighting
- b. Ad-ID
- c. Attention
- d. Interactive urinal communicator

Guidance: level 1

:: Promotion and marketing communications ::

A _____ is the intended audience or readership of a publication, advertisement, or other message. In marketing and advertising, it is a particular group of consumers within the predetermined target market, identified as the targets or recipients for a particular advertisement or message. Businesses that have a wide target market will focus on a specific _____ for certain messages to send, such as The Body Shops Mother's Day advertisements, which were aimed at the children and spouses of women, rather than the whole market which would have included the women themselves.

Exam Probability: **High**

34. *Answer choices:*

(see index for correct answer)

- a. Shop fitting
- b. Target audience
- c. Air Miles
- d. Media guide

Guidance: level 1

:: ::

_____ is a term frequently used in marketing. It is a measure of how products and services supplied by a company meet or surpass customer expectation. _____ is defined as "the number of customers, or percentage of total customers, whose reported experience with a firm, its products, or its services exceeds specified satisfaction goals."

Exam Probability: **Low**

35. *Answer choices:*

(see index for correct answer)

- a. interpersonal communication
- b. Sarbanes-Oxley act of 2002
- c. empathy
- d. imperative

Guidance: level 1

:: ::

> _____ s uses different marketing channels and tools in combination: _____ channels focus on any way a business communicates a message to its desired market, or the market in general. A _____ tool can be anything from: advertising, personal selling, direct marketing, sponsorship, communication, and promotion to public relations.

Exam Probability: **Low**

36. *Answer choices:*

(see index for correct answer)

- a. co-culture
- b. functional perspective

- c. information systems assessment
- d. Sarbanes-Oxley act of 2002

Guidance: level 1

:: Electronic feedback ::

> _____ occurs when outputs of a system are routed back as inputs as part of a chain of cause-and-effect that forms a circuit or loop. The system can then be said to feed back into itself. The notion of cause-and-effect has to be handled carefully when applied to _____ systems.

Exam Probability: **High**

37. *Answer choices:*

(see index for correct answer)

- a. Positive feedback
- b. Feedback

Guidance: level 1

:: ::

An _____ is a contingent motivator. Traditional _____ s are extrinsic motivators which reward actions to yield a desired outcome. The effectiveness of traditional _____ s has changed as the needs of Western society have evolved. While the traditional _____ model is effective when there is a defined procedure and goal for a task, Western society started to require a higher volume of critical thinkers, so the traditional model became less effective. Institutions are now following a trend in implementing strategies that rely on intrinsic motivations rather than the extrinsic motivations that the traditional _____ s foster.

Exam Probability: **High**

38. *Answer choices:*

(see index for correct answer)

- a. open system
- b. co-culture
- c. Incentive
- d. similarity-attraction theory

Guidance: level 1

:: Direct selling ::

_____ consists of two main business models: single-level marketing, in which a direct seller makes money by buying products from a parent organization and selling them directly to customers, and multi-level marketing, in which the direct seller may earn money from both direct sales to customers and by sponsoring new direct sellers and potentially earning a commission from their efforts.

Exam Probability: **Low**

39. *Answer choices:*

(see index for correct answer)

- a. Direct Selling News
- b. Direct Selling Association
- c. The Longaberger Company
- d. CVSL

Guidance: level 1

:: Data collection ::

A _____ is an utterance which typically functions as a request for information. _____ s can thus be understood as a kind of illocutionary act in the field of pragmatics or as special kinds of propositions in frameworks of formal semantics such as alternative semantics or inquisitive semantics. The information requested is expected to be provided in the form of an answer. _____ s are often conflated with interrogatives, which are the grammatical forms typically used to achieve them. Rhetorical _____ s, for example, are interrogative in form but may not be considered true _____ s as they are not expected to be answered. Conversely, non-interrogative grammatical structures may be considered _____ s as in the case of the imperative sentence "tell me your name".

Exam Probability: **Medium**

40. *Answer choices:*

(see index for correct answer)

- a. Question
- b. BanxQuote
- c. Datalogix
- d. Relational data mining

Guidance: level 1

:: Marketing ::

_____ is a growth strategy that identifies and develops new market segments for current products. A _____ strategy targets non-buying customers in currently targeted segments. It also targets new customers in new segments.

Exam Probability: **High**

41. *Answer choices:*

(see index for correct answer)

- a. Product literature
- b. Next-best-action marketing
- c. Brandjacking
- d. Cumulative prospect theory

Guidance: level 1

:: Generally Accepted Accounting Principles ::

Expenditure is an outflow of money to another person or group to pay for an item or service, or for a category of costs. For a tenant, rent is an _____. For students or parents, tuition is an _____. Buying food, clothing, furniture or an automobile is often referred to as an _____. An _____ is a cost that is "paid" or "remitted", usually in exchange for something of value. Something that seems to cost a great deal is "expensive". Something that seems to cost little is "inexpensive". "_____ s of the table" are _____ s of dining, refreshments, a feast, etc.

Exam Probability: **Medium**

42. *Answer choices:*

(see index for correct answer)

- a. Fin 48
- b. net realisable value
- c. Expense
- d. Goodwill

Guidance: level 1

:: Advertising ::

A _____ is a large outdoor advertising structure, typically found in high-traffic areas such as alongside busy roads. _____ s present large advertisements to passing pedestrians and drivers. Typically showing witty slogans and distinctive visuals, _____ s are highly visible in the top designated market areas.

Exam Probability: **High**

43. *Answer choices:*

(see index for correct answer)

- a. Privilege sign
- b. Logojet

- c. Billboard
- d. Reply marketing

Guidance: level 1

:: Marketing ::

A business can use a variety of _____ when selling a product or service. The price can be set to maximize profitability for each unit sold or from the market overall. It can be used to defend an existing market from new entrants, to increase market share within a market or to enter a new market.

Exam Probability: **Medium**

44. *Answer choices:*

(see index for correct answer)

- a. Customer insight
- b. Call centre
- c. Preference-rank translation
- d. Pricing strategies

Guidance: level 1

:: Marketing ::

_____ is "commercial competition characterized by the repeated cutting of prices below those of competitors". One competitor will lower its price, then others will lower their prices to match. If one of them reduces their price again, a new round of reductions starts. In the short term, _____s are good for buyers, who can take advantage of lower prices. Often they are not good for the companies involved because the lower prices reduce profit margins and can threaten their survival.

Exam Probability: **High**

45. *Answer choices:*

(see index for correct answer)

- a. Behance
- b. Customer dynamics
- c. Market segmentation index
- d. Price war

Guidance: level 1

:: Marketing by medium ::

_____ or viral advertising is a business strategy that uses existing social networks to promote a product. Its name refers to how consumers spread information about a product with other people in their social networks, much in the same way that a virus spreads from one person to another. It can be delivered by word of mouth or enhanced by the network effects of the Internet and mobile networks.

Exam Probability: **Medium**

46. *Answer choices:*

(see index for correct answer)

- a. New media marketing
- b. Viral marketing
- c. Brand infiltration
- d. Social intelligence architect

Guidance: level 1

:: Economic globalization ::

_____ is an agreement in which one company hires another company to be responsible for a planned or existing activity that is or could be done internally, and sometimes involves transferring employees and assets from one firm to another.

Exam Probability: **Medium**

47. *Answer choices:*

(see index for correct answer)

- a. Outsourcing
- b. global financial

Guidance: level 1

:: Data management ::

> _____ is a form of intellectual property that grants the creator of an original creative work an exclusive legal right to determine whether and under what conditions this original work may be copied and used by others, usually for a limited term of years. The exclusive rights are not absolute but limited by limitations and exceptions to _____ law, including fair use. A major limitation on _____ on ideas is that _____ protects only the original expression of ideas, and not the underlying ideas themselves.

Exam Probability: **High**

48. *Answer choices:*

(see index for correct answer)

- a. BBC Archives
- b. Consistency
- c. Control break
- d. Operational historian

Guidance: level 1

:: Brand management ::

In marketing, _____ is the analysis and planning on how a brand is perceived in the market. Developing a good relationship with the target market is essential for _____. Tangible elements of _____ include the product itself; its look, price, and packaging, etc. The intangible elements are the experiences that the consumers share with the brand, and also the relationships they have with the brand. A brand manager would oversee all aspects of the consumer's brand association as well as relationships with members of the supply chain.

Exam Probability: **Medium**

49. *Answer choices:*

(see index for correct answer)

- a. Integrated marketing
- b. BrandActive
- c. Postmodern marketing
- d. Brand management

Guidance: level 1

:: Television terminology ::

A _____ organization, also known as a non-business entity, not-for-profit organization, or _____ institution, is dedicated to furthering a particular social cause or advocating for a shared point of view. In economic terms, it is an organization that uses its surplus of the revenues to further achieve its ultimate objective, rather than distributing its income to the organization's shareholders, leaders, or members. _____s are tax exempt or charitable, meaning they do not pay income tax on the money that they receive for their organization. They can operate in religious, scientific, research, or educational settings.

Exam Probability: **High**

50. *Answer choices:*

(see index for correct answer)

- a. distance learning
- b. not-for-profit
- c. multiplexing
- d. Nonprofit

Guidance: level 1

:: Marketing terminology ::

_____ is used in marketing to describe the inability to assess the value gained from engaging in an activity using any tangible evidence. It is often used to describe services where there is no tangible product that the customer can purchase, that can be seen or touched.

Exam Probability: **Low**

51. *Answer choices:*

(see index for correct answer)

- a. Unique visitor
- b. Oscar bait
- c. Intangibility
- d. Customer value maximization

Guidance: level 1

:: Survey methodology ::

A _____ is the procedure of systematically acquiring and recording information about the members of a given population. The term is used mostly in connection with national population and housing _____ es; other common _____ es include agriculture, business, and traffic _____ es. The United Nations defines the essential features of population and housing _____ es as "individual enumeration, universality within a defined territory, simultaneity and defined periodicity", and recommends that population _____ es be taken at least every 10 years. United Nations recommendations also cover _____ topics to be collected, official definitions, classifications and other useful information to co-ordinate international practice.

Exam Probability: **Medium**

52. *Answer choices:*

(see index for correct answer)

- a. Self-report
- b. Self-report study
- c. Scale analysis
- d. Census

Guidance: level 1

:: Market research ::

> An _____ or lighthouse customer is an early customer of a given company, product, or technology. The term originates from Everett M. Rogers' Diffusion of Innovations .

Exam Probability: **High**

53. *Answer choices:*

(see index for correct answer)

- a. Early adopter
- b. Coolhunting
- c. Mendelsohn Affluent Survey
- d. Central location test

Guidance: level 1

:: Direct marketing ::

_____ is a form of direct marketing using databases of customers or potential customers to generate personalized communications in order to promote a product or service for marketing purposes. The method of communication can be any addressable medium, as in direct marketing.

Exam Probability: **High**

54. *Answer choices:*
(see index for correct answer)

- a. Database marketing
- b. Mailing list
- c. Ed Valenti
- d. CornerWorld

Guidance: level 1

:: ::

_____ is an abstract concept of management of complex systems according to a set of rules and trends. In systems theory, these types of rules exist in various fields of biology and society, but the term has slightly different meanings according to context. For example.

Exam Probability: **Low**

55. Answer choices:

(see index for correct answer)

- a. deep-level diversity
- b. Regulation
- c. corporate values
- d. personal values

Guidance: level 1

:: ::

A _____ is a professional who provides expert advice in a particular area such as security, management, education, accountancy, law, human resources, marketing, finance, engineering, science or any of many other specialized fields.

Exam Probability: **Medium**

56. Answer choices:

(see index for correct answer)

- a. imperative
- b. Consultant
- c. deep-level diversity
- d. personal values

Guidance: level 1

:: Promotion and marketing communications ::

> _____ is one of the elements of the promotional mix. . _____ uses both media and non-media marketing communications for a pre-determined, limited time to increase consumer demand, stimulate market demand or improve product availability. Examples include contests, coupons, freebies, loss leaders, point of purchase displays, premiums, prizes, product samples, and rebates.

Exam Probability: **High**

57. *Answer choices:*

(see index for correct answer)

- a. Sales promotion
- b. Thomas Register
- c. Radio advertisement
- d. Communication planning

Guidance: level 1

:: Business economics ::

In economics, _____ is demand for a factor of production or intermediate good that occurs as a result of the demand for another intermediate or final good. In essence, the demand for, say, a factor of production by a firm is dependent on the demand by consumers for the product produced by the firm. The term was first introduced by Alfred Marshall in his Principles of Economics in 1890.

Exam Probability: **Low**

58. *Answer choices:*

(see index for correct answer)

- a. Wear and tear
- b. Leontief production function
- c. Derived demand
- d. Risk financing

Guidance: level 1

:: Decision theory ::

A _____ is a deliberate system of principles to guide decisions and achieve rational outcomes. A _____ is a statement of intent, and is implemented as a procedure or protocol. Policies are generally adopted by a governance body within an organization. Policies can assist in both subjective and objective decision making. Policies to assist in subjective decision making usually assist senior management with decisions that must be based on the relative merits of a number of factors, and as a result are often hard to test objectively, e.g. work-life balance _____ . In contrast policies to assist in objective decision making are usually operational in nature and can be objectively tested, e.g. password _____ .

Exam Probability: **Medium**

59. *Answer choices:*

(see index for correct answer)

- a. Health management system
- b. Policy
- c. Belief structure
- d. Trained incapacity

Guidance: level 1

Manufacturing

Manufacturing is the production of merchandise for use or sale using labor and machines, tools, chemical and biological processing, or formulation. The term may refer to a range of human activity, from handicraft to high tech, but is most commonly applied to industrial design, in which raw materials are transformed into finished goods on a large scale. Such finished goods may be sold to other manufacturers for the production of other, more complex products, such as aircraft, household appliances, furniture, sports equipment or automobiles, or sold to wholesalers, who in turn sell them to retailers, who then sell them to end users and consumers.

:: Procurement ::

A _____ is a standard business process whose purpose is to invite suppliers into a bidding process to bid on specific products or services. RfQ generally means the same thing as Call for bids and Invitation for bid.

Exam Probability: **Medium**

1. *Answer choices:*

(see index for correct answer)

- a. Request for quotation
- b. Building Schools for the Future
- c. Tender board
- d. FAPPO

Guidance: level 1

:: Project management ::

In economics, _____ is the assignment of available resources to various uses. In the context of an entire economy, resources can be allocated by various means, such as markets or central planning.

Exam Probability: **Low**

2. *Answer choices:*

(see index for correct answer)

- a. Big Hairy Audacious Goal
- b. Resource allocation
- c. PM Declaration of Interdependence
- d. ISO 31000

Guidance: level 1

:: Costs ::

In microeconomic theory, the _____ , or alternative cost, of making a particular choice is the value of the most valuable choice out of those that were not taken. In other words, opportunity that will require sacrifices.

Exam Probability: **Low**

3. *Answer choices:*

(see index for correct answer)

- a. Opportunity cost
- b. Social cost
- c. Economic cost
- d. Implicit cost

Guidance: level 1

:: Knowledge representation ::

_____ s are causal diagrams created by Kaoru Ishikawa that show the causes of a specific event.

Exam Probability: **Medium**

4. *Answer choices:*

(see index for correct answer)

- a. Faceted classification
- b. Defeasible reasoning
- c. Ramification problem
- d. Ishikawa diagram

Guidance: level 1

:: Costs ::

_____ is the process used by companies to reduce their costs and increase their profits. Depending on a company's services or product, the strategies can vary. Every decision in the product development process affects cost.

Exam Probability: **Medium**

5. *Answer choices:*

(see index for correct answer)

- a. Cost per paper
- b. Cost reduction
- c. Incremental cost-effectiveness ratio
- d. Average cost

Guidance: level 1

:: Commerce ::

A _____ is an employee within a company, business or other organization who is responsible at some level for buying or approving the acquisition of goods and services needed by the company. Responsible for buying the best quality products, goods and services for their company at the most competitive prices, _____ s work in a wide range of sectors for many different organizations. The position responsibilities may be the same as that of a buyer or purchasing agent, or may include wider supervisory or managerial responsibilities. A _____ may oversee the acquisition of materials needed for production, general supplies for offices and facilities, equipment, or construction contracts. A _____ often supervises purchasing agents and buyers, but in small companies the _____ may also be the purchasing agent or buyer. The _____ position may also carry the title "Procurement Manager" or in the public sector, "Procurement Officer". He or she can come from both an Engineering or Economics background.

Exam Probability: **Low**

6. *Answer choices:*

(see index for correct answer)

- a. RFM

- b. Perfect tender rule
- c. Shipping list
- d. Purchasing manager

Guidance: level 1

:: Waste ::

_____ are unwanted or unusable materials. _____ is any substance which is discarded after primary use, or is worthless, defective and of no use. A by-product by contrast is a joint product of relatively minor economic value. A _____ product may become a by-product, joint product or resource through an invention that raises a _____ product's value above zero.

Exam Probability: **Medium**

7. *Answer choices:*

(see index for correct answer)

- a. Pocket litter
- b. Post-consumer waste
- c. Waste
- d. Green waste

Guidance: level 1

:: Business process ::

A _____ or business method is a collection of related, structured activities or tasks by people or equipment which in a specific sequence produce a service or product for a particular customer or customers. _____ es occur at all organizational levels and may or may not be visible to the customers. A _____ may often be visualized as a flowchart of a sequence of activities with interleaving decision points or as a process matrix of a sequence of activities with relevance rules based on data in the process. The benefits of using _____ es include improved customer satisfaction and improved agility for reacting to rapid market change. Process-oriented organizations break down the barriers of structural departments and try to avoid functional silos.

Exam Probability: **Low**

8. *Answer choices:*

(see index for correct answer)

- a. Information technology outsourcing
- b. IBM Blueworks Live
- c. Business process
- d. A Guide to the Business Analysis Body of Knowledge

Guidance: level 1

:: E-commerce ::

_____ is the business-to-business or business-to-consumer or business-to-government purchase and sale of supplies, work, and services through the Internet as well as other information and networking systems, such as electronic data interchange and enterprise resource planning.

Exam Probability: **High**

9. *Answer choices:*

(see index for correct answer)

- a. APazari
- b. Ven
- c. Mobilpenge
- d. E-procurement

Guidance: level 1

:: Costs ::

The _____ is computed by dividing the total cost of goods available for sale by the total units available for sale. This gives a weighted-average unit cost that is applied to the units in the ending inventory.

Exam Probability: **Low**

10. *Answer choices:*

(see index for correct answer)

- a. Explicit cost
- b. Joint cost
- c. Customer Cost
- d. Sliding scale

Guidance: level 1

:: Quality ::

A _____ is an initiating cause of either a condition or a causal chain that leads to an outcome or effect of interest. The term denotes the earliest, most basic, `deepest`, cause for a given behavior; most often a fault. The idea is that you can only see an error by its manifest signs. Those signs can be widespread, multitudinous, and convoluted, whereas the _____ leading to them often is a lot simpler.

Exam Probability: **Low**

11. *Answer choices:*

(see index for correct answer)

- a. Ringtest
- b. Cleaning validation
- c. Independent test organization
- d. European Organization for Quality

Guidance: level 1

:: Product management ::

_____ is the state of being which occurs when an object, service, or practice is no longer wanted even though it may still be in good working order; however, the international standard EN62402 _____ Management - Application Guide defines _____ as being the "transition from availability of products by the original manufacturer or supplier to unavailability". _____ frequently occurs because a replacement has become available that has, in sum, more advantages compared to the disadvantages incurred by maintaining or repairing the original. Obsolete also refers to something that is already disused or discarded, or antiquated. Typically, _____ is preceded by a gradual decline in popularity.

Exam Probability: **Low**

12. *Answer choices:*

(see index for correct answer)

- a. Scarcity Development Cycle
- b. Diffusion of innovations
- c. Obsolescence
- d. Product information

Guidance: level 1

:: Debt ::

_____ is the trust which allows one party to provide money or resources to another party wherein the second party does not reimburse the first party immediately , but promises either to repay or return those resources at a later date. In other words, _____ is a method of making reciprocity formal, legally enforceable, and extensible to a large group of unrelated people.

Exam Probability: **High**

13. *Answer choices:*

(see index for correct answer)

- a. Credit
- b. Cohort default rate
- c. Christians Against Poverty
- d. Debt management plan

Guidance: level 1

:: Unit operations ::

_____ is a discipline of thermal engineering that concerns the generation, use, conversion, and exchange of thermal energy between physical systems. _____ is classified into various mechanisms, such as thermal conduction, thermal convection, thermal radiation, and transfer of energy by phase changes. Engineers also consider the transfer of mass of differing chemical species, either cold or hot, to achieve _____ . While these mechanisms have distinct characteristics, they often occur simultaneously in the same system.

Exam Probability: **Medium**

14. *Answer choices:*

(see index for correct answer)

- a. Settling
- b. Separation process
- c. Distillation
- d. Heat transfer

Guidance: level 1

:: Costs ::

In economics, _____ is the total economic cost of production and is made up of variable cost, which varies according to the quantity of a good produced and includes inputs such as labour and raw materials, plus fixed cost, which is independent of the quantity of a good produced and includes inputs that cannot be varied in the short term: fixed costs such as buildings and machinery, including sunk costs if any. Since cost is measured per unit of time, it is a flow variable.

Exam Probability: **High**

15. *Answer choices:*

(see index for correct answer)

- a. Total cost

- b. Total cost of acquisition
- c. Average cost
- d. Road Logistics Costing in South Africa

Guidance: level 1

:: Product management ::

_____ s, also known as Shewhart charts or process-behavior charts, are a statistical process control tool used to determine if a manufacturing or business process is in a state of control.

Exam Probability: **Medium**

16. *Answer choices:*

(see index for correct answer)

- a. Product information
- b. Control chart
- c. Promise Index
- d. Trademark distinctiveness

Guidance: level 1

:: Planning ::

_____ is a high level plan to achieve one or more goals under conditions of uncertainty. In the sense of the "art of the general," which included several subsets of skills including tactics, siegecraft, logistics etc., the term came into use in the 6th century C.E. in East Roman terminology, and was translated into Western vernacular languages only in the 18th century. From then until the 20th century, the word "_____" came to denote "a comprehensive way to try to pursue political ends, including the threat or actual use of force, in a dialectic of wills" in a military conflict, in which both adversaries interact.

Exam Probability: **High**

17. *Answer choices:*

(see index for correct answer)

- a. Event scheduling
- b. Concept driven strategy
- c. Strategic communication
- d. Territorialist School

Guidance: level 1

:: Business planning ::

_____ is a critical component to the successful delivery of any project, programme or activity. A stakeholder is any individual, group or organization that can affect, be affected by, or perceive itself to be affected by a programme.

Exam Probability: **High**

18. *Answer choices:*

(see index for correct answer)

- a. Business war games
- b. Strategic planning
- c. operational planning
- d. Stakeholder management

Guidance: level 1

:: Project management ::

> Some scenarios associate "this kind of planning" with learning "life skills". _____s are necessary, or at least useful, in situations where individuals need to know what time they must be at a specific location to receive a specific service, and where people need to accomplish a set of goals within a set time period.

Exam Probability: **Low**

19. *Answer choices:*

(see index for correct answer)

- a. Time limit
- b. Project management 2.0

- c. Fast-track construction
- d. Gold plating

Guidance: level 1

:: Materials science ::

An _____ is a polymer with viscoelasticity and very weak intermolecular forces, and generally low Young's modulus and high failure strain compared with other materials. The term, a portmanteau of elastic polymer, is often used interchangeably with rubber, although the latter is preferred when referring to vulcanisates. Each of the monomers which link to form the polymer is usually a compound of several elements among carbon, hydrogen, oxygen and silicon. _____ s are amorphous polymers maintained above their glass transition temperature, so that considerable molecular reconformation, without breaking of covalent bonds, is feasible. At ambient temperatures, such rubbers are thus relatively soft and deformable. Their primary uses are for seals, adhesives and molded flexible parts. Application areas for different types of rubber are manifold and cover segments as diverse as tires, soles for shoes, and damping and insulating elements. The importance of these rubbers can be judged from the fact that global revenues are forecast to rise to US$56 billion in 2020.

Exam Probability: **Low**

20. *Answer choices:*

(see index for correct answer)

- a. Tribometer
- b. Pole figure

- c. Conditioner
- d. LIGA

Guidance: level 1

:: Management ::

> _____ is a method of quality control which employs statistical methods to monitor and control a process. This helps to ensure that the process operates efficiently, producing more specification-conforming products with less waste . SPC can be applied to any process where the "conforming product" output can be measured. Key tools used in SPC include run charts, control charts, a focus on continuous improvement, and the design of experiments. An example of a process where SPC is applied is manufacturing lines.

Exam Probability: **Low**

21. *Answer choices:*

(see index for correct answer)

- a. Narcissistic leadership
- b. Managerial prerogative
- c. Statistical process control
- d. Marketing management

Guidance: level 1

:: Inventory ::

The _____ is the level of inventory which triggers an action to replenish that particular inventory stock. It is a minimum amount of an item which a firm holds in stock, such that, when stock falls to this amount, the item must be reordered. It is normally calculated as the forecast usage during the replenishment lead time plus safety stock. In the EOQ model, it was assumed that there is no time lag between ordering and procuring of materials. Therefore the _____ for replenishing the stocks occurs at that level when the inventory level drops to zero and because instant delivery by suppliers, the stock level bounce back.

Exam Probability: **High**

22. *Answer choices:*

(see index for correct answer)

- a. Consignment stock
- b. Reorder point
- c. Phantom inventory
- d. Spare part

Guidance: level 1

:: Non-parametric statistics ::

A _____ is an accurate representation of the distribution of numerical data. It is an estimate of the probability distribution of a continuous variable and was first introduced by Karl Pearson. It differs from a bar graph, in the sense that a bar graph relates two variables, but a _____ relates only one. To construct a _____ , the first step is to "bin" the range of values—that is, divide the entire range of values into a series of intervals—and then count how many values fall into each interval. The bins are usually specified as consecutive, non-overlapping intervals of a variable. The bins must be adjacent, and are often of equal size.

Exam Probability: **Medium**

23. *Answer choices:*

(see index for correct answer)

- a. ANOVA on ranks
- b. Van der Waerden test
- c. Friedman test
- d. Histogram

Guidance: level 1

:: ::

The _____ is a project plan of how the production budget will be spent over a given timescale, for every phase of a business project.

Exam Probability: **High**

24. Answer choices:

(see index for correct answer)

- a. deep-level diversity
- b. hierarchical
- c. surface-level diversity
- d. empathy

Guidance: level 1

:: Gas technologies ::

A _____ is a rotary mechanical device that extracts energy from a fluid flow and converts it into useful work. The work produced by a _____ can be used for generating electrical power when combined with a generator. A _____ is a turbomachine with at least one moving part called a rotor assembly, which is a shaft or drum with blades attached. Moving fluid acts on the blades so that they move and impart rotational energy to the rotor. Early _____ examples are windmills and waterwheels.

Exam Probability: **Medium**

25. Answer choices:

(see index for correct answer)

- a. Turbine
- b. Clamond basket
- c. Wobbe index

- d. Bicycle pump

Guidance: level 1

:: Sensitivity analysis ::

_____ is the study of how the uncertainty in the output of a mathematical model or system can be divided and allocated to different sources of uncertainty in its inputs. A related practice is uncertainty analysis, which has a greater focus on uncertainty quantification and propagation of uncertainty; ideally, uncertainty and _____ should be run in tandem.

Exam Probability: **Low**

26. *Answer choices:*

(see index for correct answer)

- a. Fourier amplitude sensitivity testing
- b. Elementary effects method
- c. Sensitivity analysis
- d. Tornado diagram

Guidance: level 1

:: Production and manufacturing ::

_____ consists of organization-wide efforts to "install and make permanent climate where employees continuously improve their ability to provide on demand products and services that customers will find of particular value." "Total" emphasizes that departments in addition to production are obligated to improve their operations; "management" emphasizes that executives are obligated to actively manage quality through funding, training, staffing, and goal setting. While there is no widely agreed-upon approach, TQM efforts typically draw heavily on the previously developed tools and techniques of quality control. TQM enjoyed widespread attention during the late 1980s and early 1990s before being overshadowed by ISO 9000, Lean manufacturing, and Six Sigma.

Exam Probability: **High**

27. *Answer choices:*

(see index for correct answer)

- a. Fab lab
- b. Shop foreman
- c. Total quality management
- d. Multi-Point Interface

Guidance: level 1

:: Product development ::

In business and engineering, _____ covers the complete process of bringing a new product to market. A central aspect of NPD is product design, along with various business considerations. _____ is described broadly as the transformation of a market opportunity into a product available for sale. The product can be tangible or intangible, though sometimes services and other processes are distinguished from "products." NPD requires an understanding of customer needs and wants, the competitive environment, and the nature of the market. Cost, time and quality are the main variables that drive customer needs. Aiming at these three variables, innovative companies develop continuous practices and strategies to better satisfy customer requirements and to increase their own market share by a regular development of new products. There are many uncertainties and challenges which companies must face throughout the process. The use of best practices and the elimination of barriers to communication are the main concerns for the management of the NPD.

Exam Probability: **Medium**

28. *Answer choices:*

(see index for correct answer)

- a. Material selection
- b. Product optimization
- c. New product development
- d. Design for assembly

Guidance: level 1

:: Outsourcing ::

____ is an institutional procurement process that continuously improves and re-evaluates the purchasing activities of a company. In the services industry, ____ refers to a service solution, sometimes called a strategic partnership, which is specifically customized to meet the client's individual needs. In a production environment, it is often considered one component of supply chain management. Modern supply chain management professionals have placed emphasis on defining the distinct differences between ____ and procurement. Procurement operations support tactical day-to-day transactions such as issuing Purchase Orders to suppliers, whereas ____ represents to strategic planning, supplier development, contract negotiation, supply chain infrastructure, and outsourcing models.

Exam Probability: **Low**

29. *Answer choices:*

(see index for correct answer)

- a. Strategic sourcing
- b. Editorial process outsourcing
- c. Pillsbury Winthrop Shaw Pittman
- d. Virtual airline

Guidance: level 1

:: Fault-tolerant computer systems ::

_____ decision-making is a group decision-making process in which group members develop, and agree to support a decision in the best interest of the whole group or common goal. _____ may be defined professionally as an acceptable resolution, one that can be supported, even if not the "favourite" of each individual. It has its origin in the Latin word consensus, which is from consentio meaning literally feel together. It is used to describe both the decision and the process of reaching a decision. _____ decision-making is thus concerned with the process of deliberating and finalizing a decision, and the social, economic, legal, environmental and political effects of applying this process.

Exam Probability: **Medium**

30. *Answer choices:*

(see index for correct answer)

- a. Round-robin DNS
- b. Raft
- c. Superstabilization
- d. Single point of failure

Guidance: level 1

:: Production economics ::

_____ is the joint use of a resource or space. It is also the process of dividing and distributing. In its narrow sense, it refers to joint or alternating use of inherently finite goods, such as a common pasture or a shared residence. Still more loosely, "_____" can actually mean giving something as an outright gift: for example, to "share" one's food really means to give some of it as a gift. _____ is a basic component of human interaction, and is responsible for strengthening social ties and ensuring a person's well-being.

Exam Probability: **High**

31. *Answer choices:*

(see index for correct answer)

- a. Producer's risk
- b. Returns to scale
- c. Socially optimal firm size
- d. HMI quality

Guidance: level 1

:: Asset ::

In financial accounting, an _____ is any resource owned by the business. Anything tangible or intangible that can be owned or controlled to produce value and that is held by a company to produce positive economic value is an _____ . Simply stated, _____ s represent value of ownership that can be converted into cash . The balance sheet of a firm records the monetary value of the _____ s owned by that firm. It covers money and other valuables belonging to an individual or to a business.

Exam Probability: **High**

32. *Answer choices:*

(see index for correct answer)

- a. Current asset
- b. Asset

Guidance: level 1

:: Management ::

_____ is the practice of initiating, planning, executing, controlling, and closing the work of a team to achieve specific goals and meet specific success criteria at the specified time.

Exam Probability: **Low**

33. *Answer choices:*

(see index for correct answer)

- a. Executive compensation
- b. Event management
- c. Success trap
- d. Project management

Guidance: level 1

:: ::

> An _____ is a company that produces parts and equipment that may be marketed by another manufacturer. For example, Foxconn, a Taiwanese electronics contract manufacturing company, which produces a variety of parts and equipment for companies such as Apple Inc., Dell, Google, Huawei, Nintendo, etc., is the largest OEM company in the world by both scale and revenue.

Exam Probability: **High**

34. *Answer choices:*

(see index for correct answer)

- a. open system
- b. information systems assessment
- c. Original equipment manufacturer
- d. hierarchical

Guidance: level 1

:: Quality awards ::

The _____ recognizes U.S. organizations in the business, health care, education, and nonprofit sectors for performance excellence. The Baldrige Award is the only formal recognition of the performance excellence of both public and private U.S. organizations given by the President of the United States. It is administered by the Baldrige Performance Excellence Program, which is based at and managed by the National Institute of Standards and Technology, an agency of the U.S. Department of Commerce.

Exam Probability: **Low**

35. *Answer choices:*

(see index for correct answer)

- a. Canada Awards for Excellence
- b. EFQM Excellence Award
- c. Malcolm Baldrige National Quality Award
- d. Philippine Quality Award

Guidance: level 1

:: Process management ::

_____ is a statistics package developed at the Pennsylvania State University by researchers Barbara F. Ryan, Thomas A. Ryan, Jr., and Brian L. Joiner in 1972. It began as a light version of OMNITAB 80, a statistical analysis program by NIST. Statistical analysis software such as _____ automates calculations and the creation of graphs, allowing the user to focus more on the analysis of data and the interpretation of results. It is compatible with other _____ , Inc. software.

Exam Probability: **High**

36. *Answer choices:*

(see index for correct answer)

- a. Ideal tasks
- b. Tampering
- c. Business triage
- d. Proactive contracting

Guidance: level 1

:: Project management ::

In economics and business decision-making, a sunk cost is a cost that has already been incurred and cannot be recovered.

Exam Probability: **Medium**

37. *Answer choices:*

(see index for correct answer)

- a. Sunk costs
- b. Feature-driven development
- c. Grandfather principle
- d. Gantt chart

Guidance: level 1

:: Management ::

Business _____ is a discipline in operations management in which people use various methods to discover, model, analyze, measure, improve, optimize, and automate business processes. BPM focuses on improving corporate performance by managing business processes. Any combination of methods used to manage a company's business processes is BPM. Processes can be structured and repeatable or unstructured and variable. Though not required, enabling technologies are often used with BPM.

Exam Probability: **Low**

38. *Answer choices:*

(see index for correct answer)

- a. Process management
- b. DMSMS
- c. Private defense agency

- d. Success trap

Guidance: level 1

:: Quality assurance ::

Organizations that issue credentials or certify third parties against official standards are themselves formally accredited by _____ bodies ; hence they are sometimes known as "accredited certification bodies". The _____ process ensures that their certification practices are acceptable, typically meaning that they are competent to test and certify third parties, behave ethically and employ suitable quality assurance.

Exam Probability: **High**

39. *Answer choices:*
(see index for correct answer)

- a. State Acceptance of Production
- b. Accreditation
- c. Commission on Accreditation of Rehabilitation Facilities
- d. International healthcare accreditation

Guidance: level 1

:: ::

In production, research, retail, and accounting, a _____ is the value of money that has been used up to produce something or deliver a service, and hence is not available for use anymore. In business, the _____ may be one of acquisition, in which case the amount of money expended to acquire it is counted as _____. In this case, money is the input that is gone in order to acquire the thing. This acquisition _____ may be the sum of the _____ of production as incurred by the original producer, and further _____ s of transaction as incurred by the acquirer over and above the price paid to the producer. Usually, the price also includes a mark-up for profit over the _____ of production.

Exam Probability: **Low**

40. *Answer choices:*

(see index for correct answer)

- a. Cost
- b. interpersonal communication
- c. information systems assessment
- d. corporate values

Guidance: level 1

:: Packaging materials ::

_____ is a thin material produced by pressing together moist fibres of cellulose pulp derived from wood, rags or grasses, and drying them into flexible sheets. It is a versatile material with many uses, including writing, printing, packaging, cleaning, decorating, and a number of industrial and construction processes. _____ s are essential in legal or non-legal documentation.

Exam Probability: **High**

41. *Answer choices:*

(see index for correct answer)

- a. Greensulate
- b. Wrapping tissue
- c. Tear tape
- d. Hessian

Guidance: level 1

:: Project management ::

A _____ is a source or supply from which a benefit is produced and it has some utility. _____ s can broadly be classified upon their availability—they are classified into renewable and non-renewable _____ s. Examples of non renewable _____ s are coal, crude oil natural gas nuclear energy etc. Examples of renewable _____ s are air, water, wind, solar energy etc. They can also be classified as actual and potential on the basis of level of development and use, on the basis of origin they can be classified as biotic and abiotic, and on the basis of their distribution, as ubiquitous and localized. An item becomes a _____ with time and developing technology. Typically, _____ s are materials, energy, services, staff, knowledge, or other assets that are transformed to produce benefit and in the process may be consumed or made unavailable. Benefits of _____ utilization may include increased wealth, proper functioning of a system, or enhanced well-being. From a human perspective a natural _____ is anything obtained from the environment to satisfy human needs and wants. From a broader biological or ecological perspective a _____ satisfies the needs of a living organism.

Exam Probability: **High**

42. *Answer choices:*

(see index for correct answer)

- a. Total project control
- b. Concept note
- c. Starmad
- d. Aggregate project plan

Guidance: level 1

:: Production and manufacturing ::

_____ is a comprehensive and rigorous industrial process by which a previously sold, leased, used, worn or non-functional product or part is returned to a 'like-new' or 'better-than-new' condition, from both a quality and performance perspective, through a controlled, reproducible and sustainable process.

Exam Probability: **Medium**

43. *Answer choices:*

(see index for correct answer)

- a. Report generator
- b. Detailed division of labor
- c. Turret lathe
- d. Remanufacturing

Guidance: level 1

:: Management ::

A supply-chain network is an evolution of the basic supply chain. Due to rapid technological advancement, organisations with a basic supply chain can develop this chain into a more complex structure involving a higher level of interdependence and connectivity between more organisations, this constitutes a supply-chain network.

Exam Probability: **High**

44. *Answer choices:*

(see index for correct answer)

- a. Unified interoperability
- b. Double linking
- c. Telescopic observations strategic framework
- d. Operations management

Guidance: level 1

:: Management ::

_____ is a term used in business and Information Technology to describe the in-depth process of capturing customer's expectations, preferences and aversions. Specifically, the _____ is a market research technique that produces a detailed set of customer wants and needs, organized into a hierarchical structure, and then prioritized in terms of relative importance and satisfaction with current alternatives. _____ studies typically consist of both qualitative and quantitative research steps. They are generally conducted at the start of any new product, process, or service design initiative in order to better understand the customer's wants and needs, and as the key input for new product definition, Quality Function Deployment, and the setting of detailed design specifications.

Exam Probability: **Low**

45. *Answer choices:*

(see index for correct answer)

- a. Voice of the customer
- b. Management styles
- c. Shamrock Organization
- d. Private defense agency

Guidance: level 1

:: Project management ::

Rolling-wave planning is the process of project planning in waves as the project proceeds and later details become clearer; similar to the techniques used in agile software development approaches like Scrum..

Exam Probability: **Medium**

46. *Answer choices:*
(see index for correct answer)

- a. Terms of reference
- b. Project charter
- c. Project appraisal
- d. Rolling Wave planning

Guidance: level 1

:: Business ::

The seller, or the provider of the goods or services, completes a sale in response to an acquisition, appropriation, requisition or a direct interaction with the buyer at the point of sale. There is a passing of title of the item, and the settlement of a price, in which agreement is reached on a price for which transfer of ownership of the item will occur. The seller, not the purchaser typically executes the sale and it may be completed prior to the obligation of payment. In the case of indirect interaction, a person who sells goods or service on behalf of the owner is known as a _____ man or _____ woman or _____ person, but this often refers to someone selling goods in a store/shop, in which case other terms are also common, including _____ clerk, shop assistant, and retail clerk.

Exam Probability: **Medium**

47. *Answer choices:*

(see index for correct answer)

- a. Citizenship for life
- b. Ansoff Matrix
- c. Gray ceiling
- d. Sales

Guidance: level 1

:: ::

_____ refers to a business or organization attempting to acquire goods or services to accomplish its goals. Although there are several organizations that attempt to set standards in the _____ process, processes can vary greatly between organizations. Typically the word "_____" is not used interchangeably with the word "procurement", since procurement typically includes expediting, supplier quality, and transportation and logistics in addition to _____.

Exam Probability: **Medium**

48. *Answer choices:*

(see index for correct answer)

- a. personal values
- b. surface-level diversity
- c. Purchasing
- d. empathy

Guidance: level 1

:: Risk analysis ::

Supply-chain risk management is "the implementation of strategies to manage both everyday and exceptional risks along the supply chain based on continuous risk assessment with the objective of reducing vulnerability and ensuring continuity".

Exam Probability: **High**

49. Answer choices:

(see index for correct answer)

- a. Society for Risk Analysis
- b. Supply chain risk management
- c. The PRS Group, Inc.
- d. Murphy's Law

Guidance: level 1

:: Project management ::

A _____ is a professional in the field of project management. _____ s have the responsibility of the planning, procurement and execution of a project, in any undertaking that has a defined scope, defined start and a defined finish; regardless of industry. _____ s are first point of contact for any issues or discrepancies arising from within the heads of various departments in an organization before the problem escalates to higher authorities. Project management is the responsibility of a _____ . This individual seldom participates directly in the activities that produce the end result, but rather strives to maintain the progress, mutual interaction and tasks of various parties in such a way that reduces the risk of overall failure, maximizes benefits, and minimizes costs.

Exam Probability: **High**

50. Answer choices:

(see index for correct answer)

- a. Graphical path method
- b. Project management triangle
- c. Theory Z of Ouchi
- d. Vertical slice

Guidance: level 1

:: Production and manufacturing ::

> _____ is the process of determining the production capacity needed by an organization to meet changing demands for its products. In the context of _____ , design capacity is the maximum amount of work that an organization is capable of completing in a given period. Effective capacity is the maximum amount of work that an organization is capable of completing in a given period due to constraints such as quality problems, delays, material handling, etc.

Exam Probability: **Low**

51. *Answer choices:*

(see index for correct answer)

- a. Simatic S5 PLC
- b. Direct Clustering Algorithm
- c. Capacity planning
- d. Original design manufacturer

Guidance: level 1

:: Quality assurance ::

The _____ is a United States-based nonprofit tax-exempt 501 organization that accredits more than 21,000 US health care organizations and programs. The international branch accredits medical services from around the world. A majority of US state governments recognize _____ accreditation as a condition of licensure for the receipt of Medicaid and Medicare reimbursements.

Exam Probability: **Low**

52. *Answer choices:*
(see index for correct answer)

- a. Silk mobile
- b. State Acceptance of Production
- c. SUBSAFE
- d. Community Health Accreditation Program

Guidance: level 1

:: Production and manufacturing ::

_____ is a systematic method to improve the "value" of goods or products and services by using an examination of function. Value, as defined, is the ratio of function to cost. Value can therefore be manipulated by either improving the function or reducing the cost. It is a primary tenet of _____ that basic functions be preserved and not be reduced as a consequence of pursuing value improvements.

Exam Probability: **Low**

53. *Answer choices:*

(see index for correct answer)

- a. Nesting
- b. STEP-NC
- c. Common Industrial Protocol
- d. Original design manufacturer

Guidance: level 1

:: Distribution, retailing, and wholesaling ::

The _____ is a distribution channel phenomenon in which forecasts yield supply chain inefficiencies. It refers to increasing swings in inventory in response to shifts in customer demand as one moves further up the supply chain. The concept first appeared in Jay Forrester's Industrial Dynamics and thus it is also known as the Forrester effect. The _____ was named for the way the amplitude of a whip increases down its length. The further from the originating signal, the greater the distortion of the wave pattern. In a similar manner, forecast accuracy decreases as one moves upstream along the supply chain. For example, many consumer goods have fairly consistent consumption at retail but this signal becomes more chaotic and unpredictable as the focus moves away from consumer purchasing behavior.

Exam Probability: **High**

54. *Answer choices:*

(see index for correct answer)

- a. Bullwhip effect
- b. Cycle count
- c. Chicago Review Press
- d. New Leaf Distributing Company

Guidance: level 1

:: Quality control tools ::

A _____ is a type of diagram that represents an algorithm, workflow or process. _____ can also be defined as a diagramatic representation of an algorithm .

Exam Probability: **Medium**

55. *Answer choices:*

(see index for correct answer)

- a. Cause-and-effect diagram
- b. Scatter diagram
- c. EWMA chart
- d. Robust parameter design

Guidance: level 1

:: Insulators ::

A _____ is a piece of soft cloth large enough either to cover or to enfold a great portion of the user's body, usually when sleeping or otherwise at rest, thereby trapping radiant bodily heat that otherwise would be lost through convection, and so keeping the body warm.

Exam Probability: **Medium**

56. *Answer choices:*

(see index for correct answer)

- a. Nansulate
- b. Malter effect
- c. Blanket

- d. Vacuum insulated panel

Guidance: level 1

:: ::

_____ refers to the confirmation of certain characteristics of an object, person, or organization. This confirmation is often, but not always, provided by some form of external review, education, assessment, or audit. Accreditation is a specific organization's process of _____ . According to the National Council on Measurement in Education, a _____ test is a credentialing test used to determine whether individuals are knowledgeable enough in a given occupational area to be labeled "competent to practice" in that area.

Exam Probability: **Medium**

57. *Answer choices:*

(see index for correct answer)

- a. Certification
- b. co-culture
- c. similarity-attraction theory
- d. personal values

Guidance: level 1

:: Management ::

_____ is a category of business activity made possible by software tools that aim to provide customers with both independence from vendors and better means for engaging with vendors. These same tools can also apply to individuals' relations with other institutions and organizations.

Exam Probability: **Medium**

58. *Answer choices:*

(see index for correct answer)

- a. Personal offshoring
- b. PhD in management
- c. Quality control
- d. Vendor relationship management

Guidance: level 1

:: Help desk ::

A high-explosive anti-tank warhead is a type of shaped charge explosive that uses the Munroe effect to penetrate thick tank armor. The warhead functions by having the explosive charge collapse a metal liner inside the warhead into a high-velocity superplastic jet. This superplastic jet is capable of penetrating armor steel to a depth of seven or more times the diameter of the charge but is usually used to immobilize or destroy tanks. Due to the way they work, they do not have to be fired as fast as an armor piercing shell, allowing less recoil. Contrary to a widespread misconception, the jet does not melt its way through armor, as its effect is purely kinetic in nature. The _____ warhead has become less effective against tanks and other armored vehicles due to the use of composite armor, explosive-reactive armor, and active protection systems which destroy the _____ warhead before it hits the tank. Even though _____ rounds are less effective against the heavy armor found on 2010s main battle tanks, _____ warheads remain a threat against less-armored parts of a main battle tank and against lighter armored vehicles or unarmored vehicles and helicopters.

Exam Probability: **Low**

59. *Answer choices:*

(see index for correct answer)

- a. Supportworks
- b. HEAT
- c. Virtual help desk
- d. Technical support

Guidance: level 1

Commerce

Commerce relates to "the exchange of goods and services, especially on a large scale." It includes legal, economic, political, social, cultural and technological systems that operate in any country or internationally.

:: ::

In logic and philosophy, an _____ is a series of statements, called the premises or premisses, intended to determine the degree of truth of another statement, the conclusion. The logical form of an _____ in a natural language can be represented in a symbolic formal language, and independently of natural language formally defined "_____ s" can be made in math and computer science.

Exam Probability: **Medium**

1. *Answer choices:*

(see index for correct answer)

- a. hierarchical perspective
- b. process perspective
- c. functional perspective
- d. Argument

Guidance: level 1

:: Regulators ::

A _____ is a public authority or government agency responsible for exercising autonomous authority over some area of human activity in a regulatory or supervisory capacity. An independent _____ is a _____ that is independent from other branches or arms of the government.

Exam Probability: **Medium**

2. *Answer choices:*

(see index for correct answer)

- a. Croatian Regulatory Authority for Network Industries
- b. Energy and Utilities Board
- c. Regulatory agency

- d. Alberta Energy Regulator

Guidance: level 1

:: Manufacturing ::

A _____ is an object used to extend the ability of an individual to modify features of the surrounding environment. Although many animals use simple _____ s, only human beings, whose use of stone _____ s dates back hundreds of millennia, use _____ s to make other _____ s. The set of _____ s needed to perform different tasks that are part of the same activity is called gear or equipment.

Exam Probability: **High**

3. *Answer choices:*
(see index for correct answer)

- a. Boutique manufacturing
- b. Supplier Risk Management
- c. Tool
- d. Parts book

Guidance: level 1

:: ::

_____ is a marketing communication that employs an openly sponsored, non-personal message to promote or sell a product, service or idea. Sponsors of _____ are typically businesses wishing to promote their products or services. _____ is differentiated from public relations in that an advertiser pays for and has control over the message. It differs from personal selling in that the message is non-personal, i.e., not directed to a particular individual. _____ is communicated through various mass media, including traditional media such as newspapers, magazines, television, radio, outdoor _____ or direct mail; and new media such as search results, blogs, social media, websites or text messages. The actual presentation of the message in a medium is referred to as an advertisement, or "ad" or advert for short.

Exam Probability: **Low**

4. *Answer choices:*

(see index for correct answer)

- a. levels of analysis
- b. interpersonal communication
- c. surface-level diversity
- d. personal values

Guidance: level 1

:: Market structure and pricing ::

_____ has historically emerged in two separate types of discussions in economics, that of Adam Smith on the one hand, and that of Karl Marx on the other hand. Adam Smith in his writing on economics stressed the importance of laissez-faire principles outlining the operation of the market in the absence of dominant political mechanisms of control, while Karl Marx discussed the working of the market in the presence of a controlled economy sometimes referred to as a command economy in the literature. Both types of _____ have been in historical evidence throughout the twentieth century and twenty-first century.

Exam Probability: **High**

5. *Answer choices:*

(see index for correct answer)

- a. Open source
- b. Liberalization
- c. Installed base
- d. industry concentration

Guidance: level 1

:: ::

_____ is a means of protection from financial loss. It is a form of risk management, primarily used to hedge against the risk of a contingent or uncertain loss

Exam Probability: **High**

6. *Answer choices:*

(see index for correct answer)

- a. deep-level diversity
- b. cultural
- c. Sarbanes-Oxley act of 2002
- d. Insurance

Guidance: level 1

:: ::

A _____ is an individual or institution that legally owns one or more shares of stock in a public or private corporation. _____ s may be referred to as members of a corporation. Legally, a person is not a _____ in a corporation until their name and other details are entered in the corporation's register of _____ s or members.

Exam Probability: **High**

7. *Answer choices:*

(see index for correct answer)

- a. Shareholder
- b. similarity-attraction theory

- c. process perspective
- d. Sarbanes-Oxley act of 2002

Guidance: level 1

:: Consortia ::

A _____ is an association of two or more individuals, companies, organizations or governments with the objective of participating in a common activity or pooling their resources for achieving a common goal.

Exam Probability: **High**

8. *Answer choices:*

(see index for correct answer)

- a. Open Source Development Labs
- b. Y Chromosome Consortium
- c. AACS LA
- d. DAVIC

Guidance: level 1

:: Stock market ::

The _____ of a corporation is all of the shares into which ownership of the corporation is divided. In American English, the shares are commonly known as "_____ s". A single share of the _____ represents fractional ownership of the corporation in proportion to the total number of shares. This typically entitles the _____ holder to that fraction of the company's earnings, proceeds from liquidation of assets , or voting power, often dividing these up in proportion to the amount of money each _____ holder has invested. Not all _____ is necessarily equal, as certain classes of _____ may be issued for example without voting rights, with enhanced voting rights, or with a certain priority to receive profits or liquidation proceeds before or after other classes of shareholders.

Exam Probability: **High**

9. *Answer choices:*

(see index for correct answer)

- a. Stop catching
- b. GXG Markets
- c. Stock
- d. International Retail Service

Guidance: level 1

:: ::

The _____ is a U.S. business-focused, English-language international daily newspaper based in New York City. The Journal, along with its Asian and European editions, is published six days a week by Dow Jones & Company, a division of News Corp. The newspaper is published in the broadsheet format and online. The Journal has been printed continuously since its inception on July 8, 1889, by Charles Dow, Edward Jones, and Charles Bergstresser.

Exam Probability: **High**

10. *Answer choices:*

(see index for correct answer)

- a. Sarbanes-Oxley act of 2002
- b. hierarchical
- c. cultural
- d. information systems assessment

Guidance: level 1

:: Game theory ::

To _____ is to make a deal between different parties where each party gives up part of their demand. In arguments, _____ is a concept of finding agreement through communication, through a mutual acceptance of terms—often involving variations from an original goal or desires.

Exam Probability: **High**

11. *Answer choices:*

(see index for correct answer)

- a. Impunity game
- b. Compromise
- c. Game Description Language
- d. Strictly determined game

Guidance: level 1

:: Direct marketing ::

_____ is a form of advertising where organizations communicate directly to customers through a variety of media including cell phone text messaging, email, websites, online adverts, database marketing, fliers, catalog distribution, promotional letters, targeted television, newspapers, magazine advertisements, and outdoor advertising. Among practitioners, it is also known as direct response marketing.

Exam Probability: **Medium**

12. *Answer choices:*

(see index for correct answer)

- a. Large-group awareness training
- b. Cold calling
- c. Direct mail fundraising
- d. Direct marketing

Guidance: level 1

:: Project management ::

_____ is the right to exercise power, which can be formalized by a state and exercised by way of judges, appointed executives of government, or the ecclesiastical or priestly appointed representatives of a God or other deities.

Exam Probability: **High**

13. *Answer choices:*

(see index for correct answer)

- a. Small-scale project management
- b. Authority
- c. Karol Adamiecki
- d. Assumption-based planning

Guidance: level 1

:: International trade ::

A _____ is a document issued by a carrier to acknowledge receipt of cargo for shipment. Although the term historically related only to carriage by sea, a _____ may today be used for any type of carriage of goods.

Exam Probability: **Low**

14. *Answer choices:*

(see index for correct answer)

- a. Bill of lading
- b. Bilateral trade
- c. Trade finance
- d. financial account

Guidance: level 1

:: Dot-com bubble ::

_____ was an online grocery business that filed bankruptcy in 2001 after 3 years of operation and was later folded into Amazon.com. It was headquartered in Foster City, California, United States. It delivered products to customers' homes within a 30-minute window of their choosing. At its peak, it offered service in ten US markets: the San Francisco Bay Area; Dallas; Sacramento; San Diego; Los Angeles; Orange County, California; Chicago; Seattle; Portland, Oregon; and Atlanta, Georgia. The company had hoped to expand to 26 cities by 2001.

Exam Probability: **High**

15. *Answer choices:*

(see index for correct answer)

- a. Webvan
- b. Dot-com company
- c. GeoCities
- d. Cyberian Outpost

Guidance: level 1

:: Confidence tricks ::

_____ is the fraudulent attempt to obtain sensitive information such as usernames, passwords and credit card details by disguising oneself as a trustworthy entity in an electronic communication. Typically carried out by email spoofing or instant messaging, it often directs users to enter personal information at a fake website which matches the look and feel of the legitimate site.

Exam Probability: **Medium**

16. *Answer choices:*

(see index for correct answer)

- a. Phishing
- b. Spanish Prisoner
- c. Private investment capital subscription
- d. Television Preview

Guidance: level 1

:: ::

_____ , or auditory perception, is the ability to perceive sounds by detecting vibrations, changes in the pressure of the surrounding medium through time, through an organ such as the ear. The academic field concerned with _____ is auditory science.

Exam Probability: **Low**

17. *Answer choices:*

(see index for correct answer)

- a. Sarbanes-Oxley act of 2002
- b. Character
- c. Hearing
- d. personal values

Guidance: level 1

:: Industry ::

_____, also known as flow production or continuous production, is the production of large amounts of standardized products, including and especially on assembly lines. Together with job production and batch production, it is one of the three main production methods.

Exam Probability: **Low**

18. *Answer choices:*

(see index for correct answer)

- a. United Nations Industrial Development Organization
- b. Modelling of particle breakage
- c. AS-Interface
- d. Mass production

Guidance: level 1

:: ::

A _____ manages, commands, directs, or regulates the behavior of other devices or systems using control loops. It can range from a single home heating controller using a thermostat controlling a domestic boiler to large Industrial _____ s which are used for controlling processes or machines.

Exam Probability: **High**

19. *Answer choices:*

(see index for correct answer)

- a. Control system
- b. process perspective
- c. corporate values
- d. levels of analysis

Guidance: level 1

:: ::

Advertising is a marketing communication that employs an openly sponsored, non-personal message to promote or sell a product, service or idea. Sponsors of advertising are typically businesses wishing to promote their products or services. Advertising is differentiated from public relations in that an advertiser pays for and has control over the message. It differs from personal selling in that the message is non-personal, i.e., not directed to a particular individual.Advertising is communicated through various mass media, including traditional media such as newspapers, magazines, television, radio, outdoor advertising or direct mail; and new media such as search results, blogs, social media, websites or text messages. The actual presentation of the message in a medium is referred to as an _____ , or "ad" or advert for short.

Exam Probability: **Medium**

20. *Answer choices:*

(see index for correct answer)

- a. levels of analysis

- b. deep-level diversity
- c. process perspective
- d. cultural

Guidance: level 1

:: Monopoly (economics) ::

A _____ exists when a specific person or enterprise is the only supplier of a particular commodity. This contrasts with a monopsony which relates to a single entity's control of a market to purchase a good or service, and with oligopoly which consists of a few sellers dominating a market. Monopolies are thus characterized by a lack of economic competition to produce the good or service, a lack of viable substitute goods, and the possibility of a high _____ price well above the seller's marginal cost that leads to a high _____ profit. The verb monopolise or monopolize refers to the process by which a company gains the ability to raise prices or exclude competitors. In economics, a _____ is a single seller. In law, a _____ is a business entity that has significant market power, that is, the power to charge overly high prices. Although monopolies may be big businesses, size is not a characteristic of a _____. A small business may still have the power to raise prices in a small industry.

Exam Probability: **Medium**

21. *Answer choices:*

(see index for correct answer)

- a. Monopoly
- b. Third-party access

- c. Ramsey problem
- d. Building block model

Guidance: level 1

:: ::

_____ is an emotion involving pleasure, , or anxiety in considering or awaiting an expected event.

Exam Probability: **Low**

22. *Answer choices:*

(see index for correct answer)

- a. levels of analysis
- b. cultural
- c. similarity-attraction theory
- d. process perspective

Guidance: level 1

:: Management accounting ::

In economics, _____ s, indirect costs or overheads are business expenses that are not dependent on the level of goods or services produced by the business. They tend to be time-related, such as interest or rents being paid per month, and are often referred to as overhead costs. This is in contrast to variable costs, which are volume-related and unknown at the beginning of the accounting year. For a simple example, such as a bakery, the monthly rent for the baking facilities, and the monthly payments for the security system and basic phone line are _____ s, as they do not change according to how much bread the bakery produces and sells. On the other hand, the wage costs of the bakery are variable, as the bakery will have to hire more workers if the production of bread increases. Economists reckon _____ as a entry barrier for new entrepreneurs.

Exam Probability: **Medium**

23. *Answer choices:*

(see index for correct answer)

- a. Cost accounting
- b. Management accounting
- c. Invested capital
- d. Managerial risk accounting

Guidance: level 1

:: Auctioneering ::

Unlike sealed-bid auctions, an _____ is "open" or fully transparent, as the identity of all bidders is disclosed to each other during the auction. More generally, an auction mechanism is considered "English" if it involves an iterative process of adjusting the price in a direction that is unfavorable to the bidders. In contrast, a Dutch auction would adjust the price in a direction that favored the bidders.

Exam Probability: **Medium**

24. *Answer choices:*

(see index for correct answer)

- a. Unique bid auction
- b. World Livestock Auctioneer Championship
- c. Demsetz auction
- d. English auction

Guidance: level 1

:: Information technology ::

_____ is the use of computers to store, retrieve, transmit, and manipulate data, or information, often in the context of a business or other enterprise. IT is considered to be a subset of information and communications technology. An _____ system is generally an information system, a communications system or, more specifically speaking, a computer system – including all hardware, software and peripheral equipment – operated by a limited group of users.

Exam Probability: **Low**

25. *Answer choices:*

(see index for correct answer)

- a. Micro-innovation
- b. Anticipatory computing
- c. Information and communication technologies for environmental sustainability
- d. Normalized Systems

Guidance: level 1

:: ::

_____ is the amount of time someone works beyond normal working hours. The term is also used for the pay received for this time. Normal hours may be determined in several ways.

Exam Probability: **Medium**

26. *Answer choices:*

(see index for correct answer)

- a. corporate values
- b. Sarbanes-Oxley act of 2002
- c. surface-level diversity

- d. Overtime

Guidance: level 1

:: ::

Competition arises whenever at least two parties strive for a goal which cannot be shared: where one's gain is the other's loss.

Exam Probability: **High**

27. *Answer choices:*
(see index for correct answer)

- a. personal values
- b. process perspective
- c. functional perspective
- d. Competitor

Guidance: level 1

:: Theories ::

A _____ union is a type of multinational political union where negotiated power is delegated to an authority by governments of member states.

Exam Probability: **High**

28. *Answer choices:*

(see index for correct answer)

- a. incrementalism
- b. Supranational

Guidance: level 1

:: ::

A _____ is a fund into which a sum of money is added during an employee's employment years, and from which payments are drawn to support the person's retirement from work in the form of periodic payments. A _____ may be a "defined benefit plan" where a fixed sum is paid regularly to a person, or a "defined contribution plan" under which a fixed sum is invested and then becomes available at retirement age. _____ s should not be confused with severance pay; the former is usually paid in regular installments for life after retirement, while the latter is typically paid as a fixed amount after involuntary termination of employment prior to retirement.

Exam Probability: **Medium**

29. *Answer choices:*

(see index for correct answer)

- a. corporate values
- b. open system
- c. Pension
- d. imperative

Guidance: level 1

:: ::

A _____ is any person who contracts to acquire an asset in return for some form of consideration.

Exam Probability: **High**

30. *Answer choices:*

(see index for correct answer)

- a. Buyer
- b. Sarbanes-Oxley act of 2002
- c. levels of analysis
- d. co-culture

Guidance: level 1

:: Marketing ::

_____ is a concept introduced in a book of the same name in 1999 by marketing expert Seth Godin. _____ is a non-traditional marketing technique that advertises goods and services when advance consent is given.

Exam Probability: **Low**

31. *Answer choices:*

(see index for correct answer)

- a. Impulse purchase
- b. Market development
- c. Permission marketing
- d. Niche market

Guidance: level 1

:: Management ::

_____ is the process of thinking about the activities required to achieve a desired goal. It is the first and foremost activity to achieve desired results. It involves the creation and maintenance of a plan, such as psychological aspects that require conceptual skills. There are even a couple of tests to measure someone's capability of _____ well. As such, _____ is a fundamental property of intelligent behavior. An important further meaning, often just called " _____ " is the legal context of permitted building developments.

Exam Probability: **Medium**

32. *Answer choices:*

(see index for correct answer)

- a. Clean-sheet review
- b. Supervisory board
- c. Energy monitoring and targeting
- d. Planning

Guidance: level 1

:: ::

In marketing jargon, product lining is offering several related products for sale individually. Unlike product bundling, where several products are combined into one group, which is then offered for sale as a units, product lining involves offering the products for sale separately. A line can comprise related products of various sizes, types, colors, qualities, or prices. Line depth refers to the number of subcategories a category has. Line consistency refers to how closely related the products that make up the line are. Line vulnerability refers to the percentage of sales or profits that are derived from only a few products in the line.

Exam Probability: **Low**

33. *Answer choices:*

(see index for correct answer)

- a. Product mix
- b. process perspective
- c. cultural
- d. similarity-attraction theory

Guidance: level 1

:: ::

A _____ is an organization, usually a group of people or a company, authorized to act as a single entity and recognized as such in law. Early incorporated entities were established by charter. Most jurisdictions now allow the creation of new _____ s through registration.

Exam Probability: **High**

34. *Answer choices:*

(see index for correct answer)

- a. Corporation
- b. information systems assessment
- c. empathy
- d. levels of analysis

Guidance: level 1

:: Industrial automation ::

_____ is the technology by which a process or procedure is performed with minimal human assistance. _____ or automatic control is the use of various control systems for operating equipment such as machinery, processes in factories, boilers and heat treating ovens, switching on telephone networks, steering and stabilization of ships, aircraft and other applications and vehicles with minimal or reduced human intervention.

Exam Probability: **High**

35. *Answer choices:*

(see index for correct answer)

- a. Automation
- b. RAPIEnet
- c. I/Gear
- d. DirectLOGIC

Guidance: level 1

:: Economics terminology ::

_____ is the total receipts a seller can obtain from selling goods or services to buyers. It can be written as P × Q, which is the price of the goods multiplied by the quantity of the sold goods.

Exam Probability: **Low**

36. *Answer choices:*

(see index for correct answer)

- a. fungible
- b. Normal profit
- c. Total revenue
- d. Capital cost

Guidance: level 1

:: Commodities ::

In economics, a _____ is an economic good or service that has full or substantial fungibility: that is, the market treats instances of the good as equivalent or nearly so with no regard to who produced them. Most commodities are raw materials, basic resources, agricultural, or mining products, such as iron ore, sugar, or grains like rice and wheat. Commodities can also be mass-produced unspecialized products such as chemicals and computer memory.

Exam Probability: **Medium**

37. *Answer choices:*

(see index for correct answer)

- a. Commodity
- b. Commodity pathway diversion

- c. Commodity money
- d. Sample grade

Guidance: level 1

:: Management ::

A _____ is an idea of the future or desired result that a person or a group of people envisions, plans and commits to achieve. People endeavor to reach _____ s within a finite time by setting deadlines.

Exam Probability: **Medium**

38. *Answer choices:*

(see index for correct answer)

- a. Goal
- b. Identity formation
- c. Innovation management
- d. Product life-cycle management

Guidance: level 1

:: ::

In legal terminology, a _____ is any formal legal document that sets out the facts and legal reasons that the filing party or parties believes are sufficient to support a claim against the party or parties against whom the claim is brought that entitles the plaintiff to a remedy. For example, the Federal Rules of Civil Procedure that govern civil litigation in United States courts provide that a civil action is commenced with the filing or service of a pleading called a _____. Civil court rules in states that have incorporated the Federal Rules of Civil Procedure use the same term for the same pleading.

Exam Probability: **High**

39. *Answer choices:*

(see index for correct answer)

- a. co-culture
- b. Character
- c. Complaint
- d. information systems assessment

Guidance: level 1

:: International trade ::

An _____ is a good brought into a jurisdiction, especially across a national border, from an external source. The party bringing in the good is called an _____ er. An _____ in the receiving country is an export from the sending country. _____ ation and exportation are the defining financial transactions of international trade.

Exam Probability: **Medium**

40. *Answer choices:*

(see index for correct answer)

- a. Import
- b. Foreign Sales Corporation
- c. Uppsala model
- d. DataArt

Guidance: level 1

:: Land value taxation ::

_____, sometimes referred to as dry _____, is the solid surface of Earth that is not permanently covered by water. The vast majority of human activity throughout history has occurred in _____ areas that support agriculture, habitat, and various natural resources. Some life forms have developed from predecessor species that lived in bodies of water.

Exam Probability: **Medium**

41. *Answer choices:*

(see index for correct answer)

- a. Georgism
- b. Land

- c. Harry Gunnison Brown
- d. Henry George

Guidance: level 1

:: Commerce ::

_____ , Inc. is an American media-services provider headquartered in Los Gatos, California, founded in 1997 by Reed Hastings and Marc Randolph in Scotts Valley, California. The company`s primary business is its subscription-based streaming OTT service which offers online streaming of a library of films and television programs, including those produced in-house. As of April 2019, _____ had over 148 million paid subscriptions worldwide, including 60 million in the United States, and over 154 million subscriptions total including free trials. It is available almost worldwide except in mainland China as well as Syria, North Korea, and Crimea . The company also has offices in the Netherlands, Brazil, India, Japan, and South Korea. _____ is a member of the Motion Picture Association of America .

Exam Probability: **Medium**

42. *Answer choices:*
(see index for correct answer)

- a. GT Nexus
- b. Netflix
- c. Issuing bank
- d. Reseller

Guidance: level 1

:: Price fixing convictions ::

> _____ AG is a German multinational conglomerate company headquartered in Berlin and Munich and the largest industrial manufacturing company in Europe with branch offices abroad.

Exam Probability: **High**

43. *Answer choices:*

(see index for correct answer)

- a. SK Foods
- b. JJB Sports
- c. United States v. Archer Daniels Midland Co.
- d. Siemens

Guidance: level 1

:: Supply chain management ::

A _____ is a type of auction in which the traditional roles of buyer and seller are reversed. Thus, there is one buyer and many potential sellers. In an ordinary auction, buyers compete to obtain goods or services by offering increasingly higher prices. In contrast, in a _____, the sellers compete to obtain business from the buyer and prices will typically decrease as the sellers underbid each other.

Exam Probability: **Medium**

44. *Answer choices:*

(see index for correct answer)

- a. Calculating demand forecast accuracy
- b. RFTrax
- c. Reverse auction
- d. Institute for Supply Management

Guidance: level 1

:: ::

_____ refers to a business or organization attempting to acquire goods or services to accomplish its goals. Although there are several organizations that attempt to set standards in the _____ process, processes can vary greatly between organizations. Typically the word " _____ " is not used interchangeably with the word "procurement", since procurement typically includes expediting, supplier quality, and transportation and logistics in addition to _____ .

Exam Probability: **Low**

45. *Answer choices:*

(see index for correct answer)

- a. deep-level diversity
- b. hierarchical perspective
- c. Sarbanes-Oxley act of 2002
- d. levels of analysis

Guidance: level 1

:: Stochastic processes ::

_____ in its modern meaning is a "new idea, creative thoughts, new imaginations in form of device or method". _____ is often also viewed as the application of better solutions that meet new requirements, unarticulated needs, or existing market needs. Such _____ takes place through the provision of more-effective products, processes, services, technologies, or business models that are made available to markets, governments and society. An _____ is something original and more effective and, as a consequence, new, that "breaks into" the market or society. _____ is related to, but not the same as, invention, as _____ is more apt to involve the practical implementation of an invention to make a meaningful impact in the market or society, and not all _____ s require an invention. _____ often manifests itself via the engineering process, when the problem being solved is of a technical or scientific nature. The opposite of _____ is exnovation.

Exam Probability: **High**

46. *Answer choices:*

(see index for correct answer)

- a. Arcsine laws
- b. Minimal-entropy martingale measure
- c. return time
- d. Markov information source

Guidance: level 1

:: Commerce ::

A _____ is an employee within a company, business or other organization who is responsible at some level for buying or approving the acquisition of goods and services needed by the company. Responsible for buying the best quality products, goods and services for their company at the most competitive prices, _____ s work in a wide range of sectors for many different organizations. The position responsibilities may be the same as that of a buyer or purchasing agent, or may include wider supervisory or managerial responsibilities. A _____ may oversee the acquisition of materials needed for production, general supplies for offices and facilities, equipment, or construction contracts. A _____ often supervises purchasing agents and buyers, but in small companies the _____ may also be the purchasing agent or buyer. The _____ position may also carry the title "Procurement Manager" or in the public sector, "Procurement Officer". He or she can come from both an Engineering or Economics background.

Exam Probability: **Medium**

47. *Answer choices:*

(see index for correct answer)

- a. GT Nexus
- b. Purchasing manager
- c. Global Commerce Initiative
- d. International Marketmakers Combination

Guidance: level 1

:: Management ::

In business, a _____ is the attribute that allows an organization to outperform its competitors. A _____ may include access to natural resources, such as high-grade ores or a low-cost power source, highly skilled labor, geographic location, high entry barriers, and access to new technology.

Exam Probability: **Medium**

48. *Answer choices:*

(see index for correct answer)

- a. Advisory board
- b. Risk management
- c. Investment control
- d. Plan

Guidance: level 1

:: ::

A _____, or also known as foreman, overseer, facilitator, monitor, area coordinator, or sometimes gaffer, is the job title of a low level management position that is primarily based on authority over a worker or charge of a workplace. A _____ can also be one of the most senior in the staff at the place of work, such as a Professor who oversees a PhD dissertation. Supervision, on the other hand, can be performed by people without this formal title, for example by parents. The term _____ itself can be used to refer to any personnel who have this task as part of their job description.

Exam Probability: **Medium**

49. *Answer choices:*

(see index for correct answer)

- a. levels of analysis
- b. corporate values
- c. empathy
- d. Supervisor

Guidance: level 1

:: Decision theory ::

A _____ is a deliberate system of principles to guide decisions and achieve rational outcomes. A _____ is a statement of intent, and is implemented as a procedure or protocol. Policies are generally adopted by a governance body within an organization. Policies can assist in both subjective and objective decision making. Policies to assist in subjective decision making usually assist senior management with decisions that must be based on the relative merits of a number of factors, and as a result are often hard to test objectively, e.g. work-life balance _____ . In contrast policies to assist in objective decision making are usually operational in nature and can be objectively tested, e.g. password _____ .

Exam Probability: **Medium**

50. *Answer choices:*

(see index for correct answer)

- a. Dominance-based rough set approach
- b. Expected value of sample information
- c. Predispositioning theory
- d. Wild card

Guidance: level 1

:: Economic globalization ::

_____ is an agreement in which one company hires another company to be responsible for a planned or existing activity that is or could be done internally, and sometimes involves transferring employees and assets from one firm to another.

Exam Probability: **Medium**

51. Answer choices:

(see index for correct answer)

- a. reshoring
- b. Outsourcing

Guidance: level 1

:: Business law ::

A _____ is a business entity created by two or more parties, generally characterized by shared ownership, shared returns and risks, and shared governance. Companies typically pursue _____ s for one of four reasons: to access a new market, particularly emerging markets; to gain scale efficiencies by combining assets and operations; to share risk for major investments or projects; or to access skills and capabilities.

Exam Probability: **Low**

52. Answer choices:

(see index for correct answer)

- a. Legal tender
- b. Uniform Partnership Act
- c. Joint venture
- d. Process agent

Guidance: level 1

:: E-commerce ::

An _____ , or automated clearinghouse, is an electronic network for financial transactions, generally domestic low value payments. An ACH is a computer-based clearing house and settlement facility established to process the exchange of electronic transactions between participating financial institutions. It is a form of clearing house that is specifically for payments and may support both credit transfers and direct debits.

Exam Probability: **Medium**

53. *Answer choices:*
(see index for correct answer)

- a. Online Revolution
- b. E-tendering
- c. Automated Clearing House
- d. Switchwise

Guidance: level 1

:: ::

_____ are electronic transfer of money from one bank account to another, either within a single financial institution or across multiple institutions, via computer-based systems, without the direct intervention of bank staff.

Exam Probability: **Medium**

54. *Answer choices:*

(see index for correct answer)

- a. corporate values
- b. imperative
- c. Electronic funds transfer
- d. hierarchical

Guidance: level 1

:: ::

A _____ is a sworn body of people convened to render an impartial verdict officially submitted to them by a court, or to set a penalty or judgment. Modern juries tend to be found in courts to ascertain the guilt or lack thereof in a crime. In Anglophone jurisdictions, the verdict may be guilty or not guilty. The old institution of grand juries still exists in some places, particularly the United States, to investigate whether enough evidence of a crime exists to bring someone to trial.

Exam Probability: **High**

55. Answer choices:

(see index for correct answer)

- a. levels of analysis
- b. surface-level diversity
- c. Jury
- d. cultural

Guidance: level 1

:: E-commerce ::

_____ Inc. was an electronic money corporation founded by David Chaum in 1989. _____ transactions were unique in that they were anonymous due to a number of cryptographic protocols developed by its founder. _____ declared bankruptcy in 1998, and subsequently sold its assets to eCash Technologies, another digital currency company, which was acquired by InfoSpace on Feb. 19, 2002.

Exam Probability: **High**

56. Answer choices:

(see index for correct answer)

- a. Self-certifying key
- b. IzzoNet
- c. UN/CEFACT
- d. DigiCash

Guidance: level 1

:: ::

_____ is the provision of service to customers before, during and after a purchase. The perception of success of such interactions is dependent on employees "who can adjust themselves to the personality of the guest". _____ concerns the priority an organization assigns to _____ relative to components such as product innovation and pricing. In this sense, an organization that values good _____ may spend more money in training employees than the average organization or may proactively interview customers for feedback.

Exam Probability: **Low**

57. *Answer choices:*

(see index for correct answer)

- a. deep-level diversity
- b. hierarchical perspective
- c. levels of analysis
- d. Customer service

Guidance: level 1

:: Asset ::

In financial accounting, an _____ is any resource owned by the business. Anything tangible or intangible that can be owned or controlled to produce value and that is held by a company to produce positive economic value is an _____. Simply stated, _____s represent value of ownership that can be converted into cash. The balance sheet of a firm records the monetary value of the _____s owned by that firm. It covers money and other valuables belonging to an individual or to a business.

Exam Probability: **Medium**

58. *Answer choices:*
(see index for correct answer)

- a. Fixed asset
- b. Current asset

Guidance: level 1

:: E-commerce ::

Customer to customer markets provide an innovative way to allow customers to interact with each other. Traditional markets require business to customer relationships, in which a customer goes to the business in order to purchase a product or service. In customer to customer markets, the business facilitates an environment where customers can sell goods or services to each other. Other types of markets include business to business and business to customer.

Exam Probability: **Low**

59. *Answer choices:*

(see index for correct answer)

- a. Donna Hoffman
- b. Cleaning card
- c. Gazaro
- d. Wildcard certificate

Guidance: level 1

Business ethics

Business ethics (also known as corporate ethics) is a form of applied ethics or professional ethics, that examines ethical principles and moral or ethical problems that can arise in a business environment. It applies to all aspects of business conduct and is relevant to the conduct of individuals and entire organizations. These ethics originate from individuals, organizational statements or from the legal system. These norms, values, ethical, and unethical practices are what is used to guide business. They help those businesses maintain a better connection with their stakeholders.

_____ Corporation was an American energy, commodities, and services company based in Houston, Texas. It was founded in 1985 as a merger between Houston Natural Gas and InterNorth, both relatively small regional companies. Before its bankruptcy on December 3, 2001, _____ employed approximately 29,000 staff and was a major electricity, natural gas, communications and pulp and paper company, with claimed revenues of nearly $101 billion during 2000. Fortune named _____ "America's Most Innovative Company" for six consecutive years.

Exam Probability: **High**

1. *Answer choices:*

(see index for correct answer)

- a. corporate values
- b. information systems assessment
- c. Enron
- d. deep-level diversity

Guidance: level 1

:: ::

_____ is a bundle of characteristics, including ways of thinking, feeling, and acting, which humans are said to have naturally. The term is often regarded as capturing what it is to be human, or the essence of humanity. The term is controversial because it is disputed whether or not such an essence exists. Arguments about _____ have been a mainstay of philosophy for centuries and the concept continues to provoke lively philosophical debate. The concept also continues to play a role in science, with neuroscientists, psychologists and social scientists sometimes claiming that their results have yielded insight into _____ . _____ is traditionally contrasted with characteristics that vary among humans, such as characteristics associated with specific cultures. Debates about _____ are related to, although not the same as, debates about the comparative importance of genes and environment in development .

Exam Probability: **Medium**

2. *Answer choices:*

(see index for correct answer)

- a. imperative
- b. Human nature
- c. process perspective
- d. hierarchical perspective

Guidance: level 1

:: Real estate ::

_____ s serve several societal needs – primarily as shelter from weather, security, living space, privacy, to store belongings, and to comfortably live and work. A _____ as a shelter represents a physical division of the human habitat and the outside .

Exam Probability: **Medium**

3. *Answer choices:*

(see index for correct answer)

- a. Landed nobility
- b. AMP Technologies
- c. Rent control in the United States
- d. Building

Guidance: level 1

:: Business ethics ::

The _____ are the names of two corporate codes of conduct, developed by the African-American preacher Rev. Leon Sullivan, promoting corporate social responsibility.

Exam Probability: **High**

4. *Answer choices:*

(see index for correct answer)

- a. Nishkam Karma
- b. Anti-consumerism
- c. Sullivan principles
- d. CUC International

Guidance: level 1

:: Offshoring ::

A _____ is the temporary suspension or permanent termination of employment of an employee or, more commonly, a group of employees for business reasons, such as personnel management or downsizing an organization. Originally, _____ referred exclusively to a temporary interruption in work, or employment but this has evolved to a permanent elimination of a position in both British and US English, requiring the addition of "temporary" to specify the original meaning of the word. A _____ is not to be confused with wrongful termination. Laid off workers or displaced workers are workers who have lost or left their jobs because their employer has closed or moved, there was insufficient work for them to do, or their position or shift was abolished. Downsizing in a company is defined to involve the reduction of employees in a workforce. Downsizing in companies became a popular practice in the 1980s and early 1990s as it was seen as a way to deliver better shareholder value as it helps to reduce the costs of employers. Indeed, recent research on downsizing in the U.S., UK, and Japan suggests that downsizing is being regarded by management as one of the preferred routes to help declining organizations, cutting unnecessary costs, and improve organizational performance. Usually a _____ occurs as a cost cutting measure.

Exam Probability: **Medium**

5. *Answer choices:*

(see index for correct answer)

- a. Body shopping
- b. Nearshoring
- c. Layoff
- d. Advanced Contact Solutions

Guidance: level 1

:: United States law ::

The ABA _____, created by the American Bar Association, are a set of rules that prescribe baseline standards of legal ethics and professional responsibility for lawyers in the United States. They were promulgated by the ABA House of Delegates upon the recommendation of the Kutak Commission in 1983. The rules are merely recommendations, or models, and are not themselves binding. However, having a common set of Model Rules facilitates a common discourse on legal ethics, and simplifies professional responsibility training as well as the day-to-day application of such rules. As of 2015, 49 states and four territories have adopted the rules in whole or in part, of which the most recent to do so was the Commonwealth of the Northern Mariana Islands in March 2015. California is the only state that has not adopted the ABA Model Rules, while Puerto Rico is the only U.S. jurisdiction outside of confederation has not adopted them but instead has its own Código de Ética Profesional.

Exam Probability: **Medium**

6. *Answer choices:*

(see index for correct answer)

- a. judgment notwithstanding the verdict
- b. Model Rules of Professional Conduct

Guidance: level 1

:: Separation of investment and commercial banking ::

The _____ refers to § 619 of the Dodd–Frank Wall Street Reform and Consumer Protection Act. The rule was originally proposed by American economist and former United States Federal Reserve Chairman Paul Volcker to restrict United States banks from making certain kinds of speculative investments that do not benefit their customers. Volcker argued that such speculative activity played a key role in the financial crisis of 2007–2008. The rule is often referred to as a ban on proprietary trading by commercial banks, whereby deposits are used to trade on the bank's own accounts, although a number of exceptions to this ban were included in the Dodd-Frank law.

Exam Probability: **Medium**

7. *Answer choices:*
(see index for correct answer)

- a. Independent Commission on Banking
- b. Speculation
- c. Volcker Rule
- d. Depository institution

Guidance: level 1

:: Price fixing convictions ::

_____ AG is a German multinational conglomerate company headquartered in Berlin and Munich and the largest industrial manufacturing company in Europe with branch offices abroad.

Exam Probability: **Medium**

8. *Answer choices:*

(see index for correct answer)

- a. Siemens
- b. Hoffmann-La Roche
- c. Anheuser-Busch InBev
- d. AGC Glass Europe

Guidance: level 1

:: ::

In regulatory jurisdictions that provide for it, _____ is a group of laws and organizations designed to ensure the rights of consumers as well as fair trade, competition and accurate information in the marketplace. The laws are designed to prevent the businesses that engage in fraud or specified unfair practices from gaining an advantage over competitors. They may also provides additional protection for those most vulnerable in society. _____ laws are a form of government regulation that aim to protect the rights of consumers. For example, a government may require businesses to disclose detailed information about products—particularly in areas where safety or public health is an issue, such as food.

Exam Probability: **High**

9. *Answer choices:*

(see index for correct answer)

- a. open system
- b. hierarchical perspective
- c. information systems assessment
- d. imperative

Guidance: level 1

:: ::

A _____ is a set of rules, often written, with regards to clothing. _____ s are created out of social perceptions and norms, and vary based on purpose, circumstances and occasions. Different societies and cultures are likely to have different _____ s.

Exam Probability: **High**

10. *Answer choices:*

(see index for correct answer)

- a. similarity-attraction theory
- b. process perspective
- c. surface-level diversity
- d. Dress code

Guidance: level 1

:: Data management ::

_____ is a form of intellectual property that grants the creator of an original creative work an exclusive legal right to determine whether and under what conditions this original work may be copied and used by others, usually for a limited term of years. The exclusive rights are not absolute but limited by limitations and exceptions to _____ law, including fair use. A major limitation on _____ on ideas is that _____ protects only the original expression of ideas, and not the underlying ideas themselves.

Exam Probability: **Low**

11. *Answer choices:*

(see index for correct answer)

- a. Serializability

- b. Copyright
- c. Isolation
- d. Data security

Guidance: level 1

:: Electronic feedback ::

_____ occurs when outputs of a system are routed back as inputs as part of a chain of cause-and-effect that forms a circuit or loop. The system can then be said to feed back into itself. The notion of cause-and-effect has to be handled carefully when applied to _____ systems.

Exam Probability: **Medium**

12. *Answer choices:*
(see index for correct answer)

- a. Positive feedback
- b. feedback loop

Guidance: level 1

:: Writs ::

In common law, a writ of _____ is a writ whereby a private individual who assists a prosecution can receive all or part of any penalty imposed. Its name is an abbreviation of the Latin phrase _____ pro domino rege quam pro se ipso in hac parte sequitur, meaning "[he] who sues in this matter for the king as well as for himself."

Exam Probability: **High**

13. *Answer choices:*

(see index for correct answer)

- a. Writ
- b. Qui tam
- c. Writ of assistance

Guidance: level 1

:: Fraud ::

In the United States, _____ is the claiming of Medicare health care reimbursement to which the claimant is not entitled. There are many different types of _____ , all of which have the same goal: to collect money from the Medicare program illegitimately.

Exam Probability: **Medium**

14. *Answer choices:*

(see index for correct answer)

- a. Medicare fraud
- b. Overbilling
- c. Clothing scam companies
- d. Shell corporation

Guidance: level 1

:: ::

In ecology, a _____ is the type of natural environment in which a particular species of organism lives. It is characterized by both physical and biological features. A species' _____ is those places where it can find food, shelter, protection and mates for reproduction.

Exam Probability: **Medium**

15. *Answer choices:*

(see index for correct answer)

- a. process perspective
- b. Habitat
- c. levels of analysis
- d. imperative

Guidance: level 1

:: ::

The _____ of 1977 is a United States federal law known primarily for two of its main provisions: one that addresses accounting transparency requirements under the Securities Exchange Act of 1934 and another concerning bribery of foreign officials. The Act was amended in 1988 and in 1998, and has been subject to continued congressional concerns, namely whether its enforcement discourages U.S. companies from investing abroad.

Exam Probability: **Low**

16. *Answer choices:*

(see index for correct answer)

- a. Sarbanes-Oxley act of 2002
- b. corporate values
- c. Character
- d. interpersonal communication

Guidance: level 1

:: Public relations terminology ::

_____ , also called "green sheen", is a form of spin in which green PR or green marketing is deceptively used to promote the perception that an organization's products, aims or policies are environmentally friendly. Evidence that an organization is _____ often comes from pointing out the spending differences: when significantly more money or time has been spent advertising being "green" , than is actually spent on environmentally sound practices. _____ efforts can range from changing the name or label of a product to evoke the natural environment on a product that contains harmful chemicals to multimillion-dollar marketing campaigns portraying highly polluting energy companies as eco-friendly. Publicized accusations of _____ have contributed to the term's increasing use.

Exam Probability: **High**

17. *Answer choices:*

(see index for correct answer)

- a. Photo op
- b. Crisis communication
- c. Greenwashing
- d. No comment

Guidance: level 1

:: Product certification ::

_____ is food produced by methods that comply with the standards of organic farming. Standards vary worldwide, but organic farming features practices that cycle resources, promote ecological balance, and conserve biodiversity. Organizations regulating organic products may restrict the use of certain pesticides and fertilizers in the farming methods used to produce such products. _____ s typically are not processed using irradiation, industrial solvents, or synthetic food additives.

Exam Probability: **High**

18. *Answer choices:*

(see index for correct answer)

- a. TCO Certification
- b. Product certification
- c. Type approval
- d. Organic food

Guidance: level 1

:: Television terminology ::

A _____ organization, also known as a non-business entity, not-for-profit organization, or _____ institution, is dedicated to furthering a particular social cause or advocating for a shared point of view. In economic terms, it is an organization that uses its surplus of the revenues to further achieve its ultimate objective, rather than distributing its income to the organization's shareholders, leaders, or members. _____s are tax exempt or charitable, meaning they do not pay income tax on the money that they receive for their organization. They can operate in religious, scientific, research, or educational settings.

Exam Probability: **Medium**

19. *Answer choices:*

(see index for correct answer)

- a. Nonprofit
- b. multiplexing
- c. distance learning
- d. not-for-profit

Guidance: level 1

:: Human resource management ::

_____ encompasses values and behaviors that contribute to the unique social and psychological environment of a business. The _____ influences the way people interact, the context within which knowledge is created, the resistance they will have towards certain changes, and ultimately the way they share knowledge. _____ represents the collective values, beliefs and principles of organizational members and is a product of factors such as history, product, market, technology, strategy, type of employees, management style, and national culture; culture includes the organization's vision, values, norms, systems, symbols, language, assumptions, environment, location, beliefs and habits.

Exam Probability: **Medium**

20. *Answer choices:*

(see index for correct answer)

- a. Organizational culture
- b. Administrative services organization
- c. Voluntary redundancy
- d. Chartered Institute of Personnel and Development

Guidance: level 1

:: Auditing ::

_____, as defined by accounting and auditing, is a process for assuring of an organization's objectives in operational effectiveness and efficiency, reliable financial reporting, and compliance with laws, regulations and policies. A broad concept, _____ involves everything that controls risks to an organization.

Exam Probability: **Low**

21. *Answer choices:*

(see index for correct answer)

- a. Mitigating control
- b. Chartered Institute of Internal Auditors
- c. Internal control
- d. Technical audit

Guidance: level 1

:: ::

Cannabis, also known as _____ among other names, is a psychoactive drug from the Cannabis plant used for medical or recreational purposes. The main psychoactive part of cannabis is tetrahydrocannabinol, one of 483 known compounds in the plant, including at least 65 other cannabinoids. Cannabis can be used by smoking, vaporizing, within food, or as an extract.

Exam Probability: **Medium**

22. *Answer choices:*

(see index for correct answer)

- a. open system
- b. hierarchical
- c. levels of analysis
- d. surface-level diversity

Guidance: level 1

:: Cognitive biases ::

> In personality psychology, _____ is the degree to which people believe that they have control over the outcome of events in their lives, as opposed to external forces beyond their control. Understanding of the concept was developed by Julian B. Rotter in 1954, and has since become an aspect of personality studies. A person's "locus" is conceptualized as internal or external.

Exam Probability: **High**

23. *Answer choices:*

(see index for correct answer)

- a. Region-beta paradox
- b. John Henry effect
- c. Attribution bias
- d. Locus of control

Guidance: level 1

:: ::

> The _____ of 1906 was the first of a series of significant consumer protection laws which was enacted by Congress in the 20th century and led to the creation of the Food and Drug Administration. Its main purpose was to ban foreign and interstate traffic in adulterated or mislabeled food and drug products, and it directed the U.S. Bureau of Chemistry to inspect products and refer offenders to prosecutors. It required that active ingredients be placed on the label of a drug's packaging and that drugs could not fall below purity levels established by the United States Pharmacopeia or the National Formulary. The Jungle by Upton Sinclair with its graphic and revolting descriptions of unsanitary conditions and unscrupulous practices rampant in the meatpacking industry, was an inspirational piece that kept the public's attention on the important issue of unhygienic meat processing plants that later led to food inspection legislation. Sinclair quipped, "I aimed at the public's heart and by accident I hit it in the stomach," as outraged readers demanded and got the pure food law.

Exam Probability: **Medium**

24. *Answer choices:*

(see index for correct answer)

- a. levels of analysis
- b. interpersonal communication
- c. functional perspective
- d. Pure Food and Drug Act

Guidance: level 1

:: ::

An _____ is the release of a liquid petroleum hydrocarbon into the environment, especially the marine ecosystem, due to human activity, and is a form of pollution. The term is usually given to marine _____ s, where oil is released into the ocean or coastal waters, but spills may also occur on land. _____ s may be due to releases of crude oil from tankers, offshore platforms, drilling rigs and wells, as well as spills of refined petroleum products and their by-products, heavier fuels used by large ships such as bunker fuel, or the spill of any oily refuse or waste oil.

Exam Probability: **Medium**

25. *Answer choices:*

(see index for correct answer)

- a. corporate values
- b. functional perspective
- c. empathy
- d. Oil spill

Guidance: level 1

:: ::

The _____ is an American stock exchange located at 11 Wall Street, Lower Manhattan, New York City, New York. It is by far the world's largest stock exchange by market capitalization of its listed companies at US$30.1 trillion as of February 2018. The average daily trading value was approximately US$169 billion in 2013. The NYSE trading floor is located at 11 Wall Street and is composed of 21 rooms used for the facilitation of trading. A fifth trading room, located at 30 Broad Street, was closed in February 2007. The main building and the 11 Wall Street building were designated National Historic Landmarks in 1978.

Exam Probability: **Medium**

26. *Answer choices:*

(see index for correct answer)

- a. New York Stock Exchange
- b. corporate values
- c. information systems assessment
- d. deep-level diversity

Guidance: level 1

:: Natural gas ::

_____ is a naturally occurring hydrocarbon gas mixture consisting primarily of methane, but commonly including varying amounts of other higher alkanes, and sometimes a small percentage of carbon dioxide, nitrogen, hydrogen sulfide, or helium. It is formed when layers of decomposing plant and animal matter are exposed to intense heat and pressure under the surface of the Earth over millions of years. The energy that the plants originally obtained from the sun is stored in the form of chemical bonds in the gas.

Exam Probability: **Low**

27. *Answer choices:*

(see index for correct answer)

- a. Natural gas
- b. Petrochemistry
- c. Clathrate hydrate
- d. Moisture analysis

Guidance: level 1

:: Criminal law ::

_____ is the body of law that relates to crime. It proscribes conduct perceived as threatening, harmful, or otherwise endangering to the property, health, safety, and moral welfare of people inclusive of one's self. Most _____ is established by statute, which is to say that the laws are enacted by a legislature. _____ includes the punishment and rehabilitation of people who violate such laws. _____ varies according to jurisdiction, and differs from civil law, where emphasis is more on dispute resolution and victim compensation, rather than on punishment or rehabilitation. Criminal procedure is a formalized official activity that authenticates the fact of commission of a crime and authorizes punitive or rehabilitative treatment of the offender.

Exam Probability: **Medium**

28. *Answer choices:*

(see index for correct answer)

- a. Mala prohibita
- b. mitigating factor
- c. complicit
- d. Mala in se

Guidance: level 1

:: ::

_____ Ltd. is the world's 2nd largest offshore drilling contractor and is based in Vernier, Switzerland. The company has offices in 20 countries, including Switzerland, Canada, United States, Norway, Scotland, India, Brazil, Singapore, Indonesia and Malaysia.

Exam Probability: **Low**

29. *Answer choices:*

(see index for correct answer)

- a. co-culture
- b. functional perspective
- c. Transocean
- d. similarity-attraction theory

Guidance: level 1

:: ::

_____ in the United States is a federal and state program that helps with medical costs for some people with limited income and resources. _____ also offers benefits not normally covered by Medicare, including nursing home care and personal care services. The Health Insurance Association of America describes _____ as "a government insurance program for persons of all ages whose income and resources are insufficient to pay for health care." _____ is the largest source of funding for medical and health-related services for people with low income in the United States, providing free health insurance to 74 million low-income and disabled people as of 2017. It is a means-tested program that is jointly funded by the state and federal governments and managed by the states, with each state currently having broad leeway to determine who is eligible for its implementation of the program. States are not required to participate in the program, although all have since 1982. _____ recipients must be U.S. citizens or qualified non-citizens, and may include low-income adults, their children, and people with certain disabilities. Poverty alone does not necessarily qualify someone for _____ .

Exam Probability: **Medium**

30. *Answer choices:*

(see index for correct answer)

- a. Medicaid
- b. imperative
- c. empathy
- d. open system

Guidance: level 1

:: ::

Competition law is a law that promotes or seeks to maintain market competition by regulating anti-competitive conduct by companies. Competition law is implemented through public and private enforcement. Competition law is known as "_____ law" in the United States for historical reasons, and as "anti-monopoly law" in China and Russia. In previous years it has been known as trade practices law in the United Kingdom and Australia. In the European Union, it is referred to as both _____ and competition law.

Exam Probability: **Medium**

31. *Answer choices:*

(see index for correct answer)

- a. Antitrust

- b. empathy
- c. surface-level diversity
- d. deep-level diversity

Guidance: level 1

:: ::

The Ethics & Compliance Initiative was formed in 2015 and consists of three nonprofit organizations: the Ethics Research Center, the Ethics & Compliance Association, and the Ethics & Compliance Certification Institute. Based in Arlington, Virginia, United States, ECI is devoted to the advancement of high ethical standards and practices in public and private institutions, and provides research about ethical standards, workplace integrity, and compliance practices and processes.

Exam Probability: **Medium**

32. *Answer choices:*
(see index for correct answer)

- a. information systems assessment
- b. Ethics Resource Center
- c. personal values
- d. deep-level diversity

Guidance: level 1

:: Renewable energy ::

A _____ is a fuel that is produced through contemporary biological processes, such as agriculture and anaerobic digestion, rather than a fuel produced by geological processes such as those involved in the formation of fossil fuels, such as coal and petroleum, from prehistoric biological matter. If the source biomatter can regrow quickly, the resulting fuel is said to be a form of renewable energy.

Exam Probability: **High**

33. *Answer choices:*

(see index for correct answer)

- a. Copper indium gallium selenide
- b. Biomass
- c. Carbon neutrality
- d. Variable renewable energy

Guidance: level 1

:: ::

The American Recovery and Reinvestment Act of 2009, nicknamed the _____, was a stimulus package enacted by the 111th U.S. Congress and signed into law by President Barack Obama in February 2009. Developed in response to the Great Recession, the ARRA's primary objective was to save existing jobs and create new ones as soon as possible. Other objectives were to provide temporary relief programs for those most affected by the recession and invest in infrastructure, education, health, and renewable energy.

Exam Probability: **Medium**

34. *Answer choices:*

(see index for correct answer)

- a. cultural
- b. co-culture
- c. open system
- d. Recovery Act

Guidance: level 1

_____ism is a form of government characterized by strong central power and limited political freedoms. Individual freedoms are subordinate to the state and there is no constitutional accountability and rule of law under an _____ regime. _____ regimes can be autocratic with power concentrated in one person or it can be more spread out between multiple officials and government institutions. Juan Linz`s influential 1964 description of _____ism characterized _____ political systems by four qualities.

Exam Probability: **Low**

35. *Answer choices:*

(see index for correct answer)

- a. similarity-attraction theory
- b. empathy
- c. process perspective
- d. functional perspective

Guidance: level 1

:: ::

The Catholic Church, also known as the Roman Catholic Church, is the largest Christian church, with approximately 1.3 billion baptised Catholics worldwide as of 2017. As the world's oldest continuously functioning international institution, it has played a prominent role in the history and development of Western civilisation. The church is headed by the Bishop of Rome, known as the pope. Its central administration, the Holy See, is in the Vatican City, an enclave within the city of Rome in Italy.

Exam Probability: **High**

36. *Answer choices:*

(see index for correct answer)

- a. Sarbanes-Oxley act of 2002
- b. deep-level diversity
- c. empathy
- d. similarity-attraction theory

Guidance: level 1

:: ::

Oriental Nicety, formerly _____ , Exxon Mediterranean, SeaRiver Mediterranean, S/R Mediterranean, Mediterranean, and Dong Fang Ocean, was an oil tanker that gained notoriety after running aground in Prince William Sound spilling hundreds of thousands of barrels of crude oil in Alaska. On March 24, 1989, while owned by the former Exxon Shipping Company, and captained by Joseph Hazelwood and First Mate James Kunkel bound for Long Beach, California, the vessel ran aground on the Bligh Reef resulting in the second largest oil spill in United States history. The size of the spill is estimated to have been 40,900 to 120,000 m3 , or 257,000 to 750,000 barrels. In 1989, the _____ oil spill was listed as the 54th largest spill in history.

Exam Probability: **Low**

37. *Answer choices:*

(see index for correct answer)

- a. Exxon Valdez
- b. similarity-attraction theory
- c. imperative
- d. co-culture

Guidance: level 1

:: Labor rights ::

The _____ is the concept that people have a human _____, or engage in productive employment, and may not be prevented from doing so. The _____ is enshrined in the Universal Declaration of Human Rights and recognized in international human rights law through its inclusion in the International Covenant on Economic, Social and Cultural Rights, where the _____ emphasizes economic, social and cultural development.

Exam Probability: **Low**

38. *Answer choices:*

(see index for correct answer)

- a. Kate Mullany House
- b. Swift raids
- c. Kim Bobo
- d. Right to work

Guidance: level 1

:: Labour law ::

An _____ is special or specified circumstances that partially or fully exempt a person or organization from performance of a legal obligation so as to avoid an unreasonable or disproportionate burden or obstacle.

Exam Probability: **Medium**

39. *Answer choices:*

(see index for correct answer)

- a. Danish Vacation Law
- b. Works council
- c. Negligent retention
- d. Loudermill letter

Guidance: level 1

:: Ethical banking ::

A _____ or community development finance institution - abbreviated in both cases to CDFI - is a financial institution that provides credit and financial services to underserved markets and populations, primarily in the USA but also in the UK. A CDFI may be a community development bank, a community development credit union, a community development loan fund, a community development venture capital fund, a microenterprise development loan fund, or a community development corporation.

Exam Probability: **Low**

40. *Answer choices:*

(see index for correct answer)

- a. Charity Bank
- b. Reliance Bank
- c. Community development financial institution

- d. Institute for Social Banking

Guidance: level 1

:: ::

_____ is a non-governmental environmental organization with offices in over 39 countries and an international coordinating body in Amsterdam, the Netherlands. _____ was founded in 1971 by Irving Stowe, and Dorothy Stowe, Canadian and US ex-pat environmental activists. _____ states its goal is to "ensure the ability of the Earth to nurture life in all its diversity" and focuses its campaigning on worldwide issues such as climate change, deforestation, overfishing, commercial whaling, genetic engineering, and anti-nuclear issues. It uses direct action, lobbying, research, and ecotage to achieve its goals. The global organization does not accept funding from governments, corporations, or political parties, relying on three million individual supporters and foundation grants. _____ has a general consultative status with the United Nations Economic and Social Council and is a founding member of the INGO Accountability Charter, an international non-governmental organization that intends to foster accountability and transparency of non-governmental organizations.

Exam Probability: **Low**

41. *Answer choices:*

(see index for correct answer)

- a. functional perspective
- b. co-culture
- c. Greenpeace

- d. hierarchical perspective

Guidance: level 1

:: Parental leave ::

_____ , or family leave, is an employee benefit available in almost all countries. The term " _____ " may include maternity, paternity, and adoption leave; or may be used distinctively from "maternity leave" and "paternity leave" to describe separate family leave available to either parent to care for small children. In some countries and jurisdictions, "family leave" also includes leave provided to care for ill family members. Often, the minimum benefits and eligibility requirements are stipulated by law.

Exam Probability: **High**

42. *Answer choices:*

(see index for correct answer)

- a. Sara Hlupekile Longwe
- b. Motherhood penalty
- c. Pregnancy discrimination
- d. Additional Paternity Leave Regulations 2010

Guidance: level 1

:: Decentralization ::

_____ or sub _____ mainly refers to the unrestricted growth in many urban areas of housing, commercial development, and roads over large expanses of land, with little concern for urban planning. In addition to describing a particular form of urbanization, the term also relates to the social and environmental consequences associated with this development. In Continental Europe the term "peri-urbanisation" is often used to denote similar dynamics and phenomena, although the term _____ is currently being used by the European Environment Agency. There is widespread disagreement about what constitutes sprawl and how to quantify it. For example, some commentators measure sprawl only with the average number of residential units per acre in a given area. But others associate it with decentralization, discontinuity, segregation of uses, and so forth.

Exam Probability: **Low**

43. *Answer choices:*

(see index for correct answer)

- a. Urban sprawl
- b. Murray Bookchin
- c. Ministry of Interior, Public Safety and Decentralization
- d. Regions of Morocco

Guidance: level 1

:: Majority–minority relations ::

_____, also known as reservation in India and Nepal, positive discrimination / action in the United Kingdom, and employment equity in Canada and South Africa, is the policy of promoting the education and employment of members of groups that are known to have previously suffered from discrimination. Historically and internationally, support for _____ has sought to achieve goals such as bridging inequalities in employment and pay, increasing access to education, promoting diversity, and redressing apparent past wrongs, harms, or hindrances.

Exam Probability: **Medium**

44. *Answer choices:*

(see index for correct answer)

- a. cultural Relativism
- b. Affirmative action
- c. cultural dissonance

Guidance: level 1

:: Corporations law ::

A normal _____ consists of various departments that contribute to the company's overall mission and goals. Common departments include Marketing, [Finance, [[Operations managementOperations, Human Resource, and IT. These five divisions represent the major departments within a publicly traded company, though there are often smaller departments within autonomous firms. There is typically a CEO, and Board of Directors composed of the directors of each department. There are also company presidents, vice presidents, and CFOs.There is a great diversity in corporate forms as enterprises may range from single company to multi-corporate conglomerate. The four main _____ s are Functional, Divisional, Geographic, and the Matrix.Realistically, most corporations tend to have a "hybrid" structure, which is a combination of different models with one dominant strategy.

Exam Probability: **High**

45. *Answer choices:*

(see index for correct answer)

- a. Corporate structure
- b. Memorandum of association
- c. Corporate haven
- d. Quiet period

Guidance: level 1

A _____ service is an online platform which people use to build social networks or social relationship with other people who share similar personal or career interests, activities, backgrounds or real-life connections.

Exam Probability: **High**

46. *Answer choices:*

(see index for correct answer)

- a. deep-level diversity
- b. Social networking
- c. Character
- d. hierarchical perspective

Guidance: level 1

:: ::

_____ or accountancy is the measurement, processing, and communication of financial information about economic entities such as businesses and corporations. The modern field was established by the Italian mathematician Luca Pacioli in 1494. _____, which has been called the "language of business", measures the results of an organization`s economic activities and conveys this information to a variety of users, including investors, creditors, management, and regulators. Practitioners of _____ are known as accountants. The terms "_____" and "financial reporting" are often used as synonyms.

Exam Probability: **High**

47. *Answer choices:*

(see index for correct answer)

- a. cultural
- b. Accounting
- c. hierarchical
- d. Sarbanes-Oxley act of 2002

Guidance: level 1

:: ::

_____ is a naturally occurring, yellowish-black liquid found in geological formations beneath the Earth's surface. It is commonly refined into various types of fuels. Components of _____ are separated using a technique called fractional distillation, i.e. separation of a liquid mixture into fractions differing in boiling point by means of distillation, typically using a fractionating column.

Exam Probability: **High**

48. *Answer choices:*

(see index for correct answer)

- a. levels of analysis
- b. hierarchical perspective

- c. deep-level diversity
- d. Sarbanes-Oxley act of 2002

Guidance: level 1

:: Monopoly (economics) ::

The _____ of 1890 was a United States antitrust law that regulates competition among enterprises, which was passed by Congress under the presidency of Benjamin Harrison.

Exam Probability: **High**

49. *Answer choices:*
(see index for correct answer)

- a. Price-cap regulation
- b. Competition Commission
- c. Building block model
- d. State monopoly capitalism

Guidance: level 1

:: United Kingdom labour law ::

The _____ was a series of programs, public work projects, financial reforms, and regulations enacted by President Franklin D. Roosevelt in the United States between 1933 and 1936. It responded to needs for relief, reform, and recovery from the Great Depression. Major federal programs included the Civilian Conservation Corps , the Civil Works Administration , the Farm Security Administration , the National Industrial Recovery Act of 1933 and the Social Security Administration . They provided support for farmers, the unemployed, youth and the elderly. The _____ included new constraints and safeguards on the banking industry and efforts to re-inflate the economy after prices had fallen sharply. _____ programs included both laws passed by Congress as well as presidential executive orders during the first term of the presidency of Franklin D. Roosevelt.

Exam Probability: **Low**

50. *Answer choices:*

(see index for correct answer)

- a. Enterprise and Regulatory Reform Act 2013
- b. Trade Union Freedom Bill
- c. New Deal
- d. Arbitration Act 1996

Guidance: level 1

:: Business ethics ::

_____ is a persistent pattern of mistreatment from others in the workplace that causes either physical or emotional harm. It can include such tactics as verbal, nonverbal, psychological, physical abuse and humiliation. This type of workplace aggression is particularly difficult because, unlike the typical school bully, workplace bullies often operate within the established rules and policies of their organization and their society. In the majority of cases, bullying in the workplace is reported as having been by someone who has authority over their victim. However, bullies can also be peers, and occasionally subordinates. Research has also investigated the impact of the larger organizational context on bullying as well as the group-level processes that impact on the incidence and maintenance of bullying behaviour. Bullying can be covert or overt. It may be missed by superiors; it may be known by many throughout the organization. Negative effects are not limited to the targeted individuals, and may lead to a decline in employee morale and a change in organizational culture. It can also take place as overbearing supervision, constant criticism, and blocking promotions.

Exam Probability: **Medium**

51. *Answer choices:*

(see index for correct answer)

- a. Nishkam Karma
- b. Workplace bullying
- c. The FCPA Blog
- d. Electronic retailing self-regulation program

Guidance: level 1

:: ::

_____ generally refers to a focus on the needs or desires of one's self. A number of philosophical, psychological, and economic theories examine the role of _____ in motivating human action.

Exam Probability: **Medium**

52. *Answer choices:*

(see index for correct answer)

- a. open system
- b. deep-level diversity
- c. functional perspective
- d. co-culture

Guidance: level 1

:: Hazard analysis ::

Broadly speaking, a _____ is the combined effort of 1. identifying and analyzing potential events that may negatively impact individuals, assets, and/or the environment ; and 2. making judgments "on the tolerability of the risk on the basis of a risk analysis" while considering influencing factors . Put in simpler terms, a _____ analyzes what can go wrong, how likely it is to happen, what the potential consequences are, and how tolerable the identified risk is. As part of this process, the resulting determination of risk may be expressed in a quantitative or qualitative fashion. The _____ is an inherent part of an overall risk management strategy, which attempts to, after a _____ , "introduce control measures to eliminate or reduce" any potential risk-related consequences.

Exam Probability: **High**

53. *Answer choices:*

(see index for correct answer)

- a. Risk assessment
- b. Hazard identification
- c. Swiss cheese model

Guidance: level 1

:: ::

Bernard Lawrence _____ is an American former market maker, investment advisor, financier, fraudster, and convicted felon, who is currently serving a federal prison sentence for offenses related to a massive Ponzi scheme. He is the former non-executive chairman of the NASDAQ stock market, the confessed operator of the largest Ponzi scheme in world history, and the largest financial fraud in U.S. history. Prosecutors estimated the fraud to be worth $64.8 billion based on the amounts in the accounts of _____ 's 4,800 clients as of November 30, 2008.

Exam Probability: **High**

54. *Answer choices:*

(see index for correct answer)

- a. Madoff

- b. functional perspective
- c. process perspective
- d. deep-level diversity

Guidance: level 1

:: Social responsibility ::

The United Nations Global Compact is a non-binding United Nations pact to encourage businesses worldwide to adopt sustainable and socially responsible policies, and to report on their implementation. The _____ is a principle-based framework for businesses, stating ten principles in the areas of human rights, labor, the environment and anti-corruption. Under the Global Compact, companies are brought together with UN agencies, labor groups and civil society. Cities can join the Global Compact through the Cities Programme.

Exam Probability: **Medium**

55. *Answer choices:*

(see index for correct answer)

- a. Social impact
- b. Mallen Baker
- c. Strategic corporate social responsibility
- d. UN Global Compact

Guidance: level 1

:: Business ethics ::

_____ is an area of applied ethics which deals with the moral principles behind the operation and regulation of marketing. Some areas of _____ overlap with media ethics.

Exam Probability: **Low**

56. *Answer choices:*
(see index for correct answer)

- a. University of Illinois clout scandal
- b. Marketing ethics
- c. Minecode
- d. Symantec

Guidance: level 1

:: ::

_____ is the study and management of exchange relationships. _____ is the business process of creating relationships with and satisfying customers. With its focus on the customer, _____ is one of the premier components of business management.

Exam Probability: **Low**

57. *Answer choices:*

(see index for correct answer)

- a. imperative
- b. co-culture
- c. hierarchical
- d. interpersonal communication

Guidance: level 1

:: Marketing ::

_____ is the marketing of products that are presumed to be environmentally safe. It incorporates a broad range of activities, including product modification, changes to the production process, sustainable packaging, as well as modifying advertising. Yet defining _____ is not a simple task where several meanings intersect and contradict each other; an example of this will be the existence of varying social, environmental and retail definitions attached to this term. Other similar terms used are environmental marketing and ecological marketing.

Exam Probability: **High**

58. *Answer choices:*

(see index for correct answer)

- a. Target market
- b. Davie-Brown Index

- c. Green marketing
- d. Ameritest

Guidance: level 1

:: Business ::

_____, or built-in obsolescence, in industrial design and economics is a policy of planning or designing a product with an artificially limited useful life, so that it becomes obsolete after a certain period of time. The rationale behind this strategy is to generate long-term sales volume by reducing the time between repeat purchases.

Exam Probability: **Low**

59. *Answer choices:*
(see index for correct answer)

- a. Staff and line
- b. Les Vergers du Mekong
- c. Auckland Chamber of Commerce
- d. Disadvantaged business enterprise

Guidance: level 1

Accounting

Accounting or accountancy is the measurement, processing, and communication of financial information about economic entities such as businesses and corporations. The modern field was established by the Italian mathematician Luca Pacioli in 1494. Accounting, which has been called the "language of business", measures the results of an organization's economic activities and conveys this information to a variety of users, including investors, creditors, management, and regulators.

:: Banking terms ::

An _____ occurs when money is withdrawn from a bank account and the available balance goes below zero. In this situation the account is said to be "overdrawn". If there is a prior agreement with the account provider for an _____, and the amount overdrawn is within the authorized _____ limit, then interest is normally charged at the agreed rate. If the negative balance exceeds the agreed terms, then additional fees may be charged and higher interest rates may apply.

Exam Probability: **Medium**

1. *Answer choices:*

(see index for correct answer)

- a. Bank card
- b. Documentary collection
- c. Video banking
- d. Wholesale funding

Guidance: level 1

:: Generally Accepted Accounting Principles ::

Financial statements prepared and presented by a company typically follow an external standard that specifically guides their preparation. These standards vary across the globe and are typically overseen by some combination of the private accounting profession in that specific nation and the various government regulators. Variations across countries may be considerable, making cross-country evaluation of financial data challenging.

Exam Probability: **Medium**

2. *Answer choices:*

(see index for correct answer)

- a. Revenue recognition
- b. French generally accepted accounting principles
- c. Fixed investment
- d. Earnings before interest, taxes, depreciation, and amortization

Guidance: level 1

:: Financial markets ::

_____ s are monetary contracts between parties. They can be created, traded, modified and settled. They can be cash , evidence of an ownership interest in an entity , or a contractual right to receive or deliver cash .

Exam Probability: **High**

3. *Answer choices:*

(see index for correct answer)

- a. Clearing balance requirement
- b. Financial instrument
- c. Spot contract
- d. Alternative public offering

Guidance: level 1

:: Finance ::

_____ is a notional asset or liability to reflect corporate income taxation on a basis that is the same or more similar to recognition of profits than the taxation treatment. _____ liabilities can arise as a result of corporate taxation treatment of capital expenditure being more rapid than the accounting depreciation treatment. _____ assets can arise due to net loss carry-overs, which are only recorded as asset if it is deemed more likely than not that the asset will be used in future fiscal periods. Different countries may also allow or require discounting of the assets or particularly liabilities. There are often disclosure requirements for potential liabilities and assets that are not actually recognised as an asset or liability.

Exam Probability: **High**

4. *Answer choices:*

(see index for correct answer)

- a. Deferred tax
- b. Reinvestment risk
- c. Margin of safety
- d. Out-of-pocket expenses

Guidance: level 1

:: Budgets ::

A _____ is a financial plan for a defined period, often one year. It may also include planned sales volumes and revenues, resource quantities, costs and expenses, assets, liabilities and cash flows. Companies, governments, families and other organizations use it to express strategic plans of activities or events in measurable terms.

Exam Probability: **High**

5. *Answer choices:*

(see index for correct answer)

- a. Budget constraint
- b. Zero budget
- c. Budget
- d. Energy budget

Guidance: level 1

:: Foreign exchange market ::

A currency, in the most specific sense is money in any form when in use or circulation as a medium of exchange, especially circulating banknotes and coins. A more general definition is that a currency is a system of money in common use, especially for people in a nation. Under this definition, US dollars, pounds sterling, Australian dollars, European euros, Russian rubles and Indian Rupees are examples of currencies. These various currencies are recognized as stores of value and are traded between nations in foreign exchange markets, which determine the relative values of the different currencies. Currencies in this sense are defined by governments, and each type has limited boundaries of acceptance.

Exam Probability: **High**

6. *Answer choices:*

(see index for correct answer)

- a. Monetary unit
- b. Currency overlay
- c. Impossible trinity
- d. Forex scandal

Guidance: level 1

:: ::

The _____ of 1934 is a law governing the secondary trading of securities in the United States of America. A landmark of wide-ranging legislation, the Act of '34 and related statutes form the basis of regulation of the financial markets and their participants in the United States. The 1934 Act also established the Securities and Exchange Commission, the agency primarily responsible for enforcement of United States federal securities law.

Exam Probability: **Medium**

7. *Answer choices:*

(see index for correct answer)

- a. imperative
- b. Character
- c. surface-level diversity
- d. Securities Exchange Act

Guidance: level 1

:: Debt ::

A _____ is a monetary amount owed to a creditor that is unlikely to be paid and, or which the creditor is not willing to take action to collect for various reasons, often due to the debtor not having the money to pay, for example due to a company going into liquidation or insolvency. There are various technical definitions of what constitutes a _____, depending on accounting conventions, regulatory treatment and the institution provisioning. In the USA, bank loans with more than ninety days` arrears become "problem loans". Accounting sources advise that the full amount of a _____ be written off to the profit and loss account or a provision for _____ s as soon as it is foreseen.

Exam Probability: **Medium**

8. *Answer choices:*

(see index for correct answer)

- a. Debit commission
- b. Legal liability
- c. Extendible bond
- d. Cohort default rate

Guidance: level 1

:: Management accounting ::

_____ is an approach to determine a product's life-cycle cost which should be sufficient to develop specified functionality and quality, while ensuring its desired profit. It involves setting a target cost by subtracting a desired profit margin from a competitive market price. A target cost is the maximum amount of cost that can be incurred on a product, however, the firm can still earn the required profit margin from that product at a particular selling price. _____ decomposes the target cost from product level to component level. Through this decomposition, _____ spreads the competitive pressure faced by the company to product's designers and suppliers. _____ consists of cost planning in the design phase of production as well as cost control throughout the resulting product life cycle. The cardinal rule of _____ is to never exceed the target cost. However, the focus of _____ is not to minimize costs, but to achieve a desired level of cost reduction determined by the _____ process.

Exam Probability: **Low**

9. *Answer choices:*

(see index for correct answer)

- a. Construction accounting
- b. Overhead
- c. Target costing
- d. Cash and cash equivalents

Guidance: level 1

:: ::

_____ is the income that is gained by governments through taxation. Taxation is the primary source of income for a state. Revenue may be extracted from sources such as individuals, public enterprises, trade, royalties on natural resources and/or foreign aid. An inefficient collection of taxes is greater in countries characterized by poverty, a large agricultural sector and large amounts of foreign aid.

Exam Probability: **Low**

10. *Answer choices:*

(see index for correct answer)

- a. Tax revenue
- b. similarity-attraction theory
- c. empathy
- d. information systems assessment

Guidance: level 1

:: Accounting journals and ledgers ::

_____ is a daybook or journal which is used to record transactions relating to adjustment entries, opening stock, accounting errors etc. The source documents of this prime entry book are journal voucher, copy of management reports and invoices.

Exam Probability: **High**

11. *Answer choices:*

(see index for correct answer)

- a. General journal
- b. Subledger
- c. Subsidiary ledger
- d. Cash receipts journal

Guidance: level 1

:: Labor terms ::

_____, often called DI or disability income insurance, or income protection, is a form of insurance that insures the beneficiary's earned income against the risk that a disability creates a barrier for a worker to complete the core functions of their work. For example, the worker may suffer from an inability to maintain composure in the case of psychological disorders or an injury, illness or condition that causes physical impairment or incapacity to work. It encompasses paid sick leave, short-term disability benefits , and long-term disability benefits . Statistics show that in the US a disabling accident occurs, on average, once every second. In fact, nearly 18.5% of Americans are currently living with a disability, and 1 out of every 4 persons in the US workforce will suffer a disabling injury before retirement.

Exam Probability: **High**

12. *Answer choices:*

(see index for correct answer)

- a. Displaced workers
- b. Strike action
- c. Deflator
- d. Disability insurance

Guidance: level 1

:: Cash flow ::

In corporate finance, _____ or _____ to firm is a way of looking at a business's cash flow to see what is available for distribution among all the securities holders of a corporate entity. This may be useful to parties such as equity holders, debt holders, preferred stock holders, and convertible security holders when they want to see how much cash can be extracted from a company without causing issues to its operations.

Exam Probability: **Low**

13. *Answer choices:*

(see index for correct answer)

- a. Propequity
- b. Free cash flow
- c. First Chicago Method
- d. Cash flow loan

Guidance: level 1

:: Management accounting ::

In business, a _____ is a division that gains revenue from product sales or service provided. The manager in _____ is accountable for revenue only.

Exam Probability: **Low**

14. *Answer choices:*
(see index for correct answer)

- a. Responsibility center
- b. Entity-level controls
- c. Direct material usage variance
- d. Customer profitability

Guidance: level 1

:: Labour law ::

In law, _____ is to give an immediately secured right of present or future deployment. One has a vested right to an asset that cannot be taken away by any third party, even though one may not yet possess the asset. When the right, interest, or title to the present or future possession of a legal estate can be transferred to any other party, it is termed a vested interest.

Exam Probability: **Medium**

15. *Answer choices:*

(see index for correct answer)

- a. Collective agreement
- b. Victimisation
- c. Michele Tiraboschi
- d. Vesting

Guidance: level 1

:: ::

In production, research, retail, and accounting, a _____ is the value of money that has been used up to produce something or deliver a service, and hence is not available for use anymore. In business, the _____ may be one of acquisition, in which case the amount of money expended to acquire it is counted as _____ . In this case, money is the input that is gone in order to acquire the thing. This acquisition _____ may be the sum of the _____ of production as incurred by the original producer, and further _____ s of transaction as incurred by the acquirer over and above the price paid to the producer. Usually, the price also includes a mark-up for profit over the _____ of production.

Exam Probability: **Low**

16. *Answer choices:*

(see index for correct answer)

- a. imperative

- b. hierarchical perspective
- c. corporate values
- d. Cost

Guidance: level 1

:: ::

_____ is the consumption and saving opportunity gained by an entity within a specified timeframe, which is generally expressed in monetary terms. For households and individuals, " _____ is the sum of all the wages, salaries, profits, interest payments, rents, and other forms of earnings received in a given period of time."

Exam Probability: **Medium**

17. *Answer choices:*

(see index for correct answer)

- a. interpersonal communication
- b. process perspective
- c. Income
- d. imperative

Guidance: level 1

:: Management accounting ::

_____ is a managerial accounting cost concept. Under this method, manufacturing overhead is incurred in the period that a product is produced. This addresses the issue of absorption costing that allows income to rise as production rises. Under an absorption cost method, management can push forward costs to the next period when products are sold. This artificially inflates profits in the period of production by incurring less cost than would be incurred under a _____ system. _____ is generally not used for external reporting purposes. Under the Tax Reform Act of 1986, income statements must use absorption costing to comply with GAAP.

Exam Probability: **High**

18. *Answer choices:*

(see index for correct answer)

- a. Variable Costing
- b. Environmental full-cost accounting
- c. Invested capital
- d. Bridge life-cycle cost analysis

Guidance: level 1

:: Generally Accepted Accounting Principles ::

In accounting, _____ is the income that a business have from its normal business activities, usually from the sale of goods and services to customers. _____ is also referred to as sales or turnover. Some companies receive _____ from interest, royalties, or other fees. _____ may refer to business income in general, or it may refer to the amount, in a monetary unit, earned during a period of time, as in "Last year, Company X had _____ of $42 million". Profits or net income generally imply total _____ minus total expenses in a given period. In accounting, in the balance statement it is a subsection of the Equity section and _____ increases equity, it is often referred to as the "top line" due to its position on the income statement at the very top. This is to be contrasted with the "bottom line" which denotes net income.

Exam Probability: **Low**

19. *Answer choices:*

(see index for correct answer)

- a. Cost pool
- b. Deferral
- c. Earnings before interest and taxes
- d. Revenue

Guidance: level 1

:: Loans ::

In finance, a _____ is the lending of money by one or more individuals, organizations, or other entities to other individuals, organizations etc. The recipient incurs a debt, and is usually liable to pay interest on that debt until it is repaid, and also to repay the principal amount borrowed.

Exam Probability: **High**

20. *Answer choices:*
(see index for correct answer)

- a. Construction loan
- b. Small Business Lending Index
- c. Student loan
- d. Loan

Guidance: level 1

:: Accounting ::

It is the period for which books are balanced and the financial statements are prepared. Generally, the _____ consists of 12 months. However the beginning of the _____ differs according to the jurisdiction. For example, one entity may follow the regular calendar year, i.e. January to December as the accounting year, while another entity may follow April to March as the _____ .

Exam Probability: **High**

21. *Answer choices:*

(see index for correct answer)

- a. Accounting research
- b. FreeAgent
- c. Accounting period
- d. Russian GAAP

Guidance: level 1

:: Finance ::

The _____ of a corporation is the accumulated net income of the corporation that is retained by the corporation at a particular point of time, such as at the end of the reporting period. At the end of that period, the net income at that point is transferred from the Profit and Loss Account to the _____ account. If the balance of the _____ account is negative it may be called accumulated losses, retained losses or accumulated deficit, or similar terminology.

Exam Probability: **Medium**

22. *Answer choices:*

(see index for correct answer)

- a. Single deposit
- b. Treasury management
- c. Transport finance

- d. Retained earnings

Guidance: level 1

:: Employment classifications ::

> Generally, tax authorities will view a person as self-employed if the person chooses to be recognized as such, or is generating income such that the person is required to file a tax return under legislation in the relevant jurisdiction. In the real world, the critical issue for the taxing authorities is not that the person is trading but is whether the person is profitable and hence potentially taxable. In other words, the activity of trading is likely to be ignored if no profit is present, so occasional and hobby- or enthusiast-based economic activity is generally ignored by authorities.

Exam Probability: **Low**

23. *Answer choices:*
(see index for correct answer)

- a. Full-time
- b. Self-employment
- c. Gainful employment
- d. Freelancer

Guidance: level 1

:: Management accounting ::

_____ , or dollar contribution per unit, is the selling price per unit minus the variable cost per unit. "Contribution" represents the portion of sales revenue that is not consumed by variable costs and so contributes to the coverage of fixed costs. This concept is one of the key building blocks of break-even analysis.

Exam Probability: **Low**

24. *Answer choices:*
(see index for correct answer)

- a. Financial statement analysis
- b. Contribution margin
- c. Direct material total variance
- d. Entity-level controls

Guidance: level 1

:: Financial statements ::

_____ s - are the "Financial statements of a group in which the assets, liabilities, equity, income, expenses and cash flows of the parent company and its subsidiaries are presented as those of a single economic entity", according to International Accounting Standard 27 "Consolidated and separate financial statements", and International Financial Reporting Standard 10 "_____ s".

Exam Probability: **Medium**

25. *Answer choices:*

(see index for correct answer)

- a. Consolidated financial statement
- b. Quarterly finance report
- c. PnL Explained
- d. Statement of retained earnings

Guidance: level 1

:: Budgets ::

_____ is a method of budgeting in which all expenses must be justified and approved for each new period. Developed by Peter Pyhrr in the 1970s, _____ starts from a "zero base" at the beginning of every budget period, analyzing needs and costs of every function within an organization and allocating funds accordingly, regardless of how much money has previously been budgeted to any given line item.

Exam Probability: **Medium**

26. *Answer choices:*

(see index for correct answer)

- a. Film budgeting
- b. Black budget

- c. Zero-based budgeting
- d. Performance-based budgeting

Guidance: level 1

:: Bonds (finance) ::

A _____ is a fund established by an economic entity by setting aside revenue over a period of time to fund a future capital expense, or repayment of a long-term debt.

Exam Probability: **Medium**

27. *Answer choices:*

(see index for correct answer)

- a. Synthetic bond
- b. Guaranty Bond Bank
- c. Puttable bond
- d. Sinking fund

Guidance: level 1

:: Management accounting ::

_____ is the process of recording, classifying, analyzing, summarizing, and allocating costs associated with a process, after that developing various courses of action to control the costs. Its goal is to advise the management on how to optimize business practices and processes based on cost efficiency and capability. _____ provides the detailed cost information that management needs to control current operations and plan for the future.

Exam Probability: **Medium**

28. *Answer choices:*

(see index for correct answer)

- a. Dual overhead rate
- b. RCA open-source application
- c. Cost accounting
- d. Pre-determined overhead rate

Guidance: level 1

:: Banking ::

A _____ is a financial account maintained by a bank for a customer. A _____ can be a deposit account, a credit card account, a current account, or any other type of account offered by a financial institution, and represents the funds that a customer has entrusted to the financial institution and from which the customer can make withdrawals. Alternatively, accounts may be loan accounts in which case the customer owes money to the financial institution.

Exam Probability: **Low**

29. *Answer choices:*

(see index for correct answer)

- a. History of banking
- b. Numbered bank account
- c. Branch manager
- d. Bank account

Guidance: level 1

:: Retail financial services ::

A _____ is a prepaid stored-value money card, usually issued by a retailer or bank, to be used as an alternative to cash for purchases within a particular store or related businesses. _____ s are also given out by employers or organizations as rewards or gifts. They may also be distributed by retailers and marketers as part of a promotion strategy, to entice the recipient to come in or return to the store, and at times such cards are called cash cards. _____ s are generally redeemable only for purchases at the relevant retail premises and cannot be cashed out, and in some situations may be subject to an expiry date or fees. American Express, MasterCard, and Visa offer generic _____ s which need not be redeemed at particular stores, and which are widely used for cashback marketing strategies. A feature of these cards is that they are generally anonymous and are disposed of when the stored value on a card is exhausted.

Exam Probability: **Medium**

30. *Answer choices:*

(see index for correct answer)

- a. Gift card
- b. Pawnbroker
- c. BACS
- d. VantageScore

Guidance: level 1

:: Real estate ::

An _____ is to, interest in, or legal liability on real property that does not prohibit passing title to the property but that may diminish its value. _____ s can be classified in several ways. They may be financial or non-financial. Alternatively, they may be divided into those that affect title or those that affect the use or physical condition of the encumbered property. _____ s include security interests, liens, servitudes, leases, restrictions, encroachments, and air and subsurface rights. Also, those considered as potentially making the title defeasible are _____ s, for example, charging orders, building orders and structure alteration. _____ : charge upon or claim against land arising out of private grant or a contract.

Exam Probability: **High**

31. *Answer choices:*

(see index for correct answer)

- a. Encumbrance

- b. Severance
- c. Automated valuation model
- d. Shea Properties

Guidance: level 1

:: E-commerce ::

_____ is an e-commerce payment system used in the Netherlands, based on online banking. Introduced in 2005, this payment method allows customers to buy on the Internet using direct online transfers from their bank account.

Exam Probability: **Medium**

32. *Answer choices:*
(see index for correct answer)

- a. IDEAL
- b. Buyhatke
- c. Electronic Commerce Regulations 2002
- d. Over-the-top content

Guidance: level 1

:: Commercial crimes ::

_____ is the act of withholding assets for the purpose of conversion of such assets, by one or more persons to whom the assets were entrusted, either to be held or to be used for specific purposes. _____ is a type of financial fraud. For example, a lawyer might embezzle funds from the trust accounts of their clients; a financial advisor might embezzle the funds of investors; and a husband or a wife might embezzle funds from a bank account jointly held with the spouse.

Exam Probability: **Low**

33. *Answer choices:*

(see index for correct answer)

- a. Embezzlement
- b. Shanzhai
- c. United States antitrust law
- d. The Informant

Guidance: level 1

:: Actuarial science ::

The _____ is the greater benefit of receiving money now rather than an identical sum later. It is founded on time preference.

Exam Probability: **High**

34. *Answer choices:*

(see index for correct answer)

- a. Financial economics
- b. Esscher transform
- c. Embedded value
- d. Time value of money

Guidance: level 1

:: Information systems ::

An accounting as an information system is a system of collecting, storing and processing financial and accounting data that are used by decision makers. An _____ is generally a computer-based method for tracking accounting activity in conjunction with information technology resources. The resulting financial reports can be used internally by management or externally by other interested parties including investors, creditors and tax authorities. _____ s are designed to support all accounting functions and activities including auditing, financial accounting & reporting, managerial/ management accounting and tax. The most widely adopted accounting information systems are auditing and financial reporting modules.

Exam Probability: **Low**

35. *Answer choices:*

(see index for correct answer)

- a. Information Systems Journal

- b. Intelligent decision support system
- c. Notification system
- d. Accounting information system

Guidance: level 1

:: Generally Accepted Accounting Principles ::

A _____ or reacquired stock is stock which is bought back by the issuing company, reducing the amount of outstanding stock on the open market.

Exam Probability: **Medium**

36. *Answer choices:*

(see index for correct answer)

- a. Net income
- b. Treasury stock
- c. Engagement letter
- d. AICPA Statements of Position

Guidance: level 1

:: Accounting software ::

_____ describes a type of application software that records and processes accounting transactions within functional modules such as accounts payable, accounts receivable, journal, general ledger, payroll, and trial balance. It functions as an accounting information system. It may be developed in-house by the organization using it, may be purchased from a third party, or may be a combination of a third-party application software package with local modifications. _____ may be on-line based, accessed anywhere at any time with any device which is Internet enabled, or may be desktop based. It varies greatly in its complexity and cost.

Exam Probability: **Medium**

37. *Answer choices:*

(see index for correct answer)

- a. XBRL
- b. Sage 300 ERP
- c. CCH
- d. MAS 90

Guidance: level 1

:: Accounting in the United States ::

_____ were documents issued by the Committee on Accounting Procedure between 1938 and 1959 on various accounting problems. They were discontinued with the dissolution of the Committee in 1959 under a recommendation from the Special Committee on Research Program. In all, 17 bulletins were issued; however, the lack of binding authority over AICPA's membership reduced the influence of, and compliance with the content of the bulletins. The _____ have all been superseded by the Accounting Standards Codification .

Exam Probability: **Low**

38. *Answer choices:*

(see index for correct answer)

- a. Statements on Auditing Procedure
- b. Adjusted basis
- c. Cotton Plantation Record and Account Book
- d. Beta Alpha Psi

Guidance: level 1

:: Tax reform ::

_____ is the process of changing the way taxes are collected or managed by the government and is usually undertaken to improve tax administration or to provide economic or social benefits. _____ can include reducing the level of taxation of all people by the government, making the tax system more progressive or less progressive, or simplifying the tax system and making the system more understandable or more accountable.

Exam Probability: **High**

39. *Answer choices:*

(see index for correct answer)

- a. Goods and services tax in Malaysia
- b. Enterprise Value Tax
- c. Single tax
- d. Equity of condition

Guidance: level 1

:: Generally Accepted Accounting Principles ::

_____ , also referred to as the bottom line, net income, or net earnings is a measure of the profitability of a venture after accounting for all costs and taxes. It is the actual profit, and includes the operating expenses that are excluded from gross profit.

Exam Probability: **Medium**

40. *Answer choices:*

(see index for correct answer)

- a. Gross sales
- b. Insurance asset management
- c. Net profit

- d. Vendor-specific objective evidence

Guidance: level 1

:: Accounting source documents ::

_____ is a letter sent by a customer to a supplier to inform the supplier that their invoice has been paid. If the customer is paying by cheque, the _____ often accompanies the cheque. The advice may consist of a literal letter or of a voucher attached to the side or top of the cheque.

Exam Probability: **Low**

41. *Answer choices:*

(see index for correct answer)

- a. Remittance advice
- b. Parcel audit
- c. Credit memo
- d. Air waybill

Guidance: level 1

:: International taxation ::

_____ is the levying of tax by two or more jurisdictions on the same declared income, asset, or financial transaction. Double liability is mitigated in a number of ways, for example.

Exam Probability: **Low**

42. *Answer choices:*

(see index for correct answer)

- a. Double taxation
- b. Controlled foreign corporation
- c. Arm's-length transaction
- d. Advance pricing agreement

Guidance: level 1

:: Corporations law ::

_____, also referred to as the certificate of incorporation or the corporate charter, are a document or charter that establishes the existence of a corporation in the United States and Canada. They generally are filed with the Secretary of State or other company registrar.

Exam Probability: **Low**

43. *Answer choices:*

(see index for correct answer)

- a. Corporate law
- b. Articles of incorporation
- c. Creature of statute
- d. Company seal

Guidance: level 1

:: Accounting in the United States ::

_____ is the title of qualified accountants in numerous countries in the English-speaking world. In the United States, the CPA is a license to provide accounting services to the public. It is awarded by each of the 50 states for practice in that state. Additionally, almost every state has passed mobility laws to allow CPAs from other states to practice in their state. State licensing requirements vary, but the minimum standard requirements include passing the Uniform _____ Examination, 150 semester units of college education, and one year of accounting related experience.

Exam Probability: **Low**

44. *Answer choices:*

(see index for correct answer)

- a. Public Company Accounting Oversight Board
- b. Joseph Eve, Certified Public Accountants
- c. Trueblood Committee
- d. Adjusted basis

Guidance: level 1

:: Accounting terminology ::

Accounts are typically defined by an identifier and a caption or header and are coded by account type. In computerized accounting systems with computable quantity accounting, the accounts can have a quantity measure definition.

Exam Probability: **Medium**

45. *Answer choices:*

(see index for correct answer)

- a. Cash flow management
- b. revenue recognition principle
- c. Internal auditing
- d. Chart of accounts

Guidance: level 1

:: Auditing ::

An _____ is a security-relevant chronological record, set of records, and/or destination and source of records that provide documentary evidence of the sequence of activities that have affected at any time a specific operation, procedure, or event. Audit records typically result from activities such as financial transactions, scientific research and health care data transactions, or communications by individual people, systems, accounts, or other entities.

Exam Probability: **Low**

46. *Answer choices:*

(see index for correct answer)

- a. Audit trail
- b. ISACA
- c. Internal audit
- d. International Association of Airline Internal Auditors

Guidance: level 1

:: Financial accounting ::

In macroeconomics and international finance, the _____ is one of two primary components of the balance of payments, the other being the current account. Whereas the current account reflects a nation's net income, the _____ reflects net change in ownership of national assets.

Exam Probability: **Medium**

47. Answer choices:

(see index for correct answer)

- a. Hidden asset
- b. Deferred financing cost
- c. Capital account
- d. Advance payment

Guidance: level 1

:: Accounting source documents ::

> An _____, bill or tab is a commercial document issued by a seller to a buyer, relating to a sale transaction and indicating the products, quantities, and agreed prices for products or services the seller had provided the buyer.

Exam Probability: **Low**

48. Answer choices:

(see index for correct answer)

- a. Bank statement
- b. Invoice
- c. Banknote
- d. Parcel audit

Guidance: level 1

:: Taxation ::

A _____ is a person or organization subject to pay a tax. _____ s have an Identification Number, a reference number issued by a government to its citizens.

Exam Probability: **High**

49. *Answer choices:*

(see index for correct answer)

- a. Suits index
- b. Back taxes
- c. Transfer tax
- d. Taxpayer

Guidance: level 1

:: Organizational theory ::

Decentralisation is the process by which the activities of an organization, particularly those regarding planning and decision making, are distributed or delegated away from a central, authoritative location or group. Concepts of _____ have been applied to group dynamics and management science in private businesses and organizations, political science, law and public administration, economics, money and technology.

Exam Probability: **Low**

50. *Answer choices:*

(see index for correct answer)

- a. Strategic Choice Theory
- b. Formal consensus
- c. Battlefield promotion
- d. Conflict

Guidance: level 1

:: Accounting ::

_____ examines how accounting is used by individuals, organizations and government as well as the consequences that these practices have. Starting from the assumption that accounting both measures and makes visible certain economic events, _____ has studied the roles of accounting in organizations and society and the consequences that these practices have for individuals, organizations, governments and capital markets. It encompasses a broad range of topics including financial _____ , management _____ , auditing research, capital market research, accountability research, social responsibility research and taxation research.

Exam Probability: **High**

51. *Answer choices:*

(see index for correct answer)

- a. Cash sweep
- b. Accounting research
- c. amortisation
- d. Merdiban

Guidance: level 1

:: Asset ::

In accounting, a _____ is any asset which can reasonably be expected to be sold, consumed, or exhausted through the normal operations of a business within the current fiscal year or operating cycle . Typical _____ s include cash, cash equivalents, short-term investments , accounts receivable, stock inventory, supplies, and the portion of prepaid liabilities which will be paid within a year.In simple words, assets which are held for a short period are known as _____ s. Such assets are expected to be realised in cash or consumed during the normal operating cycle of the business.

Exam Probability: **Medium**

52. *Answer choices:*
(see index for correct answer)

- a. Current asset
- b. Fixed asset

Guidance: level 1

:: Expense ::

An _____ is the right to reimbursement of money spent by employees for work-related purposes. Some common _____ s are: administrative expense, amortization expense, bad debt expense, cost of goods sold, depreciation expense, freight-out, income tax expense, insurance expense, interest expense, loss on disposal of plant assets, maintenance and repairs expense, rent expense, salaries and wages expense, selling expense, supplies expense and utilities expense.

Exam Probability: **Low**

53. *Answer choices:*

(see index for correct answer)

- a. Interest expense
- b. Expense account
- c. Momentem
- d. expenditure

Guidance: level 1

:: International Financial Reporting Standards ::

_____ , usually called IFRS, are standards issued by the IFRS Foundation and the International Accounting Standards Board to provide a common global language for business affairs so that company accounts are understandable and comparable across international boundaries. They are a consequence of growing international shareholding and trade and are particularly important for companies that have dealings in several countries. They are progressively replacing the many different national accounting standards. They are the rules to be followed by accountants to maintain books of accounts which are comparable, understandable, reliable and relevant as per the users internal or external. IFRS, with the exception of IAS 29 Financial Reporting in Hyperinflationary Economies and IFRIC 7 Applying the Restatement Approach under IAS 29, are authorized in terms of the historical cost paradigm. IAS 29 and IFRIC 7 are authorized in terms of the units of constant purchasing power paradigm.IAS 2 is related to inventories in this standard we talk about the stock its production process etcIFRS began as an attempt to harmonize accounting across the European Union but the value of harmonization quickly made the concept attractive around the world. However, it has been debated whether or not de facto harmonization has occurred. Standards that were issued by IASC are still within use today and go by the name International Accounting Standards , while standards issued by IASB are called IFRS. IAS were issued between 1973 and 2001 by the Board of the International Accounting Standards Committee . On 1 April 2001, the new International Accounting Standards Board took over from the IASC the responsibility for setting International Accounting Standards. During its first meeting the new Board adopted existing IAS and Standing Interpretations Committee standards . The IASB has continued to develop standards calling the new standards " _____ ".

Exam Probability: **Low**

54. *Answer choices:*

(see index for correct answer)

- a. IAS 10
- b. IAS 39
- c. International Financial Reporting Standards

- d. International Public Sector Accounting Standards

Guidance: level 1

:: ::

The U.S. _____ is an independent agency of the United States federal government. The SEC holds primary responsibility for enforcing the federal securities laws, proposing securities rules, and regulating the securities industry, the nation's stock and options exchanges, and other activities and organizations, including the electronic securities markets in the United States.

Exam Probability: **Low**

55. *Answer choices:*

(see index for correct answer)

- a. levels of analysis
- b. open system
- c. Securities and Exchange Commission
- d. personal values

Guidance: level 1

:: SEC filings ::

_____ is a prescribed regulation under the US Securities Act of 1933 that lays out reporting requirements for various SEC filings used by public companies. Companies are also often called issuers, filers or registrants.

Exam Probability: **Medium**

56. *Answer choices:*

(see index for correct answer)

- a. Form F-4
- b. Form 8-K
- c. Form 5
- d. Form 10-K

Guidance: level 1

:: Manufacturing ::

_____ costs are all manufacturing costs that are related to the cost object but cannot be traced to that cost object in an economically feasible way.

Exam Probability: **Low**

57. *Answer choices:*

(see index for correct answer)

- a. Manufacturing overhead
- b. International Organization of Legal Metrology
- c. Direct Manufacturing
- d. Kanati Clothing Company

Guidance: level 1

:: Generally Accepted Accounting Principles ::

In accrual accounting, the revenue recognition principle states that expenses should be recorded during the period in which they are incurred, regardless of when the transfer of cash occurs. Conversely, cash basis accounting calls for the recognition of an expense when the cash is paid, regardless of when the expense was actually incurred.

Exam Probability: **High**

58. *Answer choices:*

(see index for correct answer)

- a. Matching principle
- b. Chinese accounting standards
- c. Pro forma
- d. Expense

Guidance: level 1

:: Business law ::

A _____ is an arrangement where parties, known as partners, agree to cooperate to advance their mutual interests. The partners in a _____ may be individuals, businesses, interest-based organizations, schools, governments or combinations. Organizations may partner to increase the likelihood of each achieving their mission and to amplify their reach. A _____ may result in issuing and holding equity or may be only governed by a contract.

Exam Probability: **Low**

59. *Answer choices:*

(see index for correct answer)

- a. Companies law
- b. Jurisdictional strike
- c. WIPO Copyright Treaty
- d. Partnership

Guidance: level 1

INDEX: Correct Answers

Foundations of Business

1. a: Incentive

2. c: Selling

3. : Career

4. a: Goal

5. c: Direct investment

6. d: Cooperation

7. d: Integrity

8. c: Buyer

9. d: Brainstorming

10. c: Logistics

11. b: Negotiation

12. : Case study

13. : Restructuring

14. d: Competition

15. d: Focus group

16. d: Schedule

17. c: Management

18. b: Creativity

19. c: Number

20. a: Description

21. b: Cash

22. d: Firm

23. : Market value

24. d: Benchmarking

25. : Procurement

26. : Reputation

27. b: Cultural

28. c: Accounting

29. a: Scheduling

30. c: Inventory

31. d: Resource management

32. : Partnership

33. d: Working capital

34. b: Interest

35. b: Economies of scale

36. b: Size

37. a: Joint venture

38. c: Currency

39. c: Question

40. b: Outsourcing

41. c: Contract

42. a: Planning

43. c: Office

44. c: Innovation

45. d: Subsidiary

46. a: Corporate governance

47. b: Analysis

48. d: Income statement

49. : Supply chain

50. b: Shareholders

51. d: Copyright

52. d: Economic Development

53. a: Building

54. : Balanced scorecard

55. d: Competitive advantage

56. : Dividend

57. a: Revenue

58. a: Regulation

59. a: Common stock

Management

1. a: Evaluation

2. a: Negotiation

3. d: Learning organization

4. c: Transactional leadership

5. a: Environmental scanning

6. c: Grievance

7. d: Mass customization

8. : Free trade

9. d: Control chart

10. : Halo effect

11. c: Compromise

12. c: Incentive

13. b: Firm

14. d: Performance

15. b: SWOT analysis

16. b: Facilitator

17. d: Consultant

18. : Scheduling

19. a: Forecasting

20. c: Committee

21. a: Operations management

22. a: Market research

23. b: Globalization

24. b: Socialization

25. c: Theory X

26. d: Management

27. d: Chief executive officer

28. d: Myers-Briggs type

29. d: Management process

30. c: Insurance

31. c: Competitive advantage

32. d: Market share

33. a: Certification

34. d: Sexual harassment

35. : Collective bargaining

36. c: Project

37. c: Income

38. d: Six Sigma

39. b: Organizational performance

40. b: Decentralization

41. c: Integrity

42. c: Contingency theory

43. d: Task force

44. : Interaction

45. : Customer

46. d: Chief executive

47. c: Interview

48. d: Choice

49. b: Decision tree

50. a: Autonomy

51. a: Joint venture

52. b: Self-assessment

53. : Human resources

54. d: Vendor

55. d: Workforce

56. a: Mission statement

57. a: Absenteeism

58. c: Hotel

59. d: Case study

Business law

1. c: Security interest

2. a: Resource

3. d: Buyer

4. : Procedural law

5. b: Contributory negligence

6. d: Incentive

7. a: Identity theft

8. a: Exclusionary rule

9. a: Pregnancy discrimination

10. b: Negotiable instrument

11. b: Subrogation

12. b: Restraint of trade

13. a: Contract law

14. d: Creditor

15. : Merger

16. d: Personnel

17. : Misappropriation

18. b: Firm

19. a: Mens rea

20. a: Offeror

21. d: Money laundering

22. a: Fair use

23. d: Limited liability

24. a: Negotiation

25. b: Labor relations

26. d: Punitive

27. b: Litigation

28. b: Complaint

29. b: Precedent

30. d: Rehabilitation Act

31. c: Proximate cause

32. : Cyberspace

33. a: Surety

34. d: Jury Trial

35. a: Economy

36. d: Auction

37. d: Federal government

38. : Embezzlement

39. c: Misrepresentation

40. a: Judicial review

41. c: Arbitration

42. b: Aid

43. b: Private law

44. d: Good faith

45. b: Expense

46. a: Argument

47. d: Stock

48. d: Adverse possession

49. d: Accounting

50. b: Directed verdict

51. c: Securities and Exchange Commission

52. b: Shares

53. d: Cooperative

54. b: Sherman Antitrust

55. c: Estoppel

56. b: Consumer protection

57. : Perfect tender

58. d: Income

59. b: Plaintiff

Finance

1. b: Schedule

2. a: Maturity date

3. d: Call option

4. c: Advertising

5. b: Working capital

6. c: Retained earnings

7. d: Callable bond

8. c: Capital market

9. : Chart of accounts

10. b: Face

11. b: Accrued interest

12. c: Marketing

13. b: Time value of money

14. a: Accrued liabilities

15. : Sales

16. d: Brand

17. d: Cost allocation

18. b: Fixed asset

19. a: Price

20. a: International Financial Reporting Standards

21. a: Net worth

22. b: Asset turnover

23. b: Bank of America

24. a: Raw material

25. a: Bank account

26. b: Goldman Sachs

27. : Aging

28. a: Forecasting

29. c: Income tax

30. b: Accounts payable

31. a: Residual value

32. b: Internal Revenue Service

33. d: Inventory

34. a: Manufacturing

35. c: Discounting

36. : Financial management

37. b: Cash equivalent

38. d: Going concern

39. : Capital structure

40. c: Audit

41. d: Choice

42. d: Management

43. b: Contract

44. d: Liquidation

45. b: Subsidiary ledger

46. : Current ratio

47. d: Cost driver

48. c: Yield curve

49. c: Demand

50. d: Earnings per share

51. c: Generally accepted accounting principles

52. a: Capital asset pricing model

53. d: Sole proprietorship

54. c: Fraud

55. b: Bank

56. c: Future value

57. a: Payment

58. b: Limited liability

59. d: Financial ratio

Human resource management

1. d: Predictive validity

2. a: Reinforcement

3. c: Fair Labor Standards Act

4. c: Employee engagement

5. a: Culture shock

6. c: Functional job analysis

7. : Criterion validity

8. : Discipline

9. b: Congress

10. : Employee referral

11. a: Minnesota Multiphasic Personality Inventory

12. b: Applicant tracking system

13. b: Asbestos

14. a: Local union

15. : Knowledge worker

16. c: Kelly Services

17. c: Psychological contract

18. b: Cross-training

19. b: Transformational leadership

20. b: Action learning

21. c: Reasonable person

22. c: Global sourcing

23. b: Training and development

24. c: Performance management

25. c: Referent power

26. a: Layoff

27. c: Goal setting

28. : Occupational Safety and Health Act

29. c: Human resource management

30. c: Family violence

31. : Externship

32. a: Resource management

33. a: Innovation

34. a: Recruitment advertising

35. b: Agency shop

36. b: Sick leave

37. b: Onboarding

38. b: Pay grade

39. d: Career

40. c: Job analysis

41. : Organizational structure

42. b: Social networking

43. d: Industrial relations

44. b: E-learning

45. c: Employee Polygraph Protection Act

46. a: Independent contractor

47. a: Job security

48. d: Total Quality Management

49. c: Featherbedding

50. c: Selection ratio

51. a: Behavior modification

52. : Alcoholism

53. a: Unemployment

54. : Public administration

55. a: Cross-functional team

56. c: Profit sharing

57. : Executive search

58. : Needs analysis

59. c: Expert power

Information systems

1. a: Network management

2. a: Security controls

3. a: Extensible Markup Language

4. d: Backup

5. : Password

6. a: Database

7. c: Blogger

8. c: Click-through

9. a: Common Criteria

10. d: Health Insurance Portability and Accountability Act

11. b: Yelp

12. d: Electronic data interchange

13. d: Market share

14. a: First mover advantage

15. : Mouse

16. b: Authentication protocol

17. d: Pop-up ad

18. d: Data aggregator

19. : Data security

20. : Business rule

21. : Chart

22. d: Economies of scale

23. c: Geocoding

24. c: Critical success factor

25. a: Payment card

26. c: Privacy

27. d: Semantic Web

28. a: Web analytics

29. : Data element

30. b: Search engine

31. c: Virtual team

32. : Disaster recovery plan

33. d: Disaster recovery

34. a: Availability

35. b: Competitive advantage

36. : Supply chain management

37. b: Service level agreement

38. d: Keystroke dynamics

39. a: Spyware

40. c: Enterprise systems

41. c: Business process

42. b: Interview

43. c: Government-to-citizen

44. d: Social commerce

45. a: Gmail

46. : Crowdsourcing

47. a: Data link

48. a: Database design

49. d: Google Calendar

50. a: Information privacy

51. c: Packet switching

52. d: Web page

53. a: Social media

54. d: Domain Name System

55. d: Spamming

56. : Open source

57. : Interactivity

58. b: Microprocessor

59. : Edge computing

Marketing

1. d: Innovation

2. c: Noise

3. c: Cognitive dissonance

4. a: Telemarketing

5. d: Resource

6. a: Wholesale

7. d: Tangible

8. : Marketing

9. c: Distribution channel

10. a: Household

11. b: Customer value

12. : Business marketing

13. c: Creative brief

14. b: Investment

15. b: North American Free Trade Agreement

16. d: Choice

17. a: Product concept

18. b: Data collection

19. a: Strategic alliance

20. c: Preference

21. c: Disintermediation

22. b: Green marketing

23. c: Respondent

24. : Brand equity

25. b: Logistics

26. a: Comparative advertising

27. b: Mass media

28. a: Information system

29. : Committee

30. a: Microsoft

31. : Total cost

32. : Advertisement

33. c: Attention

34. b: Target audience

35. : Customer satisfaction

36. : Marketing communication

37. b: Feedback

38. c: Incentive

39. : Direct selling

40. a: Question

41. : Market development

42. c: Expense

43. c: Billboard

44. d: Pricing strategies

45. d: Price war

46. b: Viral marketing

47. a: Outsourcing

48. : Copyright

49. d: Brand management

50. d: Nonprofit

51. c: Intangibility

52. d: Census

53. a: Early adopter

54. a: Database marketing

55. b: Regulation

56. b: Consultant

57. a: Sales promotion

58. c: Derived demand

59. b: Policy

Manufacturing

1. a: Request for quotation

2. b: Resource allocation

3. a: Opportunity cost

4. d: Ishikawa diagram

5. b: Cost reduction

6. d: Purchasing manager

7. c: Waste

8. c: Business process

9. d: E-procurement

10. : Average cost

11. : Root cause

12. c: Obsolescence

13. a: Credit

14. d: Heat transfer

15. a: Total cost

16. b: Control chart

17. : Strategy

18. d: Stakeholder management

19. : Schedule

20. : Elastomer

21. c: Statistical process control

22. b: Reorder point

23. d: Histogram

24. : Production schedule

25. a: Turbine

26. c: Sensitivity analysis

27. c: Total quality management

28. c: New product development

29. a: Strategic sourcing

30. : Consensus

31. : Sharing

32. b: Asset

33. d: Project management

34. c: Original equipment manufacturer

35. c: Malcolm Baldrige National Quality Award

36. : Minitab

37. a: Sunk costs

38. a: Process management

39. b: Accreditation

40. a: Cost

41. : Paper

42. : Resource

43. d: Remanufacturing

44. : Supply chain network

45. a: Voice of the customer

46. d: Rolling Wave planning

47. d: Sales

48. c: Purchasing

49. b: Supply chain risk management

50. : Project manager

51. c: Capacity planning

52. : Joint Commission

53. : Value engineering

54. a: Bullwhip effect

55. : Flowchart

56. c: Blanket

57. a: Certification

58. d: Vendor relationship management

59. b: HEAT

Commerce

1. d: Argument

2. c: Regulatory agency

3. c: Tool

4. : Advertising

5. : Market structure

6. d: Insurance

7. a: Shareholder

8. : Consortium

9. c: Stock

10. : Wall Street Journal

11. b: Compromise

12. d: Direct marketing

13. b: Authority

14. a: Bill of lading

15. a: Webvan

16. a: Phishing

17. c: Hearing

18. d: Mass production

19. a: Control system

20. : Advertisement

21. a: Monopoly

22. : Anticipation

23. : Fixed cost

24. d: English auction

25. : Information technology

26. d: Overtime

27. d: Competitor

28. b: Supranational

29. c: Pension

30. a: Buyer

31. c: Permission marketing

32. d: Planning

33. a: Product mix

34. a: Corporation

35. a: Automation

36. c: Total revenue

37. a: Commodity

38. a: Goal

39. c: Complaint

40. a: Import

41. b: Land

42. b: Netflix

43. d: Siemens

44. c: Reverse auction

45. : Purchasing

46. : Innovation

47. b: Purchasing manager

48. : Competitive advantage

49. d: Supervisor

50. : Policy

51. b: Outsourcing

52. c: Joint venture

53. c: Automated Clearing House

54. c: Electronic funds transfer

55. c: Jury

56. d: DigiCash

57. d: Customer service

58. c: Asset

59. : Consumer-to-consumer

Business ethics

1. c: Enron

2. b: Human nature

3. d: Building

4. c: Sullivan principles

5. c: Layoff

6. b: Model Rules of Professional Conduct

7. c: Volcker Rule

8. a: Siemens

9. : Consumer Protection

10. d: Dress code

11. b: Copyright

12. c: Feedback

13. b: Qui tam

14. a: Medicare fraud

15. b: Habitat

16. : Foreign Corrupt Practices Act

17. c: Greenwashing

18. d: Organic food

19. a: Nonprofit

20. a: Organizational culture

21. c: Internal control

22. : Marijuana

23. d: Locus of control

24. d: Pure Food and Drug Act

25. d: Oil spill

26. a: New York Stock Exchange

27. a: Natural gas

28. : Criminal law

29. c: Transocean

30. a: Medicaid

31. a: Antitrust

32. b: Ethics Resource Center

33. : Biofuel

34. d: Recovery Act

35. : Authoritarian

36. : Catholicism

37. a: Exxon Valdez

38. d: Right to work

39. : Undue hardship

40. c: Community development financial institution

41. c: Greenpeace

42. : Parental leave

43. a: Urban sprawl

44. b: Affirmative action

45. a: Corporate structure

46. b: Social networking

47. b: Accounting

48. : Petroleum

49. : Sherman Antitrust Act

50. c: New Deal

51. b: Workplace bullying

52. : Self-interest

53. a: Risk assessment

54. a: Madoff

55. d: UN Global Compact

56. b: Marketing ethics

57. : Marketing

58. c: Green marketing

59. : Planned obsolescence

Accounting

1. : Overdraft

2. : Generally Accepted Accounting Principles

3. b: Financial instrument

4. a: Deferred tax

5. c: Budget

6. a: Monetary unit

7. d: Securities Exchange Act

8. : Bad debt

9. c: Target costing

10. a: Tax revenue

11. a: General journal

12. d: Disability insurance

13. b: Free cash flow

14. : Revenue center

15. d: Vesting

16. d: Cost

17. c: Income

18. a: Variable Costing

19. d: Revenue

20. d: Loan

21. c: Accounting period

22. d: Retained earnings

23. b: Self-employment

24. b: Contribution margin

25. a: Consolidated financial statement

26. c: Zero-based budgeting

27. d: Sinking fund

28. c: Cost accounting

29. d: Bank account

30. a: Gift card

31. a: Encumbrance

32. a: IDEAL

33. a: Embezzlement

34. d: Time value of money

35. d: Accounting information system

36. b: Treasury stock

37. : Accounting software

38. : Accounting Research Bulletins

39. : Tax reform

40. c: Net profit

41. a: Remittance advice

42. a: Double taxation

43. b: Articles of incorporation

44. : Certified Public Accountant

45. d: Chart of accounts

46. a: Audit trail

47. c: Capital account

48. b: Invoice

49. d: Taxpayer

50. : Decentralization

51. b: Accounting research

52. a: Current asset

53. b: Expense account

54. c: International Financial Reporting Standards

55. c: Securities and Exchange Commission

56. : Regulation S-K

57. a: Manufacturing overhead

58. a: Matching principle

59. d: Partnership

CPSIA information can be obtained
at www.ICGtesting.com
Printed in the USA
LVHW051508301019
635718LV00003B/317/P

9 781538 849521